SOCIAL WORK VALUES AND ETHICS

· · ·

SOCIAL WORK VALUES AND ETHICS

FREDERIC G. REAMER

. . .

COLUMBIA UNIVERSITY PRESS   NEW YORK

COLUMBIA UNIVERSITY PRESS

NEW YORK   CHICHESTER, WEST SUSSEX

COPYRIGHT © 1995 COLUMBIA UNIVERSITY PRESS

ALL RIGHTS RESERVED

• • •

Library of Congress Cataloging-in-Publication Data

Reamer, Frederic G., 1953–
    Social work values and ethics / Frederic G. Reamer.
        p.   cm.
    Includes bibliographical references and index.
    ISBN 0–231–09990–8 (c). — ISBN 0–231–09991–6 (p)
    1. Social service—Moral and ethical aspects.   2. Social workers—
Professional ethics.   3. Social service—United States.   I. Title.
HV10.5.R427   1995
    361.3'2—dc20   94-38229
                                                                 CIP

Casebound editions of Columbia University Press books
are printed on permanent and durable acid-free paper.

Printed in the United States of America

c 10 9 8 7 6 5 4 3 2 1
p 10 9 8 7 6 5 4 3 2 1

FOR DEBORAH, EMMA, AND LEAH

. . .

CONTENTS

. . .

Social workers' understanding of professional values and ethics has matured considerably in recent years. During the earlier years of the profession's history, social workers' attention was focused primarily on cultivating a set of values upon which the mission of social work could be based. Over time, the profession has nurtured and refined a set of values that has given meaning and purpose to generations of social workers' careers. Social work's enduring commitment to vulnerable and oppressed populations, and its simultaneous preoccupation with individual well-being and social justice, are rooted in the profession's rich value base.

But the lens through which social workers view values and ethics has changed over time. Perhaps it is more accurate to say that social workers now look at these issues through several lenses, not just one, and that the angles of these lenses periodically shift in response to cultural developments and trends. Today's social workers face value and ethical issues that their predecessors in the profession could not possibly have imagined. What social worker, in the early twentieth century, could possibly have anticipated the magnitude of the current debate about the role of private practice in social work and its impact on the profession's values, or the ethical issues that have emerged for social workers as a result of society's AIDS crisis? What social worker in the 1930s could have forecast ethical debate about social workers' role in the use of animal organs to save a dying infant's life, or ethical problems created by technology such as computer networks?

In recent years a growing number of social work scholars and practitioners have begun studying, exploring, and debating values and ethical issues in the profession. Literature on social work values and ethics, presentations at professional conferences, and instruction on the subject in undergraduate and graduate social work programs have increased dramatically, especially since the early 1980s. Today's students and practitioners have access to vastly more knowledge and education related to social work values and ethics than did their predecessors. In fact, it is not an exaggeration to say that since the early 1980s social work's exploration of these issues has increased exponentially.

The same is true in other professions. In professions as diverse as journalism, medicine, engineering, accounting, and nursing, practitioners and scholars have devoted increasing amounts of attention to the subjects of values and ethics. For a variety of reasons, which I shall explore shortly, members of these professions have come to recognize the critical importance of these issues and their immediate relevance to practitioners' work.

Alongside the emergence of a wide variety of complicated values and ethical issues in social work and other professions has come the invention of an entire field of study whose purpose is to help identify, explore, and address the kinds of values and ethical issues that professionals encounter. The field of applied and professional ethics began to take shape in the early 1970s, primarily as a result of the explosion of ethical issues in medicine and health care. Since that time, scores of scholars and practitioners have studied the relevance of values and ethics to the professions, debated ethical problems in the professions, explored the relevance of ethical concepts and theories to the kinds of ethical dilemmas that arise in professional practice, and enhanced education and training in these phenomena.

Such has been the case in social work as well. The vast majority of literature on social work values and ethics has been written since the mid-1970s. Although many significant publications appeared prior to this period, most of the in-depth, scholarly exploration of these subjects has occurred since then. In addition, most of the presentations at professional conferences, training sessions in social service agencies, and undergraduate and graduate education on the subject have occurred since the mid-1970s.

Today's social workers thus have access to a far wider range of information and knowledge related to values and ethics than did earlier generations of practitioners. Times have changed dramatically in this respect, and the profession's literature must keep pace. Contemporary social workers must be acquainted with advancing knowledge related to the profession's values and the kinds of ethical issues and challenges that practitioners encounter.

Social Work Values and Ethics has been written with this purpose in mind. This book is designed to provide social workers with a succinct and comprehensive overview of the most critical and vital issues related to professional values and ethics: the nature of social work values; ethical dilemmas and decision making; and professional misconduct. *Social Work Values and Ethics* brings between two covers a summary of knowledge, topics, and debates that have emerged throughout the profession's history, emphasizing the issues that are most pressing in contemporary practice. The book acquaints readers with the core concepts they need to identify and investigate the wide range of compelling values and ethical issues facing today's social workers.

Chapter 1 provides a broad overview of the values and ethical issues in social work and a brief history of the profession's attempts to address them. This is followed in chapter 2 by an in-depth examination of the nature of social work's values and the relevance of the profession's value base to practice.

A significant portion of this book is devoted to ethical dilemmas in social work. These are situations where social workers are challenged by conflicting ethical duties and obligations, circumstances that generate considerable disagreement and debate. Chapter 3 provides a framework for thinking about and exploring ethical dilemmas and, ultimately, making difficult ethical decisions. This chapter includes a practical outline and concepts to help social workers approach ethical decisions.

Chapters 4 and 5 provide an overview of a wide range of specific ethical dilemmas in social work. Chapter 4 focuses on ethical dilemmas in direct practice, that is, ethical dilemmas encountered in work with individuals, families, and groups of clients. Chapter 5, in contrast, focuses on ethical dilemmas in indirect practice, that is, ethical dilemmas encountered in social work administration and community work and in social welfare policy.

An unfortunate aspect of social work values and ethics concerns the problems of unethical behavior and professional misconduct. Sadly, increasing numbers of social workers are being named in ethics complaints or lawsuits that allege some kind of ethical misconduct. The good news is that many of these problems are preventable. Thus chapter 6 provides readers with an overview of the nature of professional misconduct and of the ways in which social workers can become entangled in ethics complaints and lawsuits, a summary of the most common problems in the profession, and various prevention strategies.[*]

Social work values and ethics have come of age. It is a privilege to be able to provide readers with an introduction to what constitutes the heart of social work's noble mission.

---

[*]Case examples are provided throughout this book. With the exception of instances where case material is a matter of public record, circumstances have been altered and pseudonyms have been used to ensure anonymity.

SOCIAL WORK VALUES AND ETHICS

. . .

· · ·

Imagine that you are a social worker at a local community mental health center. You spend most of your time providing supportive and casework services to individuals and families who are experiencing some sort of difficulty. You have worked at the agency for about three years.

During the past two months you have provided counseling to Sarah Robinson and her two children, Brooks, age seven, and Frank, age four. Ms. Robinson originally sought help at the agency because of difficulty she was having managing Brooks's behavior. According to Ms. Robinson, Brooks "frequently throws temper tantrums when he's upset—he can really kick and scream." Ms. Robinson also reported that Brooks's teacher informed Ms. Robinson that she was having a great deal of difficulty controlling Brooks and wanted to discuss whether he should be transferred to a different classroom for "difficult students."

You have spent considerable time teaching Ms. Robinson various ways to handle Brooks's behavior, particularly the use of positive reinforcers. During the past few weeks Ms. Robinson has reported that his tantrums have been less frequent and that he has responded well to the positive reinforcers. Brooks's teacher has also reported that his behavior has "improved somewhat."

During the course of your relationship with Ms. Robinson, she has talked at length about some of her own difficulties—the difficulty of single parenthood, financial problems, and her struggle with alcoholism. In recent weeks Ms. Robinson has been especially eager to discuss her own problems. In your judgment, you and Ms. Robinson have developed a very constructive, trust-filled relationship.

Yesterday morning you received a telephone call from Ms. Robinson. She was clearly distraught. Ms. Robinson said she needed to see you as soon as possible, that she could not wait for her regularly scheduled appointment later in the week. She reported over the telephone that "something awful has happened and it's really bothering me. I need to talk to you fast. I know you'll understand."

You agreed to see Ms. Robinson today during the time made available by another client who canceled his appointment. Ms. Robinson came in alone and immediately started to cry. She said that two days earlier Brooks was

> throwing a terrible tantrum, one of his worst. I had just had it. I was feeling sick, and Frank was screaming for me to feed him. Brooks just wouldn't let up. I got so frustrated I grabbed him and pushed him. He tripped and fell into the radiator in the kitchen, chipping a tooth. I got him to a dentist right away. I told the dentist that Brooks was horsing around with his brother and bumped into the radiator. I just couldn't tell her the truth. I'm so ashamed. Things were getting so much better. I don't know what happened. I just lost it.

During this session you spent most of the time encouraging Ms. Robinson to express her feelings. You also talked with her about how most children who are receiving help for behavior management problems will regress some even though they are making considerable progress overall. The two of you talked about how Ms. Robinson might respond to any future tantrums.

Toward the end of the session you told Ms. Robinson that you were

> in a real pickle. I know that what happened with Brooks was an accident, that you didn't mean to hurt him. But here's the problem. The law requires me to report what happened. I know you don't think you deliberately abused Brooks, but, according to state law, I have to report to the child welfare agency the fact that Brooks was injured. I'd like you to help me report this, so we can show the state social worker how hard you've been working on your problems. Frankly, I don't think they'll do much. This is just something I'm supposed to do.

Ms. Robinson immediately started to cry and became very agitated. "I can't believe you would do this to me," she said. "I thought I could trust you. If you call the state, I'm never coming back here. I can't believe this."

In fact, you do not really *want* to report the case to state child welfare authorities. You firmly believe that Ms. Robinson did not mean to harm Brooks and that this was an isolated instance when she lost control. You have been impressed with Ms. Robinson's earnest attempt to address her problems and with her progress in recent months. You sense that reporting the incident to the child welfare authorities will do more harm than good; reporting is likely to alienate Ms. Robinson and undermine your therapeutic relationship with her. Moreover, Ms. Robinson is already receiving competent help from you; in your judgment, services from a state worker are not needed and would be counterproductive.

The bottom line, however, is that you feel compelled to obey the state law. You did your best to explain to Ms. Robinson why you felt the need to report the case. You told her you understood why she was so angry. But despite your best effort Ms. Robinson walked out quite distressed: "Do what you have to do. Just let me know what you end up doing so I can figure out what *I* need to do."

Seasoned social workers can certainly identify with this predicament. It is one that demands sophisticated clinical skills to help the client deal with his or her anger and to sustain the therapeutic relationship. Sometimes the clinical intervention is effective, and sometimes it is not.

At the center of this case, however, is a complex set of value and ethical issues. In fact, the value and ethical issues in this case scenario represent the four core issues in social work—and those on which I shall focus throughout this book:

1. the value base of the social work profession;
2. ethical dilemmas in social work;
3. ethical decision making in social work; and
4. practitioner malpractice and misconduct.

At the heart of this case is a difficult decision about core *social work values.* Social work is among the most value-based of all professions. As I shall explore more fully, social work is deeply rooted in a fundamental set of values that ultimately shapes the profession's mission and its practitioners' priorities. As the social worker in this case example you would be concerned about several key values, including Ms.

Robinson's right to self-determination (her wish for you to continue working with her without notifying state child welfare officials about the incident involving Brooks); the obligation to protect your client from harm (including Brooks *and* Ms. Robinson—the former from harm in the form of parental abuse, the latter from being deprived of meaningful help from you, and both from harm that might result from investigation by state child welfare officials); the obligation to obey the law (the law that requires social workers to report all instances of suspected child abuse and neglect); and the right to self-protection (that is, the social worker's right to avoid sanctions and penalties that might result from her or his failure to comply with the law).

Ideally, of course, the social worker would act in accord with all these values simultaneously. What social worker would not want to simultaneously respect clients' right to self-determination, protect clients from harm, obey the law, and protect her- or himself? The problem, however, is that situations sometimes arise in social work when core values in the profession conflict, and this leads to *ethical dilemmas*. An ethical dilemma is a situation where professional duties and obligations, rooted in core values, clash. These are the instances when social workers must decide which values—as expressed in various duties and obligations—will take precedence.

To make these difficult choices social workers need to be familiar with contemporary thinking about *ethical decision making*. In the Robinson case, the social worker must decide whether to comply with the state mandatory reporting law—and risk possibly jeopardizing the therapeutic alliance that has been formed with Ms. Robinson—or deliberately violate state law in an effort to sustain the meaningful, and apparently helpful, therapeutic relationship.

As I shall explore presently, the phenomenon of ethical decision making in the professions has matured considerably in recent years, particularly since the 1970s. Professionals trained today have far more access to helpful literature and concepts related to ethical decision making than did their predecessors. This is particularly true in social work, which has experienced a noticeable burgeoning of interest in ethical decision making.

Finally, social workers must be concerned about the possible ramifications of practitioners' ethical decisions and actions, particularly with the possibility of *professional malpractice and misconduct*. Is it acceptable for a social worker knowingly and willingly to violate a law, whatever the motive? What consequences should there be for a social worker who does not act in a client's best interests? What legal risks do social workers face based on their actions, in the form of criminal penalties, ethics complaints, formal adjudication by ethics disciplinary committees or state regulatory boards, and lawsuits?

• THE EVOLUTION OF SOCIAL WORK VALUES AND ETHICS

In order to explore fully the nature of contemporary values and ethics in social work, it is important to understand the historical evolution of thinking in the field with respect to the profession's value base, ethical dilemmas in practice, ethical decision making in social work, and practitioner malpractice and misconduct. The social work profession's grasp of key values and ethical issues has matured considerably in recent years. In fact, most of the profession's scholarship on this subject has been published since the mid-1970s. Nonetheless, the general topics of values and ethics have been central to social work since its formal inception. Historical accounts of the profession's development routinely focus on the compelling importance of social work's value base and ethical principles. Over the years, beliefs about social work's values and ethics have served as the foundation for the profession's mission.

Social work is, after all, a normative profession, perhaps the most normative of the so-called helping professions. In contrast to professions such as psychiatry, psychology, and counseling, social work's historical roots are firmly grounded in concepts such as justice and fairness. Throughout its history, social work's mission has been anchored primarily, although not exclusively, by conceptions of what is just and unjust and by a collective belief about what individuals in a society have a right to and owe to one another.

Although the theme of values and ethics has endured in the profession, social workers' conceptions of what these terms mean and of their influence on practice have changed over time. There have been several key stages in the evolution of social work values and ethics.

The first stage began in the late nineteenth century, when social work was formally inaugurated as a profession. During this period there was much more concern about the morality of the client than about the morality or ethics of the profession or its practitioners. Organizing relief and responding to the "curse of pauperism" (Paine 1880) were the profession's principal missions. This preoccupation often took the form of paternalistic attempts to strengthen the morality or rectitude of the poor whose "wayward" lives had gotten the best of them.

The rise of the settlement house movement and progressive era in the early twentieth century marked the beginning of a second key stage, when the aims and values orientation of many social workers shifted from concern about the morality, or immorality, of the poor to the need for dramatic social reform designed to ameliorate a wide range of social problems, for example, related to housing, health care, sanitation, employment, poverty, and education (Reamer 1992a).

Concern about the morality of the client continued to recede somewhat during the next several decades of the profession's life, as practitioners engaged in earnest attempts to establish and polish their intervention strategies and techniques, training programs, and schools of thought. Over time, concern about clients' morality was overshadowed by debate about the profession's very future, that is, the extent to which social work would stress the cultivation of expertise in psychosocial and psychiatric casework, psychotherapy, social welfare policy and administration, community organization, or social reform.

The third key stage began in the late 1940s and early 1950s, when concern about the moral dimensions of social work practice intensified, although in rather different form. Unlike the earlier preoccupation with the morality of the client, this mid-twentieth-century concern focused much more on the morality or ethics of the profession and of its practitioners. This was a significant shift. Nearly half a century after its formal inauguration, the profession began to develop ethical guidelines to enhance proper conduct among practitioners. In 1947, after several years of debate and discussion, the Delegate Conference of the American Association of Social Workers adopted a code of ethics. The profession's journals also began to publish articles on the subject with greater frequency (Hall 1952; Pumphrey 1959; Roy 1954).

This is not to say, of course, that social workers neglected the subject prior to this period. Certainly this was not the case. Social workers have always espoused concern about a core group of central values that have served as the profession's ballast, such as the dignity, uniqueness, and worth of the person, self-determination, autonomy, respect, justice, equality, and individuation (Biestek 1957; Cabot 1973; Hamilton 1951; Joseph 1989; National Association of Social Workers 1974; Richmond 1917). In addition, there were several modest efforts earlier in the twentieth century to place ethics on social workers' agenda. As early as 1919 there were attempts to draft professional codes of ethics (Elliott 1931). In 1922, the Family Welfare Association of America appointed an ethics committee in response to questions about ethical problems in the field (Joseph 1989; Elliott 1931). However, the late 1940s and early 1950s rather clearly constituted a watershed period in social work when the subject of professional ethics became a subject of study and scholarship in its own right (Frankel 1959; Reamer and Abramson 1982).

Not surprisingly, in the 1960s social workers shifted considerable attention toward the ethical constructs of social justice, rights, and reform. This was the beginning of the fourth key stage in the evolution of social work values and ethics. The public and political mood of this turbulent period infused social work training and practice with a prominent set of values focused on social equality, welfare rights, human rights, discrimination, and oppression (Emmet 1962; Lewis 1972; Plant 1970; Vigilante 1974). It is noteworthy that in 1960 the National Association of Social Workers (NASW) adopted its first code of ethics.

Perhaps the most visible expression of emerging concern about social work values and ethics was the 1976 publication of Levy's *Social Work Ethics*. Although the profession's journals had, by then, published a number of articles on social work values and ethics, Levy's book was the profession's most ambitious conceptual discussion of the subject. This had great symbolic significance. From that point on, scholarship on social work ethics has blossomed. Levy's work, contained in *Social Work Ethics* and other publications (1972, 1973), helped to turn social workers' attention toward the study of overarching values and ethical principles.

• THE EMERGENCE OF APPLIED
AND PROFESSIONAL ETHICS

Until the late 1970s, the profession focused primarily on social work's values and value base. At this point the profession underwent another significant transition in its concern about values and ethical issues—a transition to the current stage. During the 1970s there was a dramatic surge of interest in the broad subject of applied and professional ethics. Professions as diverse as medicine, law, business, journalism, engineering, nursing, and criminal justice began to devote sustained attention to the subject. Large numbers of undergraduate and graduate training programs added courses on applied and professional ethics to their curricula, professional conferences witnessed a substantial increase in presentations on the subject, and the number of publications on professional ethics increased dramatically (Callahan and Bok 1980; Reamer and Abramson 1982).

This growth of interest was due to a variety of factors. Controversial technological developments in health care and other fields certainly helped to spark ethical debate around such issues as termination of life support, organ transplantation, genetic engineering, and test-tube babies. What criteria should be used to determine which medically needy patients should receive scarce organs, such as hearts and kidneys? When is it acceptable to terminate life support that is keeping a comatose family member alive? To what extent is it appropriate to influence, through laboratory intervention, the sex of a fetus? Is it ethically justifiable to implant an animal's heart into the body of an infant born with an impaired heart?

Widespread publicity about scandals in government also triggered considerable interest in professional ethics. Beginning especially with Watergate in the early 1970s, the public has become painfully aware of various professionals who have abused their clients and patients, emotionally, physically, or financially. The media have been filled with disturbing reports of physicians, psychologists, clergy, social workers, and other professionals who have taken advantage of the people they are supposed to help. Consequently, most professions take more seriously their responsibility to educate practitioners about possible abuse and ways to prevent it.

In addition, the introduction, beginning especially in the 1960s, of terminology such as patients' rights, welfare rights, and prisoners' rights helped shape professionals' thinking about the need to attend to ethical concepts. Since the 1960s, members of many professions have been much more cognizant of the concept of rights, and this has led many training programs to broach questions about the nature of professionals' ethical duties to their clients and patients.

Contemporary professionals also have a much better appreciation of the limits of science and its ability to answer many complex questions professionals face. Although for some time, particularly around the 1930s, science was placed on a pedestal and widely regarded as the key that could unlock many of life's mysteries, modern-day professionals acknowledge that science cannot answer a variety of questions that are, fundamentally, ethical in nature (Sloan 1980).

Finally, the well-documented increase in litigation and malpractice, along with publicity about unethical professionals, has forced the professions to take a closer look at their ethics traditions and training. All professions have experienced an increase in claims and lawsuits filed against practitioners, and a substantial portion of these complaints allege some form of unethical conduct. As a result of this noteworthy and troubling trend, the professions, including social work, have enhanced their focus on ethics education (Reamer 1994b).

This burgeoning interest in professional values and ethics thus seems to be the product of a variety of circumstances. These factors have combined to produce a remarkable and sustained growth of interest in the subject across professions, one that has fundamentally changed the way professionals are educated and trained. I now turn to a systematic review of the key components of social work values and ethics that ought to be part of every practitioner's knowledge base.

• • •

CASE 2.1

Stephanie P. recently received her M.S.W. She was about to embark on the first stage of her social work career. Stephanie P. had worked as a teacher's aide in a preschool program located in a suburb of a major city before enrolling in the M.S.W. program at a nearby university.

Stephanie P. hopes to be "a psychotherapist working with individuals, couples, and families. When I was younger, my family received counseling help from a social worker, and since then I've always wanted to be a therapist."

Stephanie P. knows that she must obtain considerable experience before venturing out on her own. She realizes that she must provide clinical services under an experienced practitioner's supervision before starting her own private practice.

Stephanie P. has been interviewing for various positions. The one concrete offer she has received is for a position as a caseworker in a family service agency located in a low-income section of the city where she lives, an area where most residents are people of color.

Stephanie P. acknowledges that the agency provides much-needed services to the local community and would provide valuable experience, but she is reluctant to accept the position. Although it is difficult for Stephanie P. to state it publicly, she admits to herself and to her closest friends that she has never felt comfortable around poor people and ethnic minorities. Stephanie P. grew up in a relatively affluent community nearby and, she says, never spent much time around people of color or ethnic minorities. She says she will feel much more comfortable working with clients "more like myself."

This case raises a number of critically important issues about core social work values and the value base of the profession. The subject of social work values has always been central to the profession (Vigilante 1974). As Aptekar (1962; cited in Levy 1973:35) notes, "The framework of social work, as we know it, is a set of values."

Values have several important attributes and perform several important functions: they are generalized, emotionally charged conceptions of what is desirable; historically created and derived from experience; shared by a population or a group within it; and they provide the means for organizing and structuring patterns of behavior (Williams 1968; cited in Meinert 1980:6).

The term *value* is difficult to define. It derives from the Latin *valere*, meaning "to be strong, to prevail, or to be of worth" (Meinert 1980:5). Over the years scholars have penned diverse definitions of value and values, including "anything capable of being appreciated"; "the object of any need"; "a conception, explicit or implicit, distinctive of an individual or characteristic of a group, of the desirable which influences the selection from available means and ends of action"; "the desirable end states which act as a guide to human endeavor or the most general statements of legitimate ends which guide social action"; and "normative standards by which human beings are influenced in their choice among the alternative courses of action which they perceive" (Rescher 1969:2). As Rescher (1969) concludes in his classic text, *Introduction to Value Theory,*

> In the English language the word is used in a somewhat loose and fluctuating way. Philosophers and social scientists concerned with value questions have long recognized the need for a more precise value terminology to facilitate the exact formulations needed in scholarly and scientific contexts. But this desideratum seems to be the only point of agreement. All workers in the field echo this complaint. Nevertheless, all their positive efforts have failed. No proposal for delineation of value terminology has been able to generate any significant degree of concurrence, let alone become a focus of settled consensus. (P. 1)

The subject of values has been popular in social work, and most practitioners recognize the critical importance of values to the profession. As Perlman (1976:389) has noted, "The need for conscious awareness of the values that influence our doing applies at every level of social work. Not only may subjective and unanalyzed values motivate the case- and group-worker, but community planners, researchers, indeed all of us are pushed and pulled by often unseen value assumptions and commitments. Only as we continuously raise these assumptions and commitments to full consciousness can we take possession of them."

Unfortunately, however, many discussions of the concept of values in social work's literature have been superficial. Authors often cite commonly embraced social work values and offer brief summaries of their relevance to practice. Rarely does one find in-depth analyses of the nature of values in general or of social work values in particular (Hunt 1978:12, 15). As Vigilante (1974) has observed,

> Although we have identified social work practice as the amalgamation of values, knowledge, and skills, and we assume a preeminence of values, most of our sparse research efforts have been directed at the knowledge and skill components. By comparison the use of values in practice has been neglected as a target for research. Values have received only superficial attention from scholars, theory builders, and curriculum designers. . . . Social workers have religiously clung to values over the . . . years of the development of the profession and have not done these values justice. We seem to cling to them intuitively, out of faith, as a symbol of our humanitarianism. We have not treated them with the seriousness befitting their role as a fulcrum of practice.   (Pp. 108, 114)

In social work, values have been important in several key respects, with regard to 1) the nature of social work's mission; 2) the relationships that social workers have with clients, colleagues, and members of the broader society; 3) the methods of intervention that social workers use in their work; and 4) the resolution of ethical dilemmas in practice.

As I shall explore more fully, social work's fundamental aims and mission are rooted in deep-seated beliefs among the profession's founders and contemporary practitioners concerning the values of helping, aiding, and assisting people who experience problems in living (Reid 1992). Social work is not mere technology; rather, it is a value-based and value-inspired effort designed to help vulnerable people through the use of sophisticated methods of intervention (Timms 1983). As Levy (1973) observed, "Social work values in short are supposed to represent neither a random nor a variable set of norms and prescriptions. Neither are they supposed to represent a mirror of societal preferences and emphases. Rather, they are supposed to represent a standardized reflection of collective responsibility, implicit in the role of social work in society" (p. 36).

Social workers' values influence the kinds of relationships they have with clients, colleagues, and members of the broader society (Hamilton 1940; Younghusband 1967). Social workers make choices about the people with whom they want to work. For example, some practitioners devote their careers to clients they perceive as victims, such as abused children and individuals born with severe physical disabilities. Others choose to work with clients perceived by many to be perpetrators, such as prison inmates convicted of serious sex offenses. Further, as I showed in the case that opened this chapter, some social workers choose to work primarily with low-income people, whereas others prefer to work with a more affluent clientele. These choices are influenced in part by social workers' values.

Social workers' values also influence their decisions about the intervention methods they will use in their work with clients—whether individuals, families, groups, communities, or organizations (McDermott 1975; Varley 1968). For example, some social workers prefer to use confrontational techniques in their work with juvenile delinquents, believing that these are the most effective means for bringing about behavior change. Other practitioners who work with this same population may be critical of confrontational methods that seem dehumanizing and, because of their values, may prefer forms of counseling that emphasize the client's right to self-determination and the building of therapeutic alliances.

Or a social worker who is an advocate for low-income housing in a poor neighborhood may prefer direct confrontation with public officials—in the form of demonstrations, rallies, and harassment—in an effort to promote affordable housing. For this practitioner, the value of providing basic shelter for poor people is paramount, and direct confrontation may be necessary to bring it about. Another practitioner may reject such tactics because of her belief in the value of collaboration and respectful exploration of differences.

This leads to another way in which values are central to social work: they are key to efforts to resolve ethical dilemmas that involve conflicts of professional duties and obligations. Ethical dilemmas ordinarily involve values that clash, as the case presented in chapter 1 revealed. In that case, the social worker was torn between the values of respecting her client's right to self-determination (the client's wish that the social worker not report the incident involving her injured son to the local child welfare authorities) and of complying with the state child abuse and neglect mandatory reporting law. Social workers' decisions when faced with such ethical dilemmas ultimately rest on their beliefs about the nature of social work values—particularly as they are translated into specific professional duties and obligations—and which values will take precedence when they conflict.

In this chapter I shall discuss the ways in which social work values have influenced the nature of social work's basic mission; the development of the profession's value base and core set of values; typologies of social work values that have emerged in social work; the relevance of clients' and social workers' cultural and religious values; and the ways that social work values are translated into action designed to help people in need. Throughout the remainder of the book I shall also explore the ways in which social work values have influenced the relationships social workers have with clients, colleagues, and members of the broader society; the methods of intervention social workers use in their work; and the resolution of ethical dilemmas in practice.

• THE NATURE OF SOCIAL WORK'S MISSION

There has been considerable debate about the nature of social work's mission and value base throughout the profession's history.[*] Every serious account of social work's evolution acknowledges the enduring tension between "case" and "cause," between amelioration of individual suffering and social change that addresses the structural flaws in the culture that foster the problems that individuals experience.

The profession's early concern with the value of charity has its roots in the Bible and religion. Acts of charity were meant to fulfill God's commandments as much as to be genuine acts of kindness (Leiby 1985).

---

[*]Portions of this discussion are adapted from Reamer 1992a.

The Elizabethan Poor Law of 1601—commonly regarded as a landmark statute that synthesized earlier welfare legislation—had its origins in a system of poor relief provided by parishes of the Church of England. However, by the late nineteenth century there was mounting criticism of religious charity and the values that it entailed, as reflected in the invention of the still-current secular phrase *social welfare*. Religious charity frequently came to be viewed as value-oriented in a negative sense, moralistic, paternalistic, and disorganized. Although traces of biblical influence can be found in the profession even today, the turn of the century marked a perceptible shift toward the secularization of welfare and a shift in its value base. It was in the midst of this era, filled with laissez-faire ideology and Social Darwinism (the survival of the fittest), that social work got its formal start. Thus it is not surprising that the earliest chapters of the profession's history focused on improving the morals of paupers. Trattner (1979) conveys this paternalistic mood in his review of the early charity organization societies:

> Friendly visiting, then, assumed the right and the duty of intervention in the lives of the poor by their social and economic betters. The poor were not inherently vicious or mean. Rather, they were wayward children who drifted astray or who were incapable of discerning their own self-interest. They required no resource so desperately, therefore, as the advice of an intelligent friend who would offer sympathy, tact, patience, cheer, and wise counsel. The visitor's job was to discern the moral lapse responsible for the problem and then supply the appropriate guidance —something, of course, they were certain they could do.   (P. 85)

The winds began to shift in the early years of the twentieth century. The events and activities associated with the Progressive and settlement house eras and the nation's severest depression helped turn social workers' values and attention toward the problems of the broader society. Practitioners could not help but recognize the need to examine the structural defects that created widespread vulnerability and dependency (Popple 1985).

The aftermath of the Great Depression signaled an important split in social work's basic values and orientation toward helping. A significant portion of the profession continued to concentrate on therapeutic work, with an emphasis on individual change (Miles 1954; cited in Woodroofe 1962:130). In contrast were the practitioners committed to advancing public welfare and other programs begun under the New Deal. Their work was conducted in public agencies charged primarily with serving the poor, disabled, and those otherwise in need. Most were decidedly uninterested in providing psychotherapy.

But following World War II the clinicians gained control of the profession and held it until the turbulent era surrounding the 1960s. Then the factions faced off again, with critics charging that social work had abandoned its core values and social action mission and was not sufficiently concerned about converting clients' private troubles into public issues that demanded creative and ambitious public policy responses (Bisno 1956; Gilbert and Specht 1974; Rein 1970). Although social workers generally embraced the Great Society and War on Poverty programs and policies, for many the grasp slipped as the public's faith in the efficacy of these initiatives declined.

The 1980s were reminiscent of the postwar years of the 1940s and 1950s, when the relative tranquility associated with peacetime and domestic calm turned the values and attention of both the nation and its professionals inward. Pursuit of individual well-being became more compelling than pursuit of the public good. This value shift was reflected especially in social work training programs. During the 1980s curricular concentrations in community organizing and social welfare policy were either abandoned or left to limp along with under-enrollment. In contrast, electives in casework and psychotherapy were filled to the brim. As Siporin (1992:83) observed in the early 1990s, "We had social activist eras from the 1930s to the early 1940s, and again from the late 1960s to the late 1970s. Between these periods, and at present, social workers have focused more on individual and family moral reform, now termed 'therapy.' "

The data are compelling. According to NASW estimates, the number of the organization's members engaged in private practice rose from approximately three thousand in 1967 to approximately nine thousand in 1976 (Specht 1991:102). Between 1972 and 1982 there was an 18 percent decline in the number of National Association of Social Workers (social work's largest professional organization) members employed in the public sector, in federal, state, and local human service agencies. In contrast, employment in private sectarian agencies and proprietary (for-profit) agencies—the vast majority of which

provide casework and psychotherapy services—increased 132 percent and 264 percent, respectively ("Membership Survey" 1983). Further, between 1975 and 1985 the number of clinical social workers in
the United States increased from approximately twenty-five thousand
to sixty thousand (an increase of 140 percent), placing social workers
first in the list of professional groups providing mental health services
—followed by psychiatrists, clinical psychologists, and marriage and
family counselors (Goleman 1985).

Of course, this shift may reflect in part the decline since the 1970s
in the government funding of social service programs and in the number of jobs available in the public sector. The migration to the private
sector of veteran government workers frustrated by bureaucratic life
may also be a factor. One also cannot assume that social workers
engaged in private practice or affiliated with private agencies are not
involved in social action, pro bono activities, and other forms of help
focused on those individuals who are most vulnerable (Alexander
1987; Barker 1991a; Brown 1990; Butler 1990; Reeser and Epstein
1990). However, the data strongly suggest that, beginning especially in
the early 1970s, there was a mounting neglect of public issues in favor
of psychotherapeutic and casework services that for many social
workers provide more rewarding, respectable, and lucrative careers
(Specht 1990). Specht (1991) argues strongly and provocatively when
he states, "Most professionals who opt for private practice remove
themselves from the problems, settings, and populations that social
work was created to deal with. Psychotherapy practiced privately is
not a bad or evil thing to do; it's just not social work" (p. 107). Keith-
Lucas (1992) uses similarly forceful language concerning those social
workers

> who abandoned the social services and set themselves up in private
> practice. To them the word "social" ceased to have anything to do with
> society as a whole—it meant only that they took societal factors into
> consideration as they diagnosed and treated their clients. Otherwise, it
> would be hard to see them as social workers (p. 62). . . .
>
> There is certainly a need for psychotherapists and clinicians in our
> society, and there is no reason why these should not work in private
> practice or agitate for professional recognition and rewards. But I wish
> they would stop calling themselves "social workers," or that those who

act from an entirely different motivation—those really concerned with the quality of life accorded the most vulnerable in our society, those called to do something about it and prepared not only to learn but to acquire the self-discipline needed to serve society—could find themselves another name. (P. 67)

Thus important aspects of social work's values have shifted during the profession's history, including the early concern about the morality of paupers, subsequent focus on issues of social reform and social justice, and, at various times, preoccupation with a clinical and psychotherapeutic agenda. In summary, six prominent orientations toward social work's basic values and ethics have been evident over the years, with varying degrees of persistence: 1) the paternalistic orientation; 2) the social justice orientation; 3) the religious orientation; 4) the clinical orientation; 5) the defensive orientation; and 6) the amoralistic orientation. Although these orientations are conceptually distinct, they are not necessarily mutually exclusive. Elements of these different orientations can be found simultaneously within individual practitioners and within various stages throughout social work's history.

PATERNALISTIC ORIENTATION • This perspective was most clearly evident during the late nineteenth and early twentieth centuries, when friendly visiting and charity organization societies proliferated. It is based on an assumption that the profession's public mission is to enhance the rectitude of its clients, enabling them to lead virtuous, wholesome, and gainful lives, independent of support from public or private coffers. The principal aim is to help the hungry, homeless, jobless, and destitute (and, in some instances, the Godless) to muster their internal resources to lead more productive lives. Those who have strayed from life's straight and narrow path are to be helped to return to it.

SOCIAL JUSTICE ORIENTATION • According to this view, dependency is primarily a function of structural flaws in the cultural and economic life that surrounds the least advantaged. Poverty, unemployment, crime, and some forms of mental illness are by-products of a culture that has lost its moral sensibilities. Over time the defects of capitalism and unchecked racism and other forms of oppression have produced an injured and scarred underclass. The casualties of this harsh reality must be addressed by fundamental social change that pursues such goals as affirmative action, equality of opportunity, redistribution of wealth, and nonpunitive, humane welfare benefits and services. Regressive taxes, unrestrained free enterprise, and robber barons must be replaced by forms of care driven by the values of fairness, decency, and compassion. Social work's involvement in the settlement house movement, the New Deal, the War on Poverty, and the Great Society era reflects these views (Davis 1967).

RELIGIOUS ORIENTATION • Features of both the paternalistic and social justice orientations are present in the religious orientation toward social work values and ethics. From this point of view, a central mission of the professional—rooted in social work's historical link with the church—is to translate his or her religious convictions into meaningful social service (Constable 1983; Marty 1980). Charity, for example, may represent Christian love, between individuals and God and among neighbors. It is not necessarily grounded in paternalism but may derive from a sense of religious obligation (Canda 1988; Joseph 1987; Judah 1985; Siporin 1992).

CLINICAL ORIENTATION • Most recently the emerging emphasis on ethical dilemmas that arise in casework with individuals, families, and groups reflects a clinical orientation toward the place of values and ethics in social work. This phenomenon—especially evident since the late 1970s—has been part of the contemporary wave of interest in professional ethics generally. Central to it are discussions about such issues as client confidentiality (for example, the duty to protect third parties, release of information, client access to records), privileged communication, informed consent, paternalism, truth telling, conflicts of interest, whistle blowing, and compliance with laws, and agency rules and regulations. Especially characteristic of this orientation is an emphasis on ethical decision making and the resolution of conflicts of professional obligation. This emphasis on value conflicts and ethical dilemmas is grounded in part in social work's enduring concern about the relationship between clients' and workers' values.

DEFENSIVE ORIENTATION • A significant portion of current interest in social work values and ethics represents what might be dubbed a defensive orientation. In contrast to the clinical orientation, whose emphasis is on enhancing the ethical practice of social work primarily for clients' benefit (including individual clients, families, communities, and the broader society), the defensive orientation focuses on the protection of the practitioner. It is based on concerns about allegations of various forms of negligence and malpractice, and it is dominated by concern about liability issues and the ever-increasing risk of lawsuits (Reamer 1994b).

AMORALISTIC ORIENTATION • This collection of perspectives on the proper place of values and ethics in social work is tempered by an amoralistic orientation, whose principal feature is the absence of value-based or normative concepts. This view is characteristic of practitioners whose approach to social work is essentially technical, that is, preoccupied with technique. For example, many practitioners who participated in the "psychiatric deluge" of the 1920s avoided the language of values and ethics, substituting psychodynamic argot that they hoped would clarify the mysteries of human behavior. Their work was not value-free, however; certainly a preoccupation with psychodynamic constructs, or with any other theory, constitutes a value orientation (Perlman 1976:384). Rather, their work was not dominated by what have come to be widely regarded as traditional social work values. Modern-day social workers whose strategies are determined largely by allegedly value-neutral considerations such as psychotherapeutic techniques, program evaluation, and cost-benefit analyses qualify as well.

• TYPOLOGIES OF VALUES IN SOCIAL WORK PRACTICE

How have the profession's values, as they have evolved over the years, influenced social work practice? There have been several attempts to define and categorize core social work values as they pertain to practice. One of the best-known attempts to outline core social work values that guide practice was made by Gordon (1965) in his classic article entitled "Knowledge and Value: Their Distinction and Relationship in Clarifying Social Work Practice." Gordon (1965:32) asserted that there are six value-based concepts that constitute the foundation of social work practice:

1. the individual is the primary concern of this society;
2. there is interdependence among individuals in this society;
3. those individuals have social responsibility for one another;
4. there are human needs common to each person, yet each person is essentially unique and different from others;
5. an essential attribute of a democratic society is the realization of the full potential of each individual and the assumption of his social responsibility through active participation in society; and
6. society has a responsibility to provide ways in which obstacles to this self-realization (i.e., disequilibrium between the individual and his or her environment) can be overcome or prevented.

Vigilante (1974) endorsed a similar view, arguing:

> The values of social work are those that fit under the broad rubric of humanitarianism. Central among these is the dignity and worth of the individual. Social work, therefore, is work with interrelationships among groups and individuals within the context of a societal goal. It is a good social responsibility. Humanitarianism is the philosophical justification. Its transmission into professional intervention creates the value-laden, "social" character of the social worker's function.
>
> (P. 109)

Another prominent formulation of core social work values appears in the *NASW Standards for the Classification of Social Work Practice* (1982; cited in Barker 1991b:246). According to this widely circulated and prominent document, basic values for the profession include:

1. commitment to the primary importance of the individual in society;
2. respect for the confidentiality of relationships with clients;
3. commitment to social change to meet socially recognized needs;
4. willingness to keep personal feelings and needs separate from professional relationships;
5. willingness to transmit knowledge and skills to others;
6. respect and appreciation for individual and group differences;

7. commitment to develop clients' ability to help themselves;
8. willingness to persist in efforts on behalf of clients despite frustration;
9. commitment to social justice and the economic, physical, and mental well-being of all members of society; and
10. commitment to high standards of personal and professional conduct.

Although these various formulations demonstrate that there is variation in the specific core values of the profession identified by different authors, there is considerable consistency as well. As Levy (1976:80) observed, social work values "rest on a fairly constant and fundamental value base with which social workers have been identified since the advent of their professionalization."

Commonly cited values are individual worth and dignity, respect of persons, valuing individuals' capacity for change, client self-determination, providing individuals with opportunity to realize their potential, seeking to meet individuals' common human needs, seeking to provide individuals with adequate resources and services to meet their basic needs, client empowerment, equal opportunity, nondiscrimination, respect for diversity, commitment to social change and social justice, confidentiality and privacy, and willingness to transmit professional knowledge and skills to others (Abbott 1988; Baer and Federico 1979; Barker 1991b; Bartlett 1970; Biestek 1957; Biestek and Gehrig 1978; Billups 1992; Compton and Galaway 1989; Goldstein 1983; Gordon 1962; Hunt 1978; A. Johnson 1955; L. Johnson 1989; Keith-Lucas 1977; Levy 1973, 1976, 1984; Morales and Sheafor 1986; NASW 1982; Plant 1970; Popple 1992; Pumphrey 1959; Reamer 1987a, 1989, 1990, 1993a, 1994a; Sheafor, Horejsi, and Horejsi 1988; Siporin 1992; Solomon 1976; Teicher 1967; Timms 1983; Varley 1968; Wilson 1978; Zastrow 1985).

Over the years a number of prominent social work scholars have formulated typologies or classifications of these specific values. In 1959, Pumphrey presented one of the earliest typologies of social work values as they pertain to practitioners' relationships, placing them into three categories of value-based objectives. The first focused on "relating the values of the profession to those operating in the culture at large" (p. 79). This area concerned the compatibility between the profession's mission—for example, regarding social justice, social change, meeting common human needs—and the broader society's values. This category included examination of the possibility that social work's value base and mission might conflict at times with the broader society's values, for example, with respect to welfare reform or universal health care (Johnson 1955). As Frankel (1969) observed:

> We are going to live a long time with problems that puzzle our minds and inflame our passions. For us, the overhanging problem is to maintain or create conditions for responsible social action in such an era of dangerous tumult. We shall need to be much clearer than we recently have been with respect to the rules of the road and the basic premises of our conduct. It is not enough to speak of "solving problems": we have to be more exact and exacting about the principles that define for us the successful solution of a problem. In particular, this means that we must decide where we stand on the issue of the relationship of professional values to the broader social values. (P. 30)

Pumphrey's second category focused on "internal relationships within the professional membership" (pp. 79–80), for example, the ways in which the profession interprets and implements its values and encourages ethical behavior. This category includes social workers' efforts to clarify their basic values and ethical principles through *intra*professional communication and policy-making procedures.

The final category focuses on "relations to the specific groups or individuals served" (p. 80), that is, understanding and responding to clients' needs in accord with core social work values. This includes analysis of the values that guide practitioners' relationships with clients, such as respecting individual worth and dignity, valuing individuals' capacity for change and right to self-determination, promoting client empowerment, and so on.

Levy (1973, 1976, 1984) has also provided two useful classifications of the values held by the social work profession. In his first framework Levy (1973, 1976) identified three primary groups of values according to social workers' conceptions of people, conceptions of the outcomes of work with people, and ways of dealing with people. The first of the three groups includes "preferred conceptions of people"

(Levy 1973:38; 1976:83), such as the belief in individuals' inherent worth and dignity, capacity and drive toward constructive change, mutual responsibility, need to belong, uniqueness, and common human needs. The second group includes "preferred outcomes for people" (Levy 1973:40; 1976:83), such as the belief in society's obligation to provide opportunities for individual growth and development, to provide resources and services to help people meet their needs and to avoid such problems as hunger, inadequate education or housing, illness, and discrimination, and to provide equal opportunity to participate in the molding of society. Levy (1973) argues that

> a value framework is necessary within which individual social workers as well as agencies and professional associations may make their action choices, whether in relation to clients or in relation to the social conditions and institutions which affect them or might affect them given a bit of organized impetus . . . . In spite of differences of opinion among social workers—sometimes based on religious or class orientations— many of these preferred outcomes are already shared. What is needed now is sufficient crystallization of a commitment to them to constitute the set of axiological rules which would serve as a series of guides, expectations, and criteria for evaluation against which the individual and collective actions of social workers may be weighed and appraised.
>
> (P. 41)

Levy's third group includes "preferred instrumentalities for dealing with people" (Levy 1973:41; 1976:83), such as the belief that people should be treated with respect and dignity, have the right to self-determination, be encouraged to participate in social change, and be recognized as unique individuals: "When a client comes to the social worker, he should be able to expect to be treated in certain ways and not in others simply on the basis of the values he should be free to ascribe to him—for example, non-judgmentally" (p. 42).

Levy's (1984) second framework for classifying social work values was based on a very different approach. Here Levy (1984:24–27) argues that core values for the profession ought to be derived from four broad and comprehensive categories of values: societal values; organizational and institutional values; professional values; and human service practice values. Below is a sampling of the particular values that fall within each category:

SOCIETAL VALUES

1. the physical, emotional, and mental health of all persons
2. the civil and legal rights of all persons
3. the social welfare of all persons
4. altruism—the accreditation of nonremunerative efforts in behalf of others and out of sheer concern and compassion for others when they experience need of one kind or another
5. the uniqueness and differences of all persons and distinguishable groups of persons, as well as their common traits and characteristics
6. the dignity of all persons
7. access to and opportunity for healthful and safe living conditions
8. maximal opportunities for all persons to use and extend their personal capacities and potentials
9. equal opportunity for education for all persons to the extent of their personal capacities, their interests, and their aspirations
10. equal opportunity for all persons for gainful and satisfying employment in accordance with their ability and availability
11. personal privacy
12. maximal opportunities for all persons for satisfying, constructive, and salutary relationships with family members and others in accordance with their own needs and preferences
13. opportunities for all persons for physical, cultural, and artistic enrichment and development
14. opportunities for all persons for responsible participation in the formulation and implementation of public and social policies and for the development of skills in relation to both

ORGANIZATIONAL AND INSTITUTIONAL VALUES

1. the existence of and timely, adequate, unbiased, nondiscriminatory, and democratic performance by organizations and institutions of their charted, legislated, or otherwise sanctioned functions
2. equal access for all persons and distinguishable groups of per-

sons to information regarding available organizational and institutional services, programs, and opportunities

3. equal access for all persons and distinguishable groups of persons to all available services, programs, and opportunities
4. the adaptation of organizations and institutions to the changing needs and aspirations of all persons for which they have been created and designed, and are by charter or other sanction responsible to serve, as well as others in need of their services, programs, and opportunities
5. fair, considerate, optimal, and creative use of organizational and institutional authority, resources, and opportunities
6. considerate and respectful treatment of all persons
7. maximum feasible participation and self-determination in all organizations and institutions for all persons served and affected by them
8. opportunities for satisfying and productive participation in neighborhood and community affairs and developments
9. organizational and institutional accountability for competent and ethical performance of sanctioned functions

PROFESSIONAL VALUES

1. the focus on human service rather than money getting or aggrandizement
2. fair, considerate, optimal, and creative use of professional power, authority, and opportunities in relation to clientele and others
3. accountability for competent, considerate, and ethical performance of professional functions
4. advocacy in relation to public and social policies concerned with or affecting their clienteles and their functions

HUMAN SERVICE PRACTICE VALUES

1. full, fair, competent, considerate, and ethical performance of professional functions
2. avoidance of personal abuse and exploitation of clients and others

3. respect for the personal dignity of clients and others
4. respect for the personal privacy of clients and others
5. honesty and credibility
6. maximum feasible participation and self-determination of clients in relation to their needs, their problems, their interests, and their aspirations
7. advocacy of public, social, organizational, and institutional policies in relation to the needs and aspirations of clients and others who share those needs and aspirations

As these typologies of social work values suggest, one of the most persistent themes in the value base of the profession concerns social workers' simultaneous commitment to individual well-being and to the welfare of the broader society. As I shall point out below in my discussion of ethical dilemmas, social workers sometimes face difficult choices between protection of clients' individual interests and protection of the broader community's interests. There is also tension between social workers' commitment to psychotherapeutic change in individuals and families and their commitment to social change related to such phenomena as inequality, discrimination, poverty, and justice (Reamer, 1992a; Rhodes 1986; Specht 1990, 1991; Wakefield 1988a, 1988b). Billups (1992:105–6), for example argues that the "reconstruction or reinvigoration of social work . . . requires the creative inclusiveness of the simultaneous dual focus on aiding people and improving their social institutions. This is not only an obligation of the profession as a whole (and here is where we become a bit radical), but of its individual practitioners as well, no matter their personal predilections or professional specializations."

• THE INFLUENCE OF SOCIAL WORK VALUES

A significant portion of the literature on social work values focuses on the need for social workers to clarify their own personal values. The assumption here is that practitioners' personal values exert considerable influence on their views of their clients, their intervention frameworks and strategies, and their definitions of successful or unsuccessful outcome. On occasion these personal values can prove troublesome, particularly if they conflict with laws or agency policy. Gordon (1965), for example, asserts that for a social worker

> to "value" something is to "prefer" it. A measure of the extent of a preference is what price, effort, or sacrifice one will make to obtain what is preferred, whether article, behavior, or state of affairs. To identify a value held by an individual or a society, therefore, requires a description of "what" is preferred and some measure of the extent of that preference, that is, the price in effort, money, or sacrifice the individual will pay to achieve his preference, or the provision a society will make or the positive or negative sanctions it will impose to enforce the preference.
>
> (P. 33)

Rokeach's (1973) classic definition of personal values in his *The Nature of Human Values* provides a useful way to conceptualize social workers' values: "an enduring belief that a specific mode or end state of existence is personally or socially preferable to an opposite or converse mode or end state of existence" (p. 5). From this perspective, it is important to distinguish among ultimate, proximate, and instrumental values. Ultimate values are broadly conceived and provide general guidance to a group's aims. In social work, values such as respect for persons, equality, and nondiscrimination constitute ultimate values. In one of the earliest and most ambitious studies of social work values, Pumphrey (1959:43–44) described the "ultimate professional values" that were widely embraced in that era and being transmitted to social workers:

1. Each human being should be regarded by all others as an object of infinite worth. He should be preserved in a state commensurate with his innate dignity and protected from suffering.
2. Human beings have large and as yet unknown capacities for developing both inner harmony and satisfaction and ability to make outward contributions to the development of others.
3. In order to realize his potentialities every human being must interact in giving and taking relationships with others, and has an equal right to opportunities to do so.
4. Human betterment is possible. Change, growth, movement,

progress, improvement are terms appearing constantly in social work value statements, inferring social work's confidence that individually and collectively, human beings have capacity to change. Thus change *per se* is not sought, but change toward personal and social ideals affirmed by the profession, is something "better."

5. Change in a positive direction, for individuals, groups, or organized societies, may be speeded by active and purposive assistance or encouragement from others. Change in a negative direction may be slowed or prevented by the intervention of others. In other words, "helping" is a process of demonstrated validity, and is a value to be respected in its own right.

6. The most effective changes cannot be imposed. Man's potentialities include his capacity to discover and direct his own destiny. This capacity, unless lacking or grossly impaired, must be respected.

7. Much concerning man is knowable. Human effort should be directed to constant search for enlarged understanding of man's needs and potentialities. What already has been discovered should be made available and utilized in devising means to enhance individual and social self-fulfillment.

8. The profession of social work is a group committed to the preservation and implementation of these values.

Proximate values, on the other hand, are more specific. In social work they might take the form of specific policies such as psychiatric patients' right to refuse certain types of treatment, welfare clients' right to a certain level of benefits, or ethnic minorities' right to quality health care. Finally, instrumental values are specifications of desirable means to valued ends. In social work, respecting clients' right to confidentiality, self-determination, and to give informed consent would be considered instrumental values (Johnson, 1989; Rokeach 1973).

Although some social work scholars have argued that the profession does not possess a unique value base (Meinert 1980), most acknowledge that an enduring value base has, indeed, emerged and evolved over time.[*] Gordon (1965) argues that several criteria must be met for social work to be able to claim a unique set of values for the profession. First, social work must embrace, "without fundamental contradiction," what the majority of the profession believes is right for social work and "thus command practitioners' preference without reservation" (p. 38). Second, such a set of values must also be "sufficiently basic and fundamental to remain useful over a substantial period of time" and provide the profession with "the highest possible sense of mission and suggest more immediate goals and objectives consistent with this purpose" (p. 38). Finally, this set of values must "accommodate and encourage substantial growth of knowledge in the service of those values and encourage the treatment of preferred but unconfirmed assertions as hypotheses whenever they contain any elements of confirmability" (p. 38). Ideally, as Levy (1973) argues, social work values would become,

> in their ultimate stage of development were that ever to be attained, a basis of expectation—a basis for predicting or assuming what social workers would do under given circumstances, as well as for determining whether there have been any deviations or offenses. . . . In that stance, the aim must be for all social workers to stand on similar value grounds whether they are practicing individually with clients or acting collectively on society and its institutions. . . . Such value grounds must continue to remain the object of scrupulous attention even if at intervals they may represent a challenge to consensus. Consensus about them, however, and their ultimate incorporation into the social work value system when they are sufficiently refined and crystallized, must continue to be the collective objective of the social work profession. (Pp. 37, 38)

• RECONCILING PERSONAL AND PROFESSIONAL VALUES

Several issues related to social work values deserve special emphasis. First, social workers occasionally face tension between their own personal values and those held by clients, employers, or the social

---

[*]Meinert (1980) offers one of the most extreme statements in the social work literature: "Social work values do not exist, and the myth that they do should not be perpetrated on students and the public any longer" (p. 15).

work profession itself. Inevitably, social workers will face such conflicts.

With regard to clients, social workers sometimes encounter clients whose values and behaviors seem immoral and abhorrent (Goldstein 1987; Hardman 1975). Social workers may have strong reactions to the ways in which some clients parent their children, violate the law, or treat spouses or partners. How social workers respond in these situations—whether they share their opinions with clients or withhold any form of judgment—depends on practitioners' views about the role of their own personal values and opinions. As Levy (1976) notes,

> It is also incumbent upon the social worker to crystallize his own value orientation with respect to planned change. Some of his dilemmas in professional practice relate to the congruity or incongruity between his value orientation and those of his clients. Their resolution will depend in great measure on the values by which he is guided in his practice and their correlation with the values that dictate his clients' responses to the personal or social change to which his practice is geared.   (P. 101)

The following case illustrates the difficulty that social workers sometimes encounter with regard to conflict between their own and clients' values.

CASE 2.2

Roger P. was a social worker at the Pikesville Community Mental Health Center. His agency has an employee assistance (EAP) contract with a local paper manufacturer. Under the contract, the agency provides counseling to company employees.

Alvin L., a worker at the factory, has been one of Roger P.'s clients for seven weeks. Alvin L. initially requested counseling because of his concern about the amount of alcohol he was consuming. Actually, Alvin L. was referred for counseling by his supervisor, who had become concerned about Alvin L.'s job performance.

Roger P. had received special training in alcoholism treatment. He and Alvin L. developed a plan to address Alvin L.'s drinking problem.

During one of the counseling sessions, Alvin L., who was married and the father of three children, casually mentioned that he was having an affair with a woman, a co-worker at the paper factory. Alvin L.

did not seem troubled by the affair and did not ask Roger P. for any help in relation to it.

However, Roger P. was deeply troubled by his client's secretive affair. Alvin L.'s behavior violated Roger P.'s own values. Roger P. was uncertain about whether to share his concerns with his client.

In contrast, in some instances the social worker's principal goal is to recognize that clients are struggling with their own value and ethical dilemmas and to help clients address them (Siporin 1992:77). Examples include clients who are overwhelmed by the moral aspects of decisions or actions related to having an affair, caring for an elderly parent, aborting a pregnancy, divorcing a spouse, and dealing with domestic violence (Goldstein 1987). As Goldstein (1987) argues, social workers must learn that clients' difficulties often contain an important moral dimension, that clients are often wrestling with the moral aspects of problems in their lives: "The conflict and anguish that clients experience frequently result from the consequences of serious moral and ethical dilemmas and from the absence of dependable solutions. Such dilemmas are related to critical choices that need to be made about special problems of living, including obligation and responsibility to others. . . . More to the point, it will be argued that an understanding of—and, therefore, practitioners' helpfulness to—clients who are in trouble or pain can be broadened and enriched by an awareness of the extent to which the condition of clients expresses a moral conflict" (pp. 181, 182). Thus to be helpful to clients, social workers must learn to view problems through an ethical lens—as well as a clinical lens—and to speak the language of ethics.

• CULTURAL AND RELIGIOUS VALUES

Value conflicts can arise especially when a social worker is providing services to a client whose cultural or religious beliefs support behaviors or activities (for example, concerning health care or the treatment of children) that run counter to the profession's or the worker's personal values (Hardman 1975; Hollis 1964; Loewenberg and Dolgoff 1992; Reamer 1990; Rhodes 1986; Timms 1983). Thus it is important for social workers to recognize the influence of their own and clients' religious and cultural values and beliefs. In a number of situations—for example, those involving a client's decision about abortion—religious beliefs exert considerable influence on clients' and practitioners' interpretation of and response to presenting problems (Canda 1988; Loewenberg 1988). Similarly, clients who seek social work counseling to address difficulties in their marriage may be influenced by religious beliefs. The social worker may conclude, after a number of treatment sessions, that it is unlikely the couple will be able to resolve their conflict and differences. The social worker may think it is appropriate for the couple to consider separation and divorce. The couple, however, may reject this possibility because their religion prohibits divorce.

Religious views can also have a more subtle influence on clients' and social workers' actions. Consider, for example, a case in which a social worker who is a community organizer encounters a group of Caucasian residents who express racist views about neighbors who are people of color. The social worker must decide whether to confront and challenge the racist comments directly or respect the individuals' right to express their views. It is conceivable that the social worker's reaction will be shaped in part by her strongly held religious beliefs and biblical injunctions concerning relationships among neighbors.

Social workers must also be mindful of possible conflicts between their personal values and clients' cultural or ethnic norms. This sort of conflict can be particularly troubling, as illustrated by the following example.

CASE 2.3

Carol S. was a social worker in the emergency room at Memorial Hospital. One afternoon an ambulance brought a nine-year-old Southeast Asian girl, whose family had recently immigrated to the United States, to the hospital. According to the emergency medical technician, the girl collapsed on her school playground during recess. The school nurse noticed a large growth behind the girl's right ear.

The emergency room physicians quickly examined the girl and began to prepare for emergency exploratory surgery and to biopsy the growth on the young girl's head.

Carol S. contacted the girl's parents at work and explained the situation. The parents rushed to the hospital, where one of the physicians explained the medical complications and planned procedures. The physician asked the parents to consent to the surgery and biopsy.

The parents refused to sign the consent form. Through an interpreter they explained to the physician and Carol S. that their culture prohibits any procedure involving penetration of the head. The parents said that, according to their traditional cultural beliefs, penetration of the head with a needle would release a spirit and that would have devastating effects on the child and other family members.

Social workers disagree about the extent to which they should share their own opinions and values with clients. Some practitioners argue that the worker's role is to provide a neutral sounding board for clients who are struggling with issues in their lives. From this perspective, the worker's values should not bias clients' efforts to resolve problems in their lives. A competing view, however, is that social workers should acknowledge with clients their own personal values, so that clients have a full understanding of the practitioner's possible biases. In spite of this enduring debate, there is considerable support in the profession for the sentiment enunciated years ago by Hollis (1964):

> Despite the fact that the concept of acceptance has been emphasized in casework for many years, it is still often misunderstood. It has to do with the worker's attitude—and hence communications—when the client is feeling guilty or for some reason unworthy of the worker's liking or respect. It is sometimes mistakenly assumed that the worker must be without an opinion about the rightness or wrongness, the advisability or inadvisability, of the client's activities. This would be impossible even if it were desirable . . . . Certainly the worker's *personal* values must not be translated into goals for the client. His *professional* norms and values, on the other hand, inevitably and quite appropriately become a factor in treatment objectives.   (Pp. 85, 208)

Value conflicts can also arise between social workers' values and those of the profession. A good example concerns the profession's position on sexual orientation. NASW has adopted a position that is embraced by most but not all of its members. According to the NASW *Code of Ethics* (1994), the social worker should not practice, condone, facilitate, or collaborate with any form of discrimination on the basis of sexual orientation (principle II.F.3). This is a policy that is troubling to a small number of social workers who, for personal and religious reasons, are opposed to homosexuality and gay rights. This value conflict can present difficult problems for social workers opposed to homosexuality and gay rights who are employed in settings that endorse the NASW policy. In these instances, practitioners must make difficult decisions about the nature of their obligations to their clients, their employers, the social work profession, and themselves. Consider the following case, for example.

CASE 2.4

Oliver M. was a caseworker at a family social service agency. His caseload included a number of students from a nearby college with which the agency had a contract to provide mental health services.

One of Oliver M.'s clients was a nineteen-year-old man, Jim P. Jim P. originally sought counseling because of his concern about anxiety symptoms he was experiencing.

At the beginning of one session, approximately three months after their relationship began, Jim P. disclosed to Oliver M. that he was beginning to realize that he was gay. Jim P. went on to explain that he was very confused about this discovery. He asked Oliver M. to help him sort out what was going on in his life and the nature of his sexual identity.

In his personal life, Oliver M. practices a religion that is firmly opposed to and condemns homosexuality. Yet, he knows that the family service agency for which he works subscribes to and actively supports the NASW Code of Ethics principle opposing discrimination on the basis of sexual orientation. Oliver M. knows that his agency's policies require him to avoid discriminating based on sexual orientation and to actively help clients who want to explore gay or lesbian life-styles. Oliver M. is eager to help Jim P., but he is confused about how to reconcile his own personal and religious beliefs with the agency's policy.

• VALUES AND THE DUTY TO AID

Another issue deserving special emphasis concerns social workers' values or beliefs related to the determinants of clients' problems. Social workers repeatedly make assumptions about the causes and malleability of clients' problems and shape intervention plans accordingly (McDermott 1975; Reamer 1983; Stalley 1975). For example, poverty may be viewed as the outcome of a grossly unjust society that harbors discrimination, exploitation of labor, and inadequate social support, or as the result of individual sloth and laziness. Similar contrast can be offered with respect to problems such as emotional distress, crime and delinquency, unemployment, and substance abuse. Whereas some social workers may assume that these problems are the result of structural determinants over which individuals have little if any control, others may assume that these problems are the by-products of individual choice (Reamer 1983).

Social workers' values in this regard are likely to have important bearing on their response and intervention. They may affect practitioners' beliefs about what kind of change is possible, how that change can be brought about, and about what kind of assistance individuals deserve. A social worker who believes that a criminal (for example, a convicted child abuser) chooses his unlawful behavior (the so-called free will view) may respond very differently from a social worker who believes that the criminal behaves as he does because of the compelling societal forces surrounding him (the determinist view). These social workers may also have different sentiments about the extent to which the offender deserves help.

Differences in social work educators' views on the free will–determinism debate are reflected in the profession's literature. Ephross and Reisch (1982), for example, found clear differences in the ideological and value orientations of introductory social work texts' authors:

> there are clear differences among the books reviewed as to social, political and economic content, and it seems that these differences are quite important for the education of professional social workers. In a sense, one can distribute these introductory textbooks over an ideological spectrum. The temptation is to visualize such a spectrum as covering a range from "Left" to "Right." These terms are used a bit unconventionally here; they do not imply that the authors adhere to all of the political views commonly associated with Left or Right positions. Rather, the idea is of a scale whose polar points describe conceptions of the relationship between societal forces and individual experiences. The Left pole, then, encompasses the position that individuals' lives are circumscribed and heavily influenced, if not determined, by political, eco-

nomic, and institutional patterns within society. The Right pole attributes to individuals and families a great deal of leeway to determine their individual and interpersonal experiences.   (P. 280)

• CHALLENGING SOCIAL WORK'S VALUES

Another key issue concerns debate about the legitimacy of some contemporary social work values. Although social work's values have been traditionally embraced throughout the profession's history, it would be a mistake to conclude that they have been entirely static and unchallenged. Siporin (1982, 1983, 1989), for example, has expressed concern about what he believes may be excessive tolerance of nonnormative, libertarian views that may lead to abandonment of personal and social responsibility. For Siporin (1989), social work is essentially a "moral enterprise" (p. 44) but an enterprise that has lost some of its moral bearings in recent years, due largely to the influence of the medical model and proprietary or entrepreneurial models of practice: "The net effect of these trends is that they have made for an erosion of social work morality, and of its ethical commitments. They have disrupted the balances that existed about conflicting values, created partisan dissension among social workers about the issues at stake, and have fragmented the consensual unity of the social work profession" (Siporin 1989:50).

It is especially important for social workers to recognize that there is an essentially "political" aspect to their identification and endorsement of core social work values. Social work emerged in the context of Western capitalism, and the profession's values, particularly those focused on individual worth and dignity, self-determination, and distributive justice, have been influenced by Western political views (Popple 1992; Rhodes 1986). In important respects, social work values reflect a particular political ideology that ultimately influences the nature of practice. For example, social workers in a capitalist society who support and attempt to promote clients' right to self-determination may be embracing a form of individualism that runs counter to values found in other political contexts, such as a socialist society that places greater emphasis on collectivism. Similarly, the rights to privacy and to give informed consent that are now so prominent in Western society may seem quite foreign in cultures that have fundamentally different views of boundaries between people and those in authority positions.

• FROM VALUES TO ACTION

Familiarity with social work values is certainly important in and of itself. After all, practitioners' belief in and endorsement of social work values are likely to provide the kind of inspiration needed to sustain a meaningful career. In addition, a firm understanding of social work values has a more instrumental purpose: to provide conceptually based and ethically sound guides to actual practice. If practice principles are to be expressions of the profession's values, social workers must be able to identify and appreciate the connections between the profession's value base and the practice principles that influence practitioners' day-to-day work. As Perlman (1976) observed,

> A value has small worth except as it is moved, or is moveable, from believing into doing, from verbal affirmation into action. A value— defined here as a cherished belief, an emotionally invested preference or desideratum—has small worth if it can not be transmuted from idea of conviction into some form, quality, or direction of behavior. The power of a value lies in its governance and guidance for action. . . . Social work's specialness, then, is at the level of proximate instrumental values. Our specialness lies in the particular knowledges, skills, and resources that we have developed or organized by which the over-arching values may be drawn upon, reached for, and actualized.
>
> (Pp. 381, 382)

In an unusually ambitious essay on the implications of social work values, Lewis (1972) suggests that there is a direct connection between social work values and the way practice is conducted. For Lewis, a number of key social work practice principles are derived directly from core values related to trust and distributive justice. According to Lewis, trust is an essential ingredient in social work practice, with respect to both the relationship between practitioners and clients and the belief among clients that they will have fair and equal access to services:

> In a helping relationship, trust functions to support dependence without fear of self-effacement; to inculcate an expectation of joint, mutually beneficial effort—despite differences in kind, frequency, and

intensity of involvement; to reinforce the belief that assigned obligations will be fulfilled and cooperative effort sustained, reassuring participants who might otherwise fear betrayal. Trust serves as an organizing device that facilitates the communication of a moral tone to a helping relationship. . . . It is crucial for the social work profession to
develop and support practice principles that will instill trust in the helping relationships associated with its services.   (P. 406)

From this view of the key role of the value of trust, Lewis (1972:406–7)
derives a series of social work practice principles concerning fair and
equal access to services. These principles are highlighted here because
they provide an unusually good example of a social work scholar's
attempt to draw direct connections between core values and practice
principles.

1. The conditions that determine the availability of service
   should be uniformly applicable to all partaking of it. Devia-
   tions from these conditions are justified only when they can
   be shown to be to everyone's advantage.
2. No more should be asked of the recipient in a service relationship than is necessary and sufficient to transact the
   intended service. Involuntary involvement of a recipient in
   service for his own protection or that of others should provide
   for the defense of the recipient's rights by persons and procedures not under the control of the service source or an agent
   pressing for such involvement.
3. The restraints implicit in the conditions for offering or making
   claims for service should not be posed as a threat. The risks
   and obligations entailed in a service relationship should not
   unfairly burden any one participant.
4. The offer of essential concrete services should include alternatives for the intended beneficiary. Lacking alternatives the
   offer should be made as a matter of right, as free of condi-
   tioning tests as possible.
5. The recipient of service should have the opportunity to experience his role in its provision as a test of its fairness and not be
   expected to assume such fairness as a precondition for service.
6. The worker should seek to enlarge on choices available to the

recipient, including those proposed by the recipient and those newly developed in the course of rendering the service.

7. Potential recipients should be informed about programs for which they are eligible. Participating recipients should know when resources sought and promised are no longer on hand. Failure to utilize a service or sustained participation in a program of service ought not be based on ignorance of the facts concerning the availability of resources.

Lewis's (1972) second core value, from which he also derives several practice principles, is distributive justice. Drawing directly on the oft-cited work of the philosopher John Rawls, author of the modern classic *A Theory of Justice* (1971), Lewis argues that, along with trust, distributive justice is an essential component of ethical practice because it entails attempts to improve the living conditions of those who are most vulnerable:

> Clients of social service programs are among the most disadvantaged persons in our society. Social workers employed in these programs normally serve such disadvantaged clients directly or work with persons interested in promoting services for them. A principal moral justification for professional social work practice is therefore to be found in the dedication of the practitioner to the improvement of the circumstances and expectations of these clients. A helping profession not based in a morality inspiring a just order risks encouraging a practice that promotes an unjust one.
>
> Distributive justice, while by no means the whole of a just order, is a particular concern of a helping profession serving the disadvantaged.
>
> (P. 410)

The specific practice principles that Lewis (1972:411–12) derives from this perspective on the value of distributive justice are as follows:

1. The profession and its associated institutions must, in the work and attitudes of their constituents, combat unfair discriminatory practices or be judged as perpetrating the disadvantages they entail.

2. In choosing program goals and purposes, it should be assumed that ability and motivation among the disadvantaged are more widespread than is opportunity.

3. Institutionalized restrictions which limit opportunities, as

well as the personal shortcomings of the client which may curtail his options, are legitimate targets for change.

4. Opportunities to participate in the development of programs, in the formulation of policies and procedures, as well as in the practice decisions directly affecting their lives, must be afforded the disadvantaged as a minimal expectation of organizations and practices intended to help them.

As Lewis's discussion illustrates, one of social workers' most challenging tasks is to convert conceptually based values, which are often worded abstractly, into concrete guidelines for day-to-day practice. As Williams (1968:283) concludes, "Values serve as criteria for selection in action. When most explicit and fully conceptualized, values become criteria for judgment, preference, and choice."

A second instrumental reason for social workers to be clear about professional values is that, in the final analysis, practitioners' judgments about the relative importance of different values will influence their decisions when professional duties and obligations conflict, the principal ingredients of an ethical dilemma (Frankel 1959:349). Levy (1976:14, 79) makes this observation succinctly: "Ethics, in effect, is values in operation. . . . On the basis of these values, social workers can decide on or plan their professional moves and evaluate them afterwards. These values can serve as a basis for regulatory and grievance procedures, designed to encourage ethical social work practice and to adjudicate charges of deviation."

In this chapter I discussed the nature of social work values and their influence on the profession's mission and intervention approaches. As I shall show in the next chapter, conflicts among these core values in social work practice periodically produce very complex ethical dilemmas requiring difficult decisions. Throughout the discussion that follows I shall illustrate how the various perspectives on social work values I have just reviewed have a direct bearing on practitioners' ethical decisions.

③ ETHICAL DILEMMAS AND DECISION MAKING

A FRAMEWORK

• • •

CASE 3.1

Hinda B., a social worker, was clinical director at the Mt. Washington Women's Shelter. The shelter provides temporary housing and counseling for women who have been battered by their partners. The shelter has room for eight women and their children.

Mary M. and her two children have been at the shelter for six weeks. This is the family's third stay at the shelter. Mary M. reports that she has been battered by her husband "off and on for about two years. He has a real serious drinking problem. When he's sober, he's not too bad. But when he gets that whiskey in him, all of us have to watch out."

Mary M. is recovering from a broken jaw she suffered as a result of the most recent beating at the hands of her husband. She says she is afraid for herself and her children.

At a staff meeting one afternoon Hinda B. says that she has a real problem with this case and needs some help:

> Mary says she knows she's got to get away from her husband. She knows he has a very serious drinking problem and that he poses a real threat to her and the kids. But she also says that she still loves her husband and hopes he will change. I'm afraid she'll go back to him. This is what we're working on.
>
> The immediate problem, however, is that Mary just confided in me that for the last three years she has been committing welfare fraud. I mean big-time welfare fraud. Mary told me she's been collecting welfare checks under three different names and that she thinks she has saved enough money for her and the kids to move out on their own.

What do I do? Am I obligated to report this to the public welfare department, or is this confidential information? Should I confront Mary? Or should I overlook this because it may be Mary's only way out of the abusive situation with her husband?

This case provides a good illustration of an ethical dilemma in social work. As discussed earlier, an ethical dilemma occurs when a social worker encounters conflict among professional duties and values and must decide which take precedence. In this instance, the social worker is torn between her inclination to respect her client's right to confidentiality and her wish to protect her client from harm. The social worker is also concerned about the illegal nature of her client's activity.

Moral philosophers and ethicists often refer to these situations as hard cases. These are cases where one is faced with a difficult choice between conflicting duties, or what the philosopher W. D. Ross (1930) referred to as conflicting *prima facie duties*—duties that, when considered by themselves, we are inclined to perform. For example, ordinarily social workers want to respect clients' right to confidentiality *and* protect them from harm. In some situations, however, it may seem difficult to do both simultaneously. Eventually, social workers must choose what Ross (1930) calls an *actual* duty from among conflicting prima facie duties.

Thus hard cases are those where prima facie duties clash, where social workers must choose between two incompatible but ordinarily appealing options or between two incompatible and ordinarily unappealing options. Either way, we seem to have to sacrifice something, and our choice sometimes reduces to what Popper (1966) refers to as the "minimization of suffering."

Many ethical issues in social work are not this complicated. We know, for example, that we should ordinarily tell clients the truth. We also know that we should avoid actions that are likely to injure clients. These are obvious duties, and most of the time they do not conflict. However, occasionally such duties do conflict, for example, when telling clients the truth (perhaps as a candid response to a direct question about the status of a client's mental health) is likely to exacerbate their emotional suffering. These are hard cases (Reamer 1989).

In this chapter I shall explore the nature of ethical dilemmas in social work practice and examine how several tools—including codes of ethics, ethical principles, and ethical theory—can help practitioners make ethical decisions. In chapters 4 and 5 I shall focus on a wide range of ethical dilemmas in more depth and apply these decision-making tools to them.

• CODES OF ETHICS

Nearly all professions have developed codes of ethics to assist practitioners who face ethical dilemmas, most within the past century. Actually, codes of ethics serve several functions in addition to providing general guidance related to ethical dilemmas; they also protect the profession from outside regulation, establish norms related to the profession's mission, and enunciate standards that can help adjudicate allegations of misconduct (Welfel and Lipsitz 1984; cited in Corey, Corey, Callanan 1988:5).

Until recently, the most visible guides to social workers' ethical decisions have been professional codes of ethics (Reamer 1995a). There are several social work codes of ethics, including the NASW Code of Ethics, the Code of Ethics of the National Association of Black Social Workers, the Code of Ethics of the National Federation of Societies for Clinical Social Work, and the Code of Ethics of the Canadian Association of Social Workers.

The best-known ethics code to which social workers in the United States subscribe is the NASW Code of Ethics. There have been several versions of the code, reflecting changes in the broader culture and in social work's own standards.

An experimental code of ethics, published in 1920, has been traced to Mary Richmond (Pumphrey 1959), making it the earliest known attempt to formulate such a code. Although several other social work organizations formulated draft codes during the early years of the profession's history—for example, the American Association for Organizing Family Social Work and several chapters of the American Association of Social Workers—it was not until 1947 that the latter group, the largest organization of social workers of that era, adopted a formal code (Johnson 1955). In 1960, NASW adopted its first code of ethics, five years after the association was formed.

The 1960 Code of Ethics consisted of a series of proclamations concerning, for example, every social worker's duty to give precedence to professional responsibility over personal interests; to respect the privacy of clients; to give appropriate professional service in public emergencies; and to contribute knowledge, skills, and support to programs of human welfare. First-person statements (such as "I give precedence to my professional responsibility over my personal interests" and "I respect the privacy of the people I serve") were preceded by a preamble that set forth social workers' responsibility to uphold humanitarian ideals, maintain and improve social work service, and develop the philosophy and skills of the profession. In 1967 a principle pledging nondiscrimination was added to the proclamations.

However, soon after the adoption of the 1960 code, NASW members began to express concern about its level of abstraction, its scope and usefulness for resolving ethical dilemmas, and its provisions for handling ethics complaints about practitioners and agencies (McCann and Cutler 1979). In 1977 the NASW Delegate Assembly established a task force to revise the profession's code of ethics and to enhance its relevance to practice. The revised code, enacted in 1979 and implemented in 1980, included six sections of brief, unannotated principles preceded by a preamble setting forth the general purpose of the code, the enduring social work values upon which it was based, and a declaration that the code's principles provided standards for the enforcement of ethical practices among social workers.

The 1979 code was revised twice. In 1990 several principles related to solicitation of clients and fee setting were modified following an inquiry into NASW policies by the U.S. Federal Trade Commission, begun in 1986, concerning possible "restraint of trade." As a result of the inquiry, principles in the code were revised in order to remove prohibitions concerning solicitation of clients from colleagues or one's agency and to modify wording related to accepting compensation for making a referral. NASW also entered into a consent agreement with the Federal Trade Commission concerning the issues raised by the inquiry.

In 1992 the president of NASW appointed a national task force, chaired by the author, to suggest several specific revisions of the code. In 1993, based on this task force's recommendations, the NASW Delegate Assembly voted to amend the code to include several new principles related to the problem of social worker impairment and the problem of inappropriate boundaries between social workers and clients, colleagues, students, and so on (these revisions took effect in 1994). The problem of impairment concerns instances when social workers' own problems interfere with their professional functioning; the problem of inappropriate boundaries concerns the need for social workers to avoid exploitative or harmful relationships with clients and others with whom they work. Also in 1993 the NASW Delegate Assembly passed a resolution authorizing substantial revision of the association's code of ethics (this task is in process).

The sections of the current NASW code set forth principles related to social workers' conduct and comportment, and to ethical responsibility to clients, colleagues, employers and employing organizations, the social work profession, and society. The code's principles are both prescriptive (with specific regard to the case involving Mary M., for example, "The social worker should respect the privacy of clients and hold in confidence all information obtained in the course of professional service," and "The social worker's primary responsibility is to clients") and proscriptive (for example, "The social worker should not participate in, condone, or be associated with dishonesty, fraud, deceit, or misrepresentation"). A number of the code's principles are concrete and specific (for example, "The social worker should under no circumstances engage in sexual activities with clients," and "The social worker should respect confidences shared by colleagues in the course of their professional relationships and transactions"), whereas others are more abstract, asserting ethical ideals (for example, "The social worker should promote the general welfare of society," and "The social worker should uphold and advance the values, ethics, knowledge, and mission of the profession").

The wide range of principles in the code indicates that it was designed to serve several purposes. The more abstract, idealistic principles concerning social justice and general welfare provide social workers with important aspirations, as opposed to enforceable standards. Other principles, however, set forth specific rules with which practitioners are expected to comply, violations of which would provide grounds for filing a formal ethics complaint. In addition, a major purpose of the code is to provide social workers with principles to help them resolve ethical dilemmas encountered in practice.

Unfortunately, many social workers do not find the NASW Code of Ethics, or any other social work code of ethics, very helpful when faced with complicated ethical issues. Although the NASW code addresses a number of important topics—such as confidentiality, sexual misconduct, and client exploitation—it does not provide concrete guidance in those instances when professional duties conflict. In the Mary M. case, for instance, the principle concerning clients' right to confidentiality conflicts with the principle prohibiting social workers from being associated with dishonesty, fraud, and deceit. As McCann and Cutler (1979) noted in their widely circulated critique of the code,

> The sources of dissatisfaction are widespread and have involved practitioners, clients, chapter committees, and, in particular, those persons directly engaged in the adjudication of complaints in which unethical behavior is charged. At a time of growing specialization and organizational differentiation, a variety of issues have surfaced centering on the nature of the code itself, its level of abstraction and ambiguity, its scope and usefulness, and its provision for the handling of ethical complaints.
>
> (P. 5)

Of course, it would be unreasonable to expect a code of ethics to provide explicit guidance in every instance when professional duties clash, creating an ethical dilemma (Corey, Corey, and Callanan 1988:5). Codes of ethics are written for several purposes, including the inspiration of professions' members, to set forth general ethical norms for professions, and to provide professions with a moral compass; too much specificity would overwhelm the code with detail (Kultgen 1982). As the preamble to the 1994 edition of the NASW code states,

> In itself, this code does not represent a set of rules that will prescribe all the behaviors of social workers in all the complexities of professional life. Rather, it offers general principles to guide conduct, and the judicious appraisal of conduct, in situations that have ethical implications. It provides the basis for making judgments about ethical actions before and after they occur. Frequently, the particular situation determines the ethical principles that apply and the manner of their application. In such cases, not only the particular ethical principles are taken into immediate consideration, but also the entire code and its spirit. Specific appli-

cations of ethical principles must be judged within the context in which they are being considered. (P. v)

• THE RESOLUTION OF ETHICAL DILEMMAS

As I discussed in chapter 1, it is only recently that social work, as well as most other professions, has devoted substantial attention to the subject of ethical dilemmas. Especially since the mid-1970s there has been a significant increase in education, training, and scholarship on the subject.

One of the more recent trends in professional education and training is to introduce students and practitioners to ethical theories and principles that may help them analyze and resolve ethical dilemmas (Callahan and Bok 1980). These include theories and principles of what moral philosophers call *metaethics* and *normative ethics.* Metaethics concerns the meaning of ethical terms or language and the derivation of ethical principles and guidelines. Typical metaethical questions include: What do we mean by the terms *right* and *wrong,* or *good* and *bad*? What criteria should we use to judge whether someone has engaged in unethical conduct? How should we go about formulating ethical principles to guide individuals who struggle with moral choices?

Some philosophers, known as *cognitivists,* believe that it is possible to identify objective criteria for determining what is ethically right and wrong, or good and bad. Others, however, question whether this is possible. These so-called *noncognitivists* argue that such criteria are necessarily subjective, and any ethical principles we create ultimately reflect our own biases and personal preferences.

Like philosophers, social workers disagree about the objectivity of ethical principles. Some, for example, believe that it is possible to establish universal principles upon which to base ethical decisions and practice, perhaps in the form of a sanctioned code of ethics or "God-given" tenets. Proponents of this point of view are known as *absolutists.* Others—known as *relativists*—reject this point of view, arguing instead that ethical standards depend on cultural practices, political climate, contemporary norms and moral standards, and other contextual considerations (Hardman 1975).

The debate between absolutists and relativists has important bearing on our examination of ethical issues in social work (Reamer 1990). If one believes that conclusions concerning ethical values and guidelines reflect only opinions about the rightness or wrongness of specific actions and that objective standards do not exist, there is no reason even to attempt to determine whether certain actions are in fact right or wrong in the ethical sense. One opinion would be considered as valid as another. In the Mary M. case, for example, the opinion of a social worker who believes that Mary M.'s welfare fraud is morally unacceptable and must be reported to authorities would be as legitimate as the opinion of another practitioner who believes that the welfare fraud should not be reported because of the special circumstances in the case (the need for Mary M. to support herself and her two children). Fraud, or deliberate violation of the law, would not be considered wrong *absolutely*.

However, if one believes that absolute ethical standards do or can in principle exist, it is sensible to attempt to identify the content of these standards and to subsequently judge the rightness and wrongness of particular actions according to them.

The popularity of relativism and absolutism has waxed and waned throughout the ages. Belief in absolutism has generally coincided with belief in the dogmas of orthodox religion; absolutism has tended to fade, with accompanying increases in the popularity of relativism, during times of widespread religious skepticism. In recent years, however, there has been a declining tolerance of relativism and a wish for ethical standards that would serve as clear moral guides for individuals who face complex ethical dilemmas.

The quest to provide a rational justification of principles that would enable people to distinguish between right and wrong has been, without question, the most challenging problem confronting moral philosophers. Philosophers such as Plato, Aristotle, Immanuel Kant, and John Stuart Mill have devoted considerable effort to the task. Others, such as Hume, Marx, and Nietzsche, have questioned whether efforts to derive ethical principles are appropriate or worthwhile. Nonetheless, many modern philosophers have made ambitious attempts to outline ethical standards and principles to guide individuals' decisions. As Gewirth (1978a:ix) observed,

In a century when the evils that man can do to man have reached unparalleled extremes of barbarism and tragedy, the philosophic concern with rational justification in ethics is more than a quest for certainty. It is also an attempt to make coherent sense of persons' deepest convictions about the principles that should govern the ways they treat one another. For not only do the divergences among philosophers reflect different views about the logical difficulties of justification in ethics; the conflicting principles they uphold, whether presented as rationally grounded or not, have drastically different implications about the right modes of individual conduct and social institutions.

Concern about the need for clear ethical standards in social work has also increased significantly in recent years. During the early years of the profession many social workers embraced and were guided by strong beliefs in Christian values. One might even argue that in later years the widespread belief in Christian values was replaced by widespread belief in secular values, in particular, those associated with the period commonly known as the "psychiatric deluge" (Woodroofe 1962).

Beginning in the 1960s, however, relativism experienced a surge of popularity in social work. Influenced in part by the unsettling effects of the civil disturbances and social unrest of that decade and by the rise of skepticism about conventional social institutions and standards, significant numbers of social workers began to question the validity of professional codes of ethics that suggested specific standards for judging right and wrong. The result was a tendency on the part of many social workers to resist espousing specific ethical standards and values and especially the temptation to impose any particular value or values upon clients, whether they be individuals, families, or communities (Hardman 1975; Siporin 1982). What had been described in earlier years as "deviance," such as single-parent families, the use of drugs, and certain sexual mores, began to be more respected or at least tolerated by many social workers as reflections of life-styles and preferences of certain age and ethnic groups that were merely "different" from those of conventional society. Social workers experienced a dramatic shift in their threshold of tolerance for unfamiliar ways of life.

It was during the 1960s that social work, along with many other professions, found itself in the midst of its closest brush with relativism.

Since this era, however, there has been a gradual resurgence of interest in the development of ethical standards. The interest in values and ethical principles has not concerned the morality of the preferences and life-styles of clients, as it did in earlier chapters of the profession's history. Rather, the concern has been focused on the ethics of practitioners—on the justifications provided for intervening or failing to intervene in clients' lives, the acceptability of specific forms and methods of intervention, and the criteria used for distributing services and resources. The willingness of practitioners to tolerate relativism and the absence of standards as they relate to their own actions and decisions has diminished significantly. Although social workers tend to acknowledge that absolute, objective ethical standards can perhaps not be derived, there is widespread belief that the actions they perform and the decisions they make frequently have ethical content that warrants thoughtful attention. The belief that relativism provides an acceptable strategy for making difficult ethical decisions has grown somewhat anachronistic. As Emmet (1962:169) has stated in her article on ethical issues in social work, "Part of our trouble is the prevalence of the idea that moral standards are personal, subjective and emotional, and so are not matters into which intelligence enters, and for which reasons, maybe good reasons, can be given and communicated to other people."

• AN OVERVIEW OF ETHICAL THEORY

In contrast to metaethics, which is often very abstract, normative ethics tends to be of special concern to social work because of its immediate relevance to practice. Normative ethics consists of attempts to apply ethical theories and principles to actual ethical dilemmas. Such guidance is especially useful when social workers face conflicts among duties they are ordinarily inclined to perform. Thus in the Mary M. example that opens this chapter, the social worker must choose between respecting her client's right to confidentiality concerning the welfare fraud—which may ultimately prevent further abuse and domestic violence—and taking steps to prevent continued dishonesty and fraud.

Theories of normative ethics are generally grouped under two main headings. *Deontological* theories (from the Greek *deontos*, "of the obligatory") are those that claim that certain actions are inherently right or wrong, or good and bad, without regard for their consequences. Thus a deontologist—the best-known being Immanuel Kant, the eighteenth-century German philosopher—might argue that telling the truth is inherently right, and thus social workers should never lie to clients, even if it appears that lying might be more beneficial to the parties involved. The same might be said about keeping promises made to colleagues, upholding contracts with vendors, obeying a mandatory reporting law, and so on. For deontologists, rules, rights, and principles are sacred and inviolable. The ends do not necessarily justify the means, particularly if they require violating some important rule, right, principle, or law (Frankena 1973; Hancock 1974; Williams 1972). In the Mary M. case, a deontologist might argue that the social worker is obligated to keep the promise she made to her client to keep information shared by the client (regarding the welfare fraud) confidential.

One well-known problem with this deontological perspective is that it is often easy to imagine conflicting arguments using similar language about inherently right (or wrong) actions. Thus one can imagine a deontologist arguing that all human beings have an inherent right to life and that it would be immoral for a social worker to be involved in an act of assisted suicide, for example, with a client who is gravely ill and wants to end his life. However, another deontologist might argue that social workers have an inherent obligation to respect clients' right to self-determination as long as the actions involved are voluntary and informed and, therefore, that it is permissible for social workers to be involved in an act of assisted suicide. In the Mary M. case, it is not hard to imagine social workers who would disagree with the conclusion that Hinda B. has an obligation to keep her promise to Mary M. to keep information shared by her client confidential, arguing instead that there is a deontological obligation to prevent or disclose deliberate violations of the law.

The second major group of theories, *teleological* theories (from the Greek *teleios*, "brought to its end or purpose"), takes a very different approach to ethical choices. From this point of view, the rightness of any action is determined by the goodness of its *consequences*. For teleologists, it is naive to make ethical choices without weighing potential consequences. To do otherwise is to engage in what the philosopher Smart (1971) refers to as "rule worship." Hence, from this perspective (sometimes known as *consequentialism*) the responsible strategy entails an attempt to anticipate the possible outcomes of various courses of action and to weigh their relative merits (Frankena 1973; Hancock 1974). Hence, the social worker in the Mary M. case should carry out a thorough analysis of the likely costs and benefits that would result from the possible courses of action. That is, what are the costs and benefits involved in respecting her client's right to confidentiality concerning the welfare fraud? How do these costs and benefits compare to those involved in preventing continued dishonesty and fraud?

There are two major teleological schools of thought: egoism and utilitarianism. *Egoism* is a form of teleology that is not typically found in social work; according to this point of view, when faced with conflicting duties people should maximize their *own* good and enhance their self-interest. Thus Hinda B.'s decision as a social worker should be determined by what would ultimately benefit her the most or be in her best interest, for example, what would minimize her aggravation in the case, her own legal liability, and her possible conflict with her client.

In contrast, *utilitarianism*, which holds that an action is right if it promotes the maximum good, has historically been the most popular teleological theory and has, at least implicitly, served as justification for many decisions made by social workers. According to the classic form of utilitarianism—as originally formulated by the English philosophers Jeremy Bentham, in the eighteenth century, and John Stuart Mill, in the nineteenth century—when faced with conflicting duties one should perform the action that will produce the greatest good. In principle, then, a social worker should engage in a calculus to determine which set of consequences will produce the greatest good. Thus in the Mary M. case, a utilitarian might argue that respecting the client's right to confidentiality in order to protect the client and her children from harm is justifiable in order to bring about a greater good (assuming, of course, that protecting clients from bodily harm is considered more compelling than preventing welfare fraud). Similarly, a strict utilitarian might argue that tearing down a section of a town's dilapidated housing and displacing its residents is justifiable if it leads to economic revival of the entire neighborhood.

One form of utilitarian theory is known as *good-aggregative utilitarianism*, according to which the most appropriate action is that which promotes the greatest total or aggregate good. Second, there is *locus-aggregative utilitarianism*, according to which the most appropriate action is that which promotes the greatest good *for the greatest number*, considering not only the total quantity of goods produced but also the number of people to whom the goods are distributed (Gewirth 1978b). The distinction between these two forms of utilitarianism is important in social work when one considers, for example, whether to distribute a fixed amount of public assistance in a way that tends to produce the greatest aggregate satisfaction (which might entail dispensing relatively large sums to relatively few people) or produces the greatest satisfaction for the greatest number (which might entail dispensing smaller sums of money to a larger number of people).

One problem with utilitarianism is that this framework, like deontology, sometimes can be used to justify competing options. For example, whereas one utilitarian might argue that protecting Hinda B.'s client from harm (future battering) by overlooking the welfare fraud would result in the greatest good—when the benefits of protection of harm are weighed against the benefits of preventing welfare fraud—another utilitarian, who assigns different weights to the possible benefits and costs involved in the options in the Mary M. case, or who might enter different variables into this complex equation, might argue that the harm involved in welfare fraud outweighs the possible risk to the client.

Some philosophers argue that it is important and helpful to distinguish between *act* and *rule* utilitarianism (Gorovitz 1971). According to act utilitarianism, the rightness of an action is determined by the goodness of the consequences produced in *that* individual case, or by that particular act. One does not need to look beyond the implications of this one instance. By contrast, rule utilitarianism takes into account the long-run consequences likely to be produced if one generalizes from the case at hand, or treats it as a precedent. Thus an act utilitarian might justify interfering with Hinda B.'s client's right to confidentiality if it can be demonstrated that this would result in greater good (for example, the large amounts of money saved by preventing future welfare fraud would be used to assist many other vulnerable individuals). A rule utilitarian, however, might argue that the precedent established by this breach of a client's right to confidentiality would generate more harm than good, regardless of the benefits produced in this one case. That is, a rule utilitarian might argue that the precedent might undermine clients' trust in social workers, particularly regarding social workers' promises to respect confidentiality, thus limiting social work's effectiveness as a profession.

Another illustration of the distinction between act and rule utilitarianism concerns the well-known mandatory reporting laws related to child abuse and neglect. According to these statutes, now found in every state in the United States, social workers and other mandated reporters are required to notify child welfare or protective service authorities whenever they suspect child abuse or neglect. As I pointed out in the Robinson case introduced in chapter 1, circumstances sometimes arise that lead social workers to conclude that a client's best interests would not be served by complying with the mandatory reporting law. In these instances, social workers believe that more harm than good would result if they obeyed the law. What these social workers are claiming, at least implicitly, is that it is permissible to violate a law when it appears that greater good would result.

This is a classic example of act utilitarianism. An act utilitarian might justify violating a mandatory reporting law if it can be demonstrated convincingly that this would result in greater good (for example, if the social worker is able to show that she would not be able to continue working with the family if she reported the suspected abuse or neglect and that her continuing to work with the family offers the greatest potential for preventing further neglect or abuse). A rule utilitarian, however, might argue that the precedent established by this deliberate violation of the law would generate more harm than good, regardless of the benefits produced by this one particular violation. A rule utilitarian might argue that the precedent established by this case might encourage other social workers to take matters into their own hands rather than report suspected abuse or neglect to local protective service officials and that this would, in the long run, be more harmful than helpful.

A key problem with utilitarianism, then, is that different people are likely to consider different factors and weigh them differently, as a result of their different life experiences, values, political ideologies, and so on. In the Mary M. case, one social worker might place considerable emphasis on the importance of client privacy, whereas another practitioner might place more value on the importance of respect for the law.

In addition, when taken to the extreme, classic utilitarianism can justify trampling on the rights of a vulnerable minority in order to benefit the majority. In principle, a callous utilitarian social worker could argue that the social costs produced by policies to protect the civil rights of mentally ill people (for example, extensive competency evaluations prior to involuntary commitment) are outweighed by the public benefit (removal of "public nuisances" from the streets). In light of countless instances throughout history in which the rights of minorities and other oppressed groups have been insensitively violated to benefit the majority, social workers have good reason to be concerned about such strict applications of utilitarian principles.

Perhaps the best-known proposed alternative to utilitarianism is presented in a book by the contemporary philosopher John Rawls (1971), *A Theory of Justice*. Rawls's theory, which has profound implications for social workers, assumes that individuals who are formulating a moral principle by which to be governed are in an "original position" of equality and that each individual is unaware of his or her own attributes and status that might produce some advantage or disadvantage. Under this "veil of ignorance" it is assumed that individuals will derive a moral framework, which Rawls calls the "difference principle," that ultimately protects the least advantaged based upon a ranked ordering of priorities. Rawls also makes another distinction that is important for social workers to consider: the distinction between *natural* duties—fundamental obligations such as helping others in dire need or not injuring other people—and *supererogatory* actions—actions that are commendable and praiseworthy, but not obligatory.

Rawls's work introduced a concept that has become critically important in ethics and in social work: the rank-ordering of values and ethical duties. For Rawls and many other moral philosophers, ethical decisions often reduce to difficult judgments about what values or duties will take precedence over others. Should a client's right to privacy or the need to protect a client from harm take precedence over the need to respect the law and avoid being associated with fraud? To use Ross's (1930) terminology, which of various conflicting prima facie duties should take precedence, that is, which should be one's *actual* duty?

Other philosophers have also offered theories about the most appropriate way to rank-order conflicting duties. The philosopher Donagan (1977) argues in *The Theory of Morality* that when choosing among duties that may result in harm, one should do that which results in the least harm. Popper (1966) calls this the minimization of suffering, and Smart (Smart and Williams 1973) calls this negative utilitarianism. According to Donagan (1977),

> What [common morality] provides depends on the fact that, although wrongness, or moral impermissibility, does not have degrees, impermissible wrongs are more or less grave. The explanation of this is simple. Any violation of the respect owed to human beings as rational is flatly and unconditionally forbidden; but the respect owed to human beings may be violated either more or less gravely. It is absolutely impermissible either to murder or to steal; but although murder is no more wrong than stealing, it is a graver wrong. There is a parallel in the criminal law, in which murder and stealing are equally felonies, but murder is a graver felony than stealing. In general, every wrong action impairs some human good, and the gravity of wrong actions varies with the human goods they impair. Although there is room for dispute in some cases as to whether or not this action is a graver wrong than that (for example, whether theft of one's reputation is worse than theft of one's purse), when they find themselves trapped . . . in a choice between wrongs, not only do most moral agents have opinions about whether these wrongs are equally grave, and if they are not, about which is the graver; but also, if they adhere to the same moral tradition, their opinions on these questions largely agree. And, given that wrongs can differ in gravity, it quite obviously follows from the fundamental principle of morality that, when through some misdeed a man is confronted with a choice between wrongs, if one of them is less grave than the others, he is to choose it. This precept is a special application of a more general principle which I shall refer to as the principle of the least evil, and which was already proverbial in Cicero's time: namely, *min-*

ima de malis eligenda—when you must choose between evils, choose
the least. (P. 152)

From this perspective, then, the social worker's obligation in the Mary
M. case is to follow that course of action that results in the least harm.
This might produce a very different result from a strategy that seeks to
produce the greatest good.

In an important work entitled *Reason and Morality*, the philosopher Gewirth (1978a) has offered a number of arguments that are particularly relevant to social workers' thinking about the rank-ordering
of conflicting duties (Reamer 1979, 1990). Gewirth's approach, which
I shall draw on extensively, also provides a useful illustration of the
ways in which moral philosophers think about ethical dilemmas. Following a series of complex—and controversial—philosophical arguments and derivations, Gewirth ultimately claims that human beings
have a fundamental right to *freedom* (very similar to social workers'
conceptualization of self-determination) and *well-being* and that
there are three core "goods" that human beings must value: *basic
goods*—those aspects of well-being that are necessary for anyone to
engage in purposeful activity (for example, life itself, health, food,
shelter, mental equilibrium); *nonsubtractive goods*—goods the loss of
which would diminish a person's ability to pursue his or her goals (for
example, as a result of being subjected to inferior living conditions or
harsh labor, or as a result of being stolen from, cheated on, or lied to);
and *additive goods*—goods that enhance a person's ability to pursue
his or her goals (for example, knowledge, self-esteem, material wealth,
education).

Like all moral philosophers, Gewirth recognizes that various duties
and rights people have sometimes conflict and that choices sometimes
need to be made among them. Gewirth argues that conflicting duties
can be rank-ordered or placed in a hierarchy based on the goods
involved. Given this hierarchy, Gewirth (1978a:342–45) claims, several principles can be derived to help make choices among conflicting
duties.

First, if one person or group violates or is about to violate the rights
of another to freedom and well-being (including basic, nonsubtractive,
and additive goods), action to prevent or remove the violation may be

justified. Whether the action to prevent or remove the violation is justified depends on the extent to which the violation jeopardizes an individual's ability to act in the future. Thus if a social worker's client discloses in confidence that he plans to harm his partner, the practitioner's duty to protect the partner from harm would override the client's right to confidentiality. The partner's right to well-being would justify violation of the client's right to self-determination and privacy.

Second, because every individual has the duty to respect others' right to the goods that are necessary for human action (freedom and well-being), one duty takes precedence over another if the good involved in the former duty is more necessary for human action and if the right to that duty cannot be protected without violating the latter duty. Hence, protection of a client's partner from violent harm that may be inflicted by the client would take precedence over the client's right to privacy, because the good involved in the former duty (protection from serious bodily injury) is more necessary for human action and functioning than is privacy.

Third, rules governing interactions among people can, in particular cases, override the duty not to coerce others. Such rules must, however, meet several conditions: any coercion permitted by the rules must be necessary to prevent undeserved coercion and serious harm; such coercion must not go beyond what is necessary for such protection; and the rules that permit occasional coercion must be imposed as a result of democratic process. Thus it would be permissible to coerce one's client (for example, forcing disclosure to authorities the fact that he has threatened to harm his partner) in order to prevent undeserved coercion (bodily assault) and serious harm. However, coercion with regard to disclosure of confidential information must not go beyond what is necessary to protect the client's partner, and public policy regarding such disclosure should be the result of democratic process (for example, public policy formed by elected legislators or judges).

In my view, Gewirth's framework is particularly helpful in addressing ethical dilemmas in social work. His concept of basic goods, for example, is consistent with social work's long-standing preoccupation with basic human needs. Further, Gewirth's rank-ordering of values,

goods, and duties provides compelling support to the social work profession's enduring commitment to addressing the needs of society's
most vulnerable members. Based on this approach to the rank-ordering of values and duties, and based on my assessment of the strengths
and limitations of the most prominent theories of normative ethics, I
have formulated a set of six guidelines to help social workers make
decisions in instances when their duties conflict (Reamer 1990). I
believe these guidelines draw on the most compelling features of both
deontological and teleological-utilitarian principles in a manner that is
consistent with widely held social work values. Although these guidelines do not provide clear-cut, unambiguous solutions to all ethical
dilemmas (no such guidelines can), they can help social workers identify the nature of the dilemmas they face in practice and organize their
thinking and related arguments about how to resolve them.

> 1. Rules against basic harms to the necessary preconditions of human
> action (such as life itself, health, food, shelter, mental equilibrium) take
> precedence over rules against harms such as lying or revealing confi-
> dential information or threats to additive goods such as recreation, edu-
> cation, and wealth.

This guideline could justify disclosure of confidential information in
order to protect a third party from serious harm (for example, if a social
worker's client has threatened to seriously injure his wife), because
protection of individuals from violent harm is more compelling than
the right to privacy, if one of these goods must be sacrificed. This
guideline would also justify spending a disproportionate percentage of
government funds on the most vulnerable (those who are poor, ill,
uneducated, and so on) as opposed to spending equal amounts of
money on services for people who are poor and those who are not. In
the Mary M. case, one might imagine a social worker arguing that the
need to protect Mary M. and her children from future abuse is more
compelling than preventing welfare fraud.

> 2. An individual's right to basic well-being (including goods that are
> essential for human action) takes precedence over another individual's
> right to self-determination.

In general, this guideline suggests that individuals have a right to self-determination and to act as they wish, consistent with social work's long-standing belief in clients' right to self-determination, unless their actions threaten the welfare of others. For example, social workers generally ought to respect clients' parenting methods and styles, even if their approach is very different from one in which the social worker believes. However, if a client's parenting approach threatens the basic well-being of a child, it would be appropriate for the social worker to take steps to interfere with the parents' right to self-determination.

In the Mary M. case, Mary M.'s right to basic well-being and to protection from harm takes precedence over her husband's right to self-determination (to abuse her as he wishes).

> 3. An individual's right to self-determination takes precedence over his or her own right to basic well-being.

In general this guideline suggests that someone who chooses to engage in self-destructive behavior should be allowed to do so *if* it can be established that the individual is making an informed, voluntary decision with knowledge of relevant circumstances and that the consequences of the decision will not threaten the well-being of others. Temporary interference with an individual who threatens to engage or actually engages in behavior that results in basic harm to him- or herself is justifiable in order to determine whether the conditions of voluntariness and informed choice have been met. The guideline requires, however, that if these conditions have been met further interference must be discontinued.

Imagine, for example, that Mary M. decides that she wants to leave the shelter and return to her abusive husband. Perhaps Mary M. believes that her husband is going to change, and she wants to give him another chance. According to this guideline, the social worker in the case, Hinda B., must respect Mary M.'s right to engage in what appears to be self-destructive behavior (returning to her husband) as long as there is evidence that Mary M.'s decision is informed and voluntary. Temporary interference may be justifiable to determine whether Mary M. is in fact acting voluntarily and to ensure that she has knowledge of the possible consequences of her decision, and whether others (her children, for example) are threatened. It would be permissible for the social worker to spend considerable time with Mary M. in an attempt to get her to see the risks involved in returning to her husband. However, if it can be established that the client's decision is voluntary and informed, and that the basic welfare of others is not threatened, interference with the client should stop. This may not be easy, because social workers' instinct is to protect people. Nonetheless, social workers must respect clients' right to engage in some forms of self-destructive behavior.

> 4. The obligation to obey laws, rules, and regulations to which one has voluntarily and freely consented ordinarily overrides one's right to engage voluntarily and freely in a manner that conflicts with these laws, rules, and regulations.

If a social worker voluntarily joins the staff of an agency that prohibits discussion of abortion with clients, for example, it would ordinarily be unethical to violate the policy deliberately. If a social worker disagrees with the policy, he or she should seek employment elsewhere or seek to change the agency's policy. Similarly, if a social worker disagrees with the mandatory reporting law related to child abuse and neglect, he or she should seek to change it through legislative process. It would be unethical for a social worker deliberately to violate the law, which was enacted as a result of democratic process. Similarly, both Mary M. and Hinda B. are obligated to obey the law (as it pertains to welfare fraud, for example).

> 5. Individuals' rights to well-being may override laws, rules, regulations, and arrangements of voluntary associations in cases of conflict.

Thus the obligation to obey laws, rules, and regulations is not absolute and has limits. Situations can arise in which, because of a threat to a client's basic well-being, a law, rule, or regulation can justifiably be violated. At what point violation is justifiable is highly debatable; social workers will disagree about the circumstances under which willful violation of a law, rule, or regulation is warranted. In the Mary M. case, for instance, one can imagine social workers disagreeing about the extent to which it is justifiable for Mary M. to violate the law in order to escape her husband's abuse. We should acknowledge, however, that, in principle, some violations of the law may be justifiable.

In addition, the rules of professional associations that have been entered into voluntarily should not be complied with if they threaten the well-being of individuals. For example, if a social worker is ordered by the director of her agency to falsify records prior to an accreditation site visit or to obtain reimbursement from a funding source, the social worker should not feel obligated to obey. To the contrary, the social worker should take steps to challenge and confront the director's unethical conduct.

> 6. The obligation to prevent basic harms such as starvation and to promote public goods such as housing, education, and public assistance overrides the right to complete control over one's property.

This guideline pertains specifically to the justification of taxation and other forms of coercion (for example, the use of the public policy of eminent domain to establish essential facilities for vulnerable populations) required to provide aid to those in need and to prevent basic harms. The guideline justifies the assessment of taxes and other measures to ensure that basic services are provided to such populations as abused children, people living in poverty and without housing or health care, the disabled, and so on.

These six guidelines can be usefully applied in instances when social workers encounter conflicts among duties. As will become evident in my subsequent discussion of actual ethical dilemmas in social work practice, these guidelines can provide useful criteria for organizing analyses and decision making.

It is important to keep in mind, however, that such guidelines, no matter how specific, cannot provide clear solutions to every dilemma. Individuals will disagree about the relative merits of the particular values, goods, and duties addressed in the guidelines. Even those social workers who agree about the relative importance of different values, goods, and duties may disagree about their relevance in individual cases. The very nature of guidelines is such that applications of them to individual cases inevitably require considerable interpretation, speculation, and inference, all of which invite and ordinarily result in some measure of disagreement. Such disagreement may concern the validity of the guidelines themselves as well as their particular application in specific cases. This is to be expected and encouraged. After all, the value of ethical guidelines is in their ability to help one organize one's thinking and to provide a systematic framework for practitioners who encounter difficult ethical dilemmas.

Having said this, I should also acknowledge that in many instances social workers will agree about the rank-ordering of competing values or duties. Although exceptions will always exist in the hard cases, it will often be clear as to which duties should take precedence when they conflict. As the moral philosopher Gert (1970) concluded in his discussion of difficulties involved in resolving conflicts among competing ethical duties,

> So it may not always be possible to decide which one of a set of tools is best. Each of them might be better in one characteristic, with no way of deciding which combination is best. All informed rational men [*sic*] may agree that A, B, and C are good tools, and that D, E, and F are bad ones. Further A and B may be preferred to C. Nonetheless there may be no agreement on whether A or B is better. . . . But the lack of complete agreement does not mean that there will not be substantial agreement. There is no agreement about whether Ted Williams, Stan Musial, or Willie Mays was the best baseball player. This does not mean that there is no agreement that all three of them are better than 99 percent of all baseball players, past or present. (P. 53)

• THE PROCESS OF ETHICAL DECISION MAKING

There is no precise formula available for resolving ethical dilemmas. Reasonable, thoughtful social workers can disagree about the ethical principles and criteria that ought to guide ethical decisions in any given case. But ethicists generally agree that it is important to approach ethical decisions systematically, to follow a series of steps to ensure that all aspects of the ethical dilemma are addressed. By following a series of clearly formulated steps social workers can enhance the quality of the ethical decisions they make. In my experience, it is helpful for social workers to follow these steps when attempting to resolve ethical dilemmas:

  1. Identify the ethical issues, including the social work values and duties that conflict.

II. Identify the individuals, groups, and organizations who are likely to be affected by the ethical decision.

III. Tentatively identify all possible courses of action and the participants involved in each, along with the possible benefits and risks for each.

IV. Thoroughly examine the reasons in favor of and opposed to each possible course of action, considering relevant:

　　a. ethical theories, principles, and guidelines (for example, deontological and teleological-utilitarian perspectives and ethical guidelines based on them);

　　b. codes of ethics and legal principles;

　　c. social work practice theory and principles;

　　d. personal values (including religious, cultural, and ethnic values and political ideology), particularly those that conflict with one's own. And

V. Consult with colleagues and appropriate experts (such as agency staff, supervisors, agency administrators, attorneys, ethics scholars).

VI. Make the decision and document the decision-making process.

VII. Monitor, evaluate, and document the decision.

We can clarify the various elements of this decision-making framework by applying it to the Mary M. case with which I opened this chapter. In this case the social worker, Hinda B., was unsure about her ethical duty with respect to Mary M., who was residing in a women's shelter, along with her two children, after having been battered by her husband. Hinda B. was concerned that Mary M. would be battered again if she decided to return to her husband. At the same time, however, Hinda B. was concerned about Mary M.'s welfare fraud. Let us now consider the various steps in the decision-making framework as they pertain to this case.

　　I. *Identify the ethical issues, including the social work values and duties that conflict.* The primary ethical issue in this case is the conflict among several core social work values and duties: the social worker's duty to respect clients' right to confidentiality; the social worker's duty to protect clients from harm; the social worker's duty to avoid being associated with dishonesty and fraud; and the social worker's duty to promote respect for the law. It is conceivable, of course, that skillful counseling would prevent the ethical dilemma. That is, it is possible that acquainting Mary M. with the risks involved in welfare fraud would lead her to decide to stop the practice. But it is also possible that mere information about these risks would not influence Mary M. and that Hinda B. would need to decide whether to respect Mary M.'s confidentiality or to take additional steps to prevent or disclose welfare fraud.

II. *Identify the individuals, groups, and organizations who are likely to be affected by the ethical decision.* A number of individuals may be affected by the decision in this case, including the clients, Mary M. and her children; Mary M.'s husband; the social worker, Hinda B.; other needy individuals who may be deprived of benefits because of the welfare fraud; and taxpayers who are affected by welfare fraud. In addition, the agency involved in the case, the women's shelter, may be affected by the outcome.

III. *Tentatively identify all possible courses of action, the participants involved in each, and the possible benefits and risks for each.* It is important to brainstorm possible courses of action to help organize subsequent analysis based on ethical and social work theories, principles, and guidelines. It may be that these analyses will generate other options and courses of action that the social worker did not think of at this stage. Nonetheless, it is helpful to engage in this preliminary brainstorming about all the conceivable options. One option in this case is for the social worker to respect her client's wish for confidentiality with regard to the welfare fraud. The possible benefits are that Mary M. would have the means to live apart from her abusive husband and would not be charged with a crime that might result in the children's

removal from her care. The possible risks are that Mary M.'s criminal activity would continue, at considerable cost to other needy individuals and to taxpayers. The social worker's and agency's failure to seek disclosure of the welfare fraud might also reinforce Mary M.'s criminal activity. In addition, the social worker and her agency may be legally vulnerable because of their knowledge of the welfare fraud.

A second option is for the social worker to insist that Mary M. terminate the welfare fraud. Hinda B. might explain that she cannot, in good conscience, sanction or condone the welfare fraud and that, if Mary M. does not cease and desist on her own, Hinda B. would be obligated to report the fraud to law enforcement officials. The possible benefits of this option are that the expensive fraud being perpetrated on taxpayers would stop and Mary M. would be sent a clear message that such fraudulent activity is unacceptable. In addition, more money would be available for other needy individuals. The possible risks are that Mary M. might be forced, for financial reasons, to return to her abusive husband. She may also be charged with a criminal offense, and conviction may mean that her children would be removed from her care.

IV. *Thoroughly examine the reasons in favor of and opposed to each possible course of action, considering relevant:*

    a. *codes of ethics and legal principles;*

    b. *ethical theories, principles, and guidelines (for example, deontological and teleological-utilitarian perspectives and ethical guidelines based on them);*

    c. *social work practice theory and principles;*

    d. *personal values (including religious values and political ideology); and*

    e. *relevant cultural and ethnic issues.*

A number of principles in the NASW Code of Ethics are relevant to this case, including:

I.A.2. *The social worker should not participate in, condone, or be*

associated with dishonesty, fraud, deceit, or misrepresentation. The social worker in this case must be concerned about her possible association with welfare fraud being perpetrated by her client.

II.F. *Primacy of Clients' Interests—The social worker's primary responsibility is to clients.* This principle suggests that the social worker must act in a way that promotes her *clients'* interests (as opposed to other parties, such as the agency's interests or the interests of other needy individuals or taxpayers).

II.F.10. *The social worker should withdraw service precipitously only under unusual circumstances, giving careful consideration to all factors in the situation and taking care to minimize possible adverse effects.* If Hinda B. should decide to withdraw her services from Mary M. (for example, if Mary M. refuses to terminate the welfare fraud and Hinda B. concludes, as a result, that she cannot continue to work with Mary M.), she should do so only after thinking through the various options and their possible impact very thoroughly.

II.G. *The social worker should make every effort to foster maximum self-determination on the part of clients.* This principle suggests that Hinda B. should respect her clients' wishes in this case, which might entail respecting Mary M.'s confidentiality with respect to the welfare fraud.

II.H. *Confidentiality and Privacy—The social worker should respect the privacy of clients and hold in confidence all information obtained in the course of professional service.* Consistent with the preceding principle, this principle clearly implies that Hinda B. should not divulge the confidential information that Mary M. shared with her concerning the welfare fraud.

II.H.1. *The social worker should share with others confidences revealed by clients, without their consent, only for compelling professional reasons.* In contrast to principle II.H., this principle states that there are limits to clients' right to confidentiality. It is thus possible that the NASW Code of Ethics would permit Hinda B. to disclose confi-

dential information shared by Mary M. if Hinda B. can identify "compelling professional reasons."

II.H.2. *The social worker should inform clients fully about the limits of confidentiality in a given situation, the purposes for which information is obtained, and how it may be used.* Thus Hinda B. should have explained to Mary M., presumably at an early point in their relationship, about the limits of clients' right to confidentiality. That would have enabled Mary M. to decide what information she wanted to share with Hinda B. and how much risk to assume concerning the possibility that Hinda B. would disclose this information without Mary M.'s consent.

V.M. *Maintaining the Integrity of the Profession—The social worker should uphold and advance the values, ethics, knowledge, and mission of the profession.* This is a vague principle. Nonetheless, we can imagine that many social workers would interpret it to mean that Hinda B. should be guided in this case by her understanding of the profession's values and ethics related to concepts such as confidentiality, self-determination, obeying the law, and so on. Exactly what the implications of this principle are for Hinda B.'s decision are not clear.

VI.P. *Promoting the General Welfare—The social worker should promote the general welfare of society.* This principle suggests that social workers should not only consider clients' interests but, in addition, should consider the potential impact of their decisions on the broader society. Hence, Hinda B. should factor into her decision the consequences of disclosure for the general public, including other needy individuals and taxpayers who are affected by welfare fraud. Hinda B. should also consider, perhaps, the effect that disclosure of confidential information without a client's permission could have on the public's perceptions and trust of social workers.

In addition to considering the principles contained in the NASW Code of Ethics and other codes, a social worker facing a difficult ethical decision should carefully consider relevant legal principles, including statutes and case law. Although ethical decisions should not necessarily be dictated by prevailing statutes and case law, social workers should always take legal precedents and principles into account. In some instances the law may reinforce social workers' ethical instincts, such as when the law permits or obligates a social worker to disclose confidential information in order to prevent serious harm to a third party. In other situations, however, the law may seem to undermine social workers' ethical beliefs, for example, if adherence to a little-known and rarely enforced statute would mean the termination of a client's much-needed welfare benefits.

Social workers should also draw on relevant ethical theories, principles, and guidelines. Ethical theories, principles, and guidelines can help social workers conceptualize more clearly the ways in which their professional duties may conflict and possible resolutions of these ethical dilemmas. For example, in this case a deontologist would consider the extent to which the social worker has inherent duties, or duties that ought to be performed for their own sake. One might argue, for example, that Hinda B. has an inherent duty to respect her client's right to self-determination and confidentiality. At the same time, however, a deontologist might argue that the social worker in this case has an inherent obligation to uphold respect for the law. Again, deontological perspectives may conflict.

What about the teleological or consequentialist perspective? As noted earlier, utilitarianism tends to be the most popular teleological perspective in social work. This is the point of view that says that when faced with an ethical conflict a social worker should do that which results in the greatest good or least harm in the aggregate or, alternatively, the greatest good or least harm for the greatest number.

An *act* utilitarian—who is primarily interested in the consequences produced by the immediate case—might argue that the social worker should respect her client's right to self-determination and wish for confidentiality because this would result in the greatest good and least harm. The good would result from the fact that Mary M. would be able to live independently and avoid further abuse that might occur if she were forced to return to her husband's residence, and from the fact that Mary M. would avoid criminal charges related to the welfare fraud that might lead to the removal of her children from her care. An act utilitarian might argue that the costs involved in the welfare fraud would be outweighed by these various benefits.

At the same time, however, one can imagine another act utilitarian who would reach a different, and opposite, conclusion. For this act utilitarian, the social worker should take steps to ensure that Mary M.'s welfare fraud is terminated. From this point of view, there are substantial costs associated with welfare fraud, including the financial cost to other needy individuals and taxpayers and the harm inflicted on the general public as a result of deliberate violation of the law.

Rule utilitarians might also have differing views in this case. In contrast to act utilitarianism, which is concerned with the consequences associated with a particular case, rule utilitarianism is concerned with the long-term consequences that would result if the actions in the immediate case were generalized to all other similar cases. Thus a rule utilitarian might concede that, consistent with one version of act utilitarianism, the greatest good and least harm in the immediate case would result from respecting the client's right to self-determination and confidentiality; however, the rule utilitarian might argue that, *in the long run*, it would be unethical to respect the client's right to self-determination and confidentiality because of the harmful consequences that would result if this practice were generalized to all similar cases. That is, a rule utilitarian might argue that while one instance of concealing welfare fraud may be permissible, because of the special circumstances in the particular case, the general practice cannot be sanctioned because of the dire consequences for the public welfare system and society as a whole. A rule utilitarian would argue that we are obligated to consider these long-term consequences and that only the action that produces the greatest good or least harm *in the long run*, if one generalizes the practice, is justifiable.

Given the contradictory conclusions produced by deontological and teleological-utilitarian theories—a common occurrence—it may help to consider the decision-making guidelines presented earlier. Several are especially relevant.

1. *Rules against basic harms to the necessary preconditions of human action (such as life itself, health, food, shelter, mental equilibrium) take precedence over rules against harms such as lying or revealing confidential information or threats to additive goods such as recreation, education, and wealth.* At first glance, this guideline sug-

gests that Mary M.'s welfare fraud may be justifiable on the grounds that harm caused by such deception is outweighed by the abuse that may be prevented if Mary M. is able to avoid returning to an abusive environment.

This might seem to be a reasonable interpretation of the guideline if there were evidence that Mary M.'s participation in the welfare fraud was the *only* way for her to avoid returning to her abusive husband. In fact, the social worker would be obligated to pursue a variety of alternative strategies, which do not depend on welfare fraud, before reaching such a conclusion. Although it may not be easy, there are other options that would need to be pursued. For example, the social worker should explore the possibility of having Mary M. and her children enroll in a transitional housing program for battered women who are seeking independent living. These programs are often designed for women in Mary M.'s situation, that is, women who need to escape an abusive situation but do not have the financial resources to do so (Carlson 1991). Such transitional housing programs are usually subsidized by public and private funds to enable low-income women and their children to participate. The programs typically require that women enroll in job training, school programs, counseling, and other services to enable them to live independently after a reasonable period of time.

Clearly, the social worker in this case should do everything in her power to discourage the blatant welfare fraud. From an act utilitarian point of view, Mary M.'s fraud may be depriving other potential recipients of needed resources. From a rule utilitarian perspective, the precedent set in this case could have far-reaching damaging consequences for the welfare system.

2. *An individual's right to basic well-being (including goods that are essential for human action) takes precedence over another individual's right to self-determination.* There are two ways to think about the relevance of this guideline. The most obvious concerns Mary M.'s right to be protected from her husband. That is, Mary M.'s right to basic well-being takes precedence over her husband's right to self-determination (to abuse his wife).

The second, and less obvious, application of this guideline concerns the rights of needy individuals to have access to a welfare program that is not undermined by welfare fraud. Ultimately, welfare fraud could threaten the viability of the entire welfare program, because disclosure of welfare fraud often leads to public cynicism and to proposals to end or sharply curtail welfare benefits. That is, one might argue that the basic well-being of needy individuals should take precedence over Mary M.'s right to self-determination (to engage in welfare fraud).

4. *The obligation to obey laws, rules, and regulations to which one has voluntarily and freely consented ordinarily overrides one's right to engage voluntarily and freely in a manner that conflicts with these laws, rules, and regulations.* The fact that Hinda B. and Mary M. live in a democratic society requires them to adhere to laws, including those that prohibit welfare fraud. As I shall point out presently, there are exceptions to this requirement; ordinarily, however, it would be unethical to engage voluntarily and freely in activities that violate laws.

5. *Individuals' rights to well-being may override laws, rules, regulations, and arrangements of voluntary associations in cases of conflict.* This guideline suggests that there are instances when it is justifiable to violate laws, particularly if such violation is necessary to safeguard an individual's right to basic well-being. To take an extreme example, most people would agree that it would be permissible to drive a car carefully through a red light in order to get a seriously injured relative to a hospital emergency room. Even though driving a car through a red light is illegal, it may be necessary, and justifiable, in order to save a life.

The civil disobedience literature is also full of instances in which violation of some statute or regulation seems justifiable in the name of social justice. For example, a number of authors have argued that illegal protests, demonstrations, and even property destruction may be justifiable to challenge immoral practices such as racial and sexual discrimination, unjust wars, inadequate funding for social services, and so on (Campbell 1991; Wasserstrom 1975).

The key question here, of course, is whether the threat to Mary M.'s basic well-being is sufficiently compelling to justify deliberate violation of laws pertaining to welfare fraud. On the surface, this does not appear to be the case. That is, the social worker would have to produce substantial and compelling evidence demonstrating that such deliberate violation of the law is the *only recourse available* to enable Mary M. to live independently of her husband. Most likely, this would be hard to do. Although it may be difficult to arrange an alternative— such as enrolling Mary M. in a transitional housing program for battered women—such alternatives must be pursued.

The social worker in this case should also consult relevant social work practice theory. It may be that literature on the phenomena of domestic violence and battering will offer useful insights. Often, skillful practice intervention in a case will help to resolve the ethical dilemma.

What social work practice theory and literature might be helpful in this case? In recent years, social workers and colleagues in allied professions have begun to develop a substantial knowledge base related to domestic violence and battering (Allen and Straus 1980; Bagarozzi and Giddings 1983; Bass and Rice 1979; Bograd 1984; Bolton and Bolton 1987; Cantoni 1981; Carlson 1991; Douglas 1987; Felthouse 1983; Fleming 1979; Goodstein and Page 1981; Henson and Schinderman 1980; Lynch and Norris 1977–78; Roberts 1984; Schechter and Gray 1988; Strube 1988; Walker 1980). This literature suggests that practitioners who work with battered women should not be overly optimistic about their ability to get the batterer to accept responsibility for his behavior (most batterers are male) and to seek help voluntarily (Bolton and Bolton 1987; Saunders 1982). Based on her extensive review of the theoretical and empirical literature, Carlson (1991) concludes that "the ideal situation is for the wife to live separately from her partner and agree to reconcile only after an extended period of time without violence—for example, six to eight months—and with conjoint counseling" (p. 490).

Although this information from social work theory and the practice literature does not resolve Hinda B.'s ethical dilemma, it does help clarify the overall treatment goal: to help her client live independently of her husband, at least for an extended period of time. It appears, however, that relying on Mary M.'s welfare fraud to reach this goal would be unethical.

Hinda B. should also incorporate her own personal values and political ideology into the ethical decision making (Levy 1976; Rhodes 1986). She should also carefully consider values and ideological viewpoints that are different from her own. Let's say, for sake of argument, that Hinda B. embraces a feminist perspective on the phenomenon of domestic violence. That is, Hinda B. views the battering of women as a manifestation of power differentials between partners; she avoids blaming the victim and seeks to empower women who are victimized by abusive men who fail to accept responsibility for their inappropriate behavior (Bograd 1982; Carlson 1991). This is a legitimate and compelling perspective, and it challenges a number of long-standing practices in social work that have located the problem in and placed substantial blame on victims.

What, however, does this ideological perspective mean with respect to Hinda B.'s ethical decision, and how does it compare with other points of view? An extreme or radical position would be that the social worker and client should pursue any steps necessary to enable the victimized client to escape her abusive situation and to become empowered. This may include deliberate violation of the law, which may seem quite secondary when a woman is being battered. A more moderate feminist position would be that Hinda B. and Mary M. should engage in counseling designed to empower Mary M. and, *using legal means*, should arrange housing and other social services that will enable Mary M. to live independently of her husband.

V. *Consult with colleagues and appropriate experts (such as agency staff, supervisors, agency administrators, attorneys, ethics scholars).* Ordinarily, social workers should not make ethical decisions by themselves. This is not to suggest that ethical decisions are always group decisions. Sometimes they are, but in many instances individual social workers ultimately make the decisions once they have had an opportunity to consult with colleagues and appropriate experts.

Typically, social workers should consider consulting with colleagues who are involved in similar work and who are likely to understand the issues—supervisors, agency administrators, attorneys, and ethics experts. Sometimes this consultation may be obtained informally, in the form of casual and spontaneous conversation with colleagues, and sometimes, particularly in agency settings, through more formal means, such as with institutional ethics committees (Reamer 1987).

The concept of institutional ethics committees (IECs) emerged most prominently in 1976, when the New Jersey Supreme Court ruled that Karen Anne Quinlan's family and physicians should consult an ethics committee in deciding whether to remove her from life-support systems (although a number of hospitals have had something resembling ethics committees since at least the 1920s). The court based its ruling in part on a seminal article that appeared in the *Baylor Law Review* in 1975, in which a pediatrician advocated the use of ethics committees in cases when health care professionals face difficult ethical choices (Teel 1975).

Ethics committees, which can include representatives from various disciplines, often provide case consultation in addition to education and training (Cohen 1988; Cranford and Doudera 1984). A large percentage of agency-based ethics committees provides nonbinding ethics consultation and can offer an opportunity for practitioners to think through case-specific issues with colleagues who have knowledge of ethical issues as a result of their experiences, familiarity with relevant ethical concepts and literature, or specialized ethics training. Although IECs are not always able to provide definitive opinions about the complex issues that are frequently brought to their attention (nor should they be expected to), they can provide a valuable forum for thorough and critical analyses of difficult ethical dilemmas.

There are two important reasons for obtaining consultation. The first is that experienced and thoughtful consultants may offer useful insights concerning the case and may raise issues the social worker had not considered. The expression "two heads are better than one" may seem trite, but it is often true.

The second reason is that such consultation may help social workers protect themselves if they are sued because of the decisions they make. The fact that a social worker sought consultation demonstrates that the practitioner approached the decision carefully and prudently, and this can help if someone alleges that the worker made an inappropriate decision hastily and carelessly.

VI. *Make the decision and document the decision-making process.* Once the social worker has carefully considered the various ethical issues, including the social work values and duties that conflict; identified the individuals, groups, and organizations who are likely to be affected by the ethical decision; tentatively identified all possible courses of action and the participants involved in each, along with the possible benefits and risks for each; thoroughly examined the reasons in favor of and opposed to each possible course of action (considering relevant ethical theories, principles, and guidelines; codes of ethics; social work practice theory and principles; and personal values); and consulted with colleagues and appropriate experts, it is time to make a decision. In some instances the decision will seem clear. Going through the decision-making process will have clarified and illuminated the issues so that the social worker's ethical obligation seems unambiguous.

In other instances, however, social workers may still feel somewhat uncertain about their ethical obligation. These are the hard cases and are not uncommon in ethical decision making. After all, situations that warrant full-scale ethical decision making, with all the steps that this entails, are, by definition, complicated. If they were not complex, these situations could have been resolved easily and simply at an earlier stage. Thus it should not be surprising that many ethical dilemmas remain controversial even after practitioners have taken the time to examine them thoroughly and systematically. Such is the nature of ethical dilemmas.

This is a critically important point. In the Mary M. case, for example, I would argue that Hinda B. must, at some point, share her concerns about the welfare fraud with Mary M. This would occur after Hinda B. makes it very clear that she wants to help Mary M. arrange to live independently, apart from her abusive husband, as long as that is what Mary M. wants. Hinda B.'s principal goal should be clear: to help her client make an informed decision about her future relationship with her husband, her housing arrangements, and so on. Once this goal has been mutually agreed upon, however, I believe it would be morally wrong for Hinda B. to ignore the issue of welfare fraud. For reasons I set forth earlier, it would be a mistake for Hinda B. tacitly to condone or sanction Mary M.'s dishonesty and fraud, especially if other resources are available to enable Mary M. and her children to live independently. In addition, Hinda B. has an obligation to other needy individuals who may not receive benefits because of Mary M.'s welfare fraud, and to taxpayers who are being harmed by the fraud. This case could set an unfortunate and damaging precedent with respect to welfare fraud. This is not to suggest or assume that the welfare system does not need serious reform, particularly with respect to the need for decent benefits that will help to discourage welfare fraud in the first place. It may very well need such reform, and Hinda B. should be encouraged to do what she can to promote it. That too is part and parcel of her responsibility as a social worker.

Hinda B. also has the right to consider the consequences for herself. That is, Hinda B. has the right to avoid a situation in which she feels as if she is actively supporting a client who is engaged in welfare fraud. Hinda B. may also feel as if she is jeopardizing her own career by knowingly working with such a client. In the final analysis, Hinda B. may feel as if her job is to present Mary M. with full information about the risks involved in the welfare fraud and to help Mary M. make a decision about this activity. Should Mary M. refuse to stop the fraud, it would be permissible for Hinda B. to terminate the relationship, as long as she does so in a manner consistent with the NASW Code of Ethics and with sound social work practice principles. The termination should not be precipitous, and Hinda B. should help Mary M. arrange for alternative services. Ideally, Mary M. would stop engaging in welfare fraud; if she does not, however, Hinda B. does not have an obligation to continue working with her.

Whether Hinda B. has an obligation to report Mary M.'s welfare fraud to departmental or law enforcement officials is a very complicated issue. On one hand, many, perhaps most, social workers are reluctant to "turn in" clients. Social workers generally recognize that their low-income clients live in dire straits and want to do whatever they can to help them. Some practitioners choose to ignore income that clients receive under the table, moderate forms of welfare fraud, and so on, when clients are genuinely needy.

On the other hand, most social workers also understand the need to comply with laws, regulations, and organizational policies. This is important in order to avoid widespread chaos in the human services.

In chapter 5 I shall address more directly the ethical issues involved in these decisions.

An important point here is that this assessment and conclusion merely reflect the product of my ethical analysis and decision making. Other practitioners may use the very same framework and reach different conclusions. This does not reveal a fundamental flaw in this decision-making framework. Rather, it highlights an unavoidable attribute of ethical decision making: complicated cases are likely to produce different assessments and conclusions, even after thorough and systematic analysis of the ethical issues.

This is not necessarily a problem. In the end, what we should be most interested in is thoughtful decision making, recognizing that reasonable people may disagree. This is a characteristic of social work practice that is generally well accepted. No one expects all clinical social workers to agree on a treatment plan when faced with a complicated case, particularly if the practitioners draw on different theoretical perspectives, personal and professional experiences, political ideologies, and so on. The same holds for a group of community organizers or social work administrators who are presented with a complex set of circumstances and asked for a recommendation. One should expect no different when the focus is on an ethical dilemma. What clients and other affected parties have a right to expect is that social workers involved in the decision will be thorough, thoughtful, sensitive, and fair.

Once the decision is made, social workers should always be careful to document the steps involved in the decision-making process. Ethical decisions are just as much a part of social work practice as clinical interventions, and they should become part of the record (Kagle 1991). This is simply sound professional practice. Both the worker involved in the case and other workers who may become involved in the case may need access to these notes at some time in the future.

In addition, it is extremely important to prepare notes on the ethical decision making in the event that the case results in legal proceedings (for example, a lawsuit filed against the social worker). As mentioned above, carefully written notes documenting the social worker's diligence can protect the worker from allegations of malpractice or negligence (Reamer 1994b).

Social workers need to decide how much detail to include in their documentation. Too much detail can be problematic, particularly if the practitioner's records are subpoenaed. Sensitive details about the client's life and circumstances may be exposed against the client's wishes. At the same time, social workers can encounter problems if their documentation is too brief and skimpy, especially if the lack of detail affects the quality of care provided in the future or by other workers. In short, social workers need to include the level of detail that facilitates the delivery of service without exposing clients unnecessarily, consistent with generally accepted standards in the profession (Kagle 1991; Wilson 1980).

VII. *Monitor, evaluate, and document the decision.* Whatever ethical decision a worker makes is not the end of the process. In some respects, it constitutes a beginning of a new stage in the problem-solving process. Social workers should always pay close attention to and evaluate the consequences of their ethical decisions. This is important in order to be accountable to clients, employers and funding sources and, if necessary, to provide documentation in the event of an ethics complaint, malpractice claim, or lawsuit. This may take the form of routine case monitoring, recording, or more extensive evaluation using the variety of research tools now available to practitioners (Blythe and Tripodi 1989; Grinnell 1993; Siegel 1984, 1988). Hence, Hinda B. might use both informal methods and standardized instruments to monitor and assess Mary M.'s functioning, self-esteem, and her feelings about the services she is receiving (especially related to Hinda B.'s handling of the ethical dilemma involving the welfare fraud).

As I noted in the preceding discussion, it would be a mistake to assume that systematic ethical decision making will always produce clear and unambiguous results. To expect this would be to misunderstand the nature of ethics. Social workers' different theoretical perspectives, personal and professional experiences, and biases will inevitably combine to produce differing points of view. This is just fine, particularly if we are confident that sustained dialogue among practitioners about the merits of their respective views is likely to enhance their understanding and insight. As in all other aspects of social work practice, the process is often what matters most. As Jonsen (1984:4) notes, ethics guidelines by themselves "are not the modern substitute for the Decalogue. They are, rather, shorthand moral education. They set out the concise definitions and the relevant distinctions that prepare the already well-disposed person to make the shrewd judgment that this or that instance is a typical case of this or that sort, and, then, decide how to act."

In this chapter I examined the nature of ethical dilemmas in social work and reviewed various ways to address them. I now turn to a more detailed discussion and analysis of ethical dilemmas in social work practice.

• • •

Social workers encounter a wide range of ethical dilemmas. In general, they fall into two groups: ethical dilemmas involving work with individual clients, families, and groups (direct practice), and ethical dilemmas involving activities such as community organizing, social policy and planning, and administration (indirect practice). In this chapter I shall focus on ethical dilemmas in direct practice and apply the decision-making framework introduced in chapter 3. Chapter 5 will focus on ethical dilemmas in indirect practice.

Ethical dilemmas in direct practice involve a number of issues. Among the most prominent themes are confidentiality and privacy; self-determination and paternalism; divided loyalties; professional boundaries; and the relationship between professional and personal values.

• CONFIDENTIALITY AND PRIVACY

Various ethical dilemmas arise in social work related to confidentiality and privacy. Common dilemmas faced by practitioners involve disclosure of confidential information 1) to protect a third party, 2) to protect or benefit a client, 3) in response to a court order, and 4) to parents or guardians concerning minor children.

CASE 4.1

Ivy T. was a member of a group private practice. She provided weekly counseling to Donald M., a forty-one-year-old insurance agent who was distressed about problems in his marriage. According to Donald

M., for about a year his wife has been "hostile and distant. She barely talks to me anymore. I just don't know what happened to us."

During one therapy session Donald M. became unusually upset and agitated. He told Ivy T. that two days earlier he found out that his wife was having an affair with another man. Donald M. talked at length about how he felt betrayed and enraged. Toward the end of the session Donald M. blurted out, "I might regret it later, but I think I'm going to kill that guy."

In the brief time remaining in their session, Ivy T. asked Donald M. specific questions about his wish to harm his wife's alleged lover. By the end of the session Ivy T. was unsure about whether Donald M. actually intended to assault the man who was apparently involved with his wife.

Many social workers have encountered instances when clients actually threaten to harm a third party (often a spouse, partner, or lover) or say something ambiguous during a counseling session suggesting that they *may* harm someone. The primary ethical issue in these instances is social workers' choice between respecting clients' right to confidentiality and self-determination, and their duty to protect other people who may be harmed by their clients.

Social workers face a difficult choice when clients object to social workers' disclosure of confidential information concerning the possible threat to a third party. Practitioners have to take into account possible physical risks to third parties who may be injured by clients. In addition, social workers have to consider possible damage to the therapeutic relationship that may result from unauthorized disclosure and the legal risks clients may face as a result of disclosure of their threat (for example, criminal prosecution). Social workers also need to consider the possible consequences for themselves, in the form of an ethics complaint or lawsuit alleging that they failed to maintain confidentiality (if filed by clients) or failed to protect a third party (if filed by injured victims).

In these situations social workers have various choices. They can attempt to intervene clinically, in an effort to prevent harm or obtain the client's consent to disclosure to protect the threatened party. If

these measures are not successful, social workers need to decide whether to uphold clients' right to confidentiality and self-determination or to disclose the information against clients' wishes.

From a deontological perspective, one might argue that social workers have an inherent obligation to respect clients' right to confidentiality and self-determination.* In contrast, an act utilitarian might claim that this is very shortsighted and that social workers' obligation to respect confidentiality and self-determination is outweighed by the need to prevent serious harm to third parties. Consistent with a deontological viewpoint, a rule utilitarian might be concerned about the long-term consequences of social workers' violation of clients' right to confidentiality and self-determination. That is, a rule utilitarian might worry that the integrity and viability of the therapeutic relationship social workers typically have with clients would be undermined if clients began to believe that social workers will not always keep information shared by them confidential. The tension between deontological and teleological-utilitarian perspectives is also reflected in the NASW Code of Ethics, which simultaneously, and appropriately, emphasizes the importance of respect for clients' right to confidentiality and to prevent harm to the general public. According to the code, "The social worker should respect the privacy of clients and hold in confidence all information obtained in the course of professional service" (principle II.H); and "The social worker should promote the general welfare of society" (principle VI.P).

This case is also one in which legal principles are relevant. The best-known legal precedent is the case of *Tarasoff v. Board of Regents of the University of California* (1976). This famous case paved the way for a number of statutes and court decisions that now influence practitioners' decisions in cases where clients pose a threat to third parties.

According to the court record, the Tarasoff case involved Prosenjit Poddar, who was receiving mental health counseling as an outpatient

---

*In my discussion of cases throughout the remainder of the book I shall make frequent use of terms such as *deontological, teleological, utilitarian, act utilitarian,* and *rule utilitarian.* I recognize that these terms are cumbersome and jargonistic. However, these are standard and widely used terms in the ethics literature. It would be difficult to create simple and clear alternatives.

at the Cowell Memorial Hospital at the University of California at Berkeley. Poddar informed his psychologist, Lawrence Moore, that he was planning to kill an unnamed woman, easily identified as Tatiana Tarasoff, upon her return to the university from her summer vacation. After the counseling session during which Poddar stated his intention, the psychologist telephoned the university police and requested that they observe Poddar because he might need hospitalization as an individual who was "dangerous to himself or others." The psychologist followed up the telephone call with a letter requesting the help of the chief of the university police.

The campus police took Poddar into custody temporarily but released him based on evidence that he was rational; the police also warned Poddar to stay away from Tarasoff. At that point Poddar moved in with Tarasoff's brother in an apartment near where Tarasoff lived with her parents. Shortly thereafter the psychologist's supervisor and the chief of the department of psychiatry, Dr. Harvey Powelson, asked the university police to return the psychologist's letter, ordered that the letter and the psychologist's case notes be destroyed, and directed that no further action be taken to hospitalize Poddar. No one warned Tarasoff or her family of Poddar's threat. Poddar never returned to treatment. Two months later he killed Tarasoff.

Tarasoff's parents sued the Board of Regents of the university, several employees of the student health service, and the chief of the campus police, along with four of his officers, because their daughter was never notified of the threat. A lower court in California dismissed the suit on the basis of immunity for the multiple defendants and the psychotherapist's need to preserve confidentiality. The parents appealed, and the California Supreme Court upheld the appeal and later reaffirmed the appellate court's decision that failure to protect the intended victim was irresponsible. The court ultimately held that a mental health professional who knows that a client plans to harm another individual has a duty to protect the intended victim.

The Tarasoff case and a number of subsequent court decisions thus suggest that social workers have a duty to disclose confidential information when doing so will prevent serious harm to a third party (Reamer 1991, 1994b). This policy is also consistent with the ethical guideline that states that measures required to prevent basic harm to life and health take precedence over rules against harms such as revealing confidential information.

CASE 4.2

Alan F. was a social worker at the Columbia Family Service Agency. He has provided marriage counseling to Peter and Doris S. The couple began counseling when Doris S. told Peter S. that she was thinking about asking for a divorce.

Both Peter S. and Doris S. agreed that Peter has a serious gambling problem. The couple is in financial trouble as a result of the gambling, and Doris recently said, "I just can't take it anymore. Either Peter gets some help and stops this gambling, or we're through. I've had it."

Peter became involved in a local chapter of Gamblers Anonymous and talked in the couple's sessions with Alan F. about how valuable GA has been and about how relieved he is that he has stopped gambling.

One afternoon Peter S. called Alan F. and told Alan F. that he needed to talk to him privately. At their meeting the next day Peter S. informed Alan F. that he had been lying about going to GA meetings, that his gambling problem was worse than ever, and he was feeling desperate. Peter S. asked Alan F. for help and pleaded with him not to tell his wife about his lying.

This case is quite different from the previous case (4.1), in which a client actually threatened to harm another individual. In the present case, a social worker has access to confidential information provided by one client that, in the practitioner's judgment, a second client may be entitled to. The first client has not verbalized a threat to harm someone else.

To what extent does the social worker in this case, Alan F., have an obligation to respect Peter S.'s explicit request for confidentiality? What obligation does he have to Doris S.? Does she have the right to be informed about her husband's lying and deception? Also, what right does Alan F. have to take his own interests into account, particularly his right to avoid involvement in Peter S.'s deliberate attempt to conceal his continued gambling problem from his wife?

Alan F.'s options include working with Peter S. to enable him to disclose his continued gambling problem to his wife, withdrawing from the case if Peter S. refuses to disclose this information, and disclosing Peter S.'s "secret" to Doris S. on his own.

Ideally, of course, Alan F. would be successful in his attempt to get Peter S. to disclose the information himself. But what if he is not successful? A deontologist might argue that Alan F. has an inherent obligation to honor his client's right to privacy. Of course, another deontologist who has a different perspective might conclude that the social worker has an inherent duty to protect Doris S. from harm being inflicted upon her by Peter S. An act utilitarian also might claim that the information should be disclosed but for different reasons, that is, for the greater good that would result from protecting Doris S. from a marriage based on active deception and from confronting Peter S.'s lying. In contrast, a rule utilitarian might argue that withholding the information may be justifiable so as not to undermine clients' trust in social workers. An ethical egoist might take the position that Alan F. has the right to withdraw from the case or disclose the information to Doris S. so that he protects himself from involvement in deception.

The NASW Code of Ethics does not seem particularly helpful here; its principles concerning clients' right to confidentiality and social workers' primary obligation to clients do not clarify Alan F.'s principal obligation. The ethical guideline presented in chapter 3 suggesting that social workers' obligation to protect individuals from basic harms to the necessary preconditions of human action overrides harms such as revealing confidential information may be helpful, if it can be shown that Doris S.'s mental health—in the form of her fundamental ability to function—is threatened by her husband's continued gambling and deception.

Although Peter S. has a prima facie right to confidentiality and self-determination, he forfeits these rights when his actions threaten other individuals. In this instance, Peter S.'s deliberate deception of his wife is unacceptable, particularly in the context of marriage counseling. Moreover, as a social worker Alan F. has a right to avoid involvement in this sort of active deception, no matter how indirect his participation. If Peter S. is not willing to stop the deception or inform his wife of his continued gambling (which could then be addressed clinically), it would be appropriate for Alan F. to explain to Peter S. that he cannot continue to counsel the couple. Alan F. would explain that it is unethical for him to continue counseling knowing that one member of a couple is actively deceiving the other, with the social worker's knowledge. Alan F. would also explain that the prospects for a marriage based to some extent on deception are not good and that he is concerned about the threat to his own peace of mind that might result from being involved in concealment of important information from Doris S. Alan F. might offer to meet with Peter S. for several sessions to help him think about how to share this information with his wife and to discuss Peter S.'s feelings about informing her of his gambling. Such a strategy would allow Peter S. an opportunity to continue in treatment and would allow him time to attempt to resolve his feelings about telling his wife about his gambling. It is a strategy designed to allow the couple to continue working on their marital problems and to avoid having Alan F. be party to a plan to deceive his wife deliberately. Handling the case in this way is justifiable on the grounds that it offers the best prospects for protecting the rights of all the parties involved in the case.

CASE 4.3

Bev E. was a caseworker with the Cheswolde Family Service Agency. She was providing counseling services to Nina C., who sought Bev E.'s help because of problems her nine-year-old son, Bobby, was having in school. According to his teacher, Bobby seemed "depressed and easily distracted" and was having difficulty completing classroom projects.

After two months, Bev E. also began to provide counseling to Nina C., who said she was feeling "overwhelmed with anxiety." Nina C. was divorced from Bobby's father, Ron. Nina and Ron C. were in the process of a custody dispute.

One day Bev E. received a subpoena to appear in court to testify in the custody proceedings. Ron C.'s attorney subpoenaed Bev E. in order to ask her questions under oath about Nina C.'s mental health and her ability to care for her son, Bobby. Nina C. did not want Bev E. to testify or to disclose information she had shared with Bev E. in confidential therapy sessions.

The ethical dilemma in this case is clear. It involves the conflict between the social worker's duty to protect clients' right to confidentiality and a court order requesting the possible disclosure of confidential information. The client in this case, Nina C., could be harmed by disclosure of the information, as a result of the revelation of personal details about her life and by the possibility that she would not retain custody of her son as a result. In contrast, Nina C.'s husband, Ron, and their son, Bobby, also stand to be affected by the social worker's response to the subpoena. In addition, if the social worker decides to withhold the information, in defiance of a court order, she could face contempt of court penalties, which could be harmful to her career.

From a deontological perspective, one might argue that social workers are obligated to obey court orders and hence that the social worker, Bev. E., should disclose the requested information. Similarly, an act utilitarian might conclude that disclosure in this one case would be justifiable if there is evidence that it would enhance the likelihood of a desirable or good outcome for the parties involved, primarily the child. This good would outweigh whatever harm results from the disclosure, for example, harm to the client-therapist relationship, harm to the social worker's reputation and career, and so on. This point of view is consistent with the ethical guideline that states that the harm involved in violating a client's right to confidentiality may be justifiable if it is necessary to prevent a basic harm, such as the child's basic mental health. A rule utilitarian, however, might argue that disclosure of confidential information against the client's wishes would be a mistake because in the long run the general practice of breaching clients' right to confidentiality would undermine clients' trust in their social workers and discourage people from seeking help.

This kind of ethical dilemma—in which social workers must decide whether to disclose confidential information in response to a court subpoena—is faced by many practitioners. In many instances the court case involves a custody dispute, where a social worker's testimony is sought in an effort to support or challenge parents' claims about their ability to care for their children. In other instances social workers are subpoenaed to testify when clients have sued another party (for example, alleging that they incurred emotional injuries as a result of employment termination or some kind of accident) or have been sued by another party.

On occasion clients do not object to their social workers' testimony, particularly when they believe that the testimony will support their side of a case. Often, however, clients do not give their social workers permission to testify, either because they believe that the testimony would be harmful in court or because the information the social workers would disclose is very personal and private.

Unfortunately, many social workers misunderstand what a subpoena requires of them. Some social workers believe that a subpoena requires them to appear in court and disclose the information requested, and that otherwise they will be found in contempt of court and be incarcerated or fined. In fact, however, a subpoena is merely an order to appear in court to respond to the request for information (information that may be presented in the form of verbal testimony or in case records). As Grossman (1973) said, "If the recipient knew how easy it was to have a subpoena issued; if he knew how readily the subpoena could demand information when there actually was no legal right to command the disclosure of information; if he knew how often an individual releases information that legally he had no right to release because of intimidation—he would view the threat of the subpoena with less fear and greater skepticism" (p. 245).

If clients have not given their social workers permission to disclose the requested information, social workers should do their best to convince the court that the information should not be disclosed. Social workers can argue that the information was shared in confidence and that disclosure in court without the client's permission would cause considerable harm. If possible, social workers should suggest alternative ways or sources through which the court can obtain the information being sought. According to Wilson (1978), "When data sought by the court can be obtained through some other source, a professional who has been subpoenaed may not have to disclose his confidential data. If the practitioner freely relinquishes his confidential though non-privileged data with little or no objection, the courts may not even check to see if the information can be obtained elsewhere. If the professional resists disclosure, however, the court may investigate to see if it can get the data from some other source" (p. 138).

It is possible that a court of law will formally order social workers to reveal subpoenaed information despite practitioners' attempts to resist disclosure of it. This may occur even in states that recognize by statute that the clients of social workers have the right of privileged communication, that is, that social workers are permitted to disclose confidential information only when clients grant them permission to do so. For example, in a well-known New York State case (*Humphrey v. Norden* 1974), a social worker whose client was presumably protected by the state's privileged communication statute was ordered to testify in a paternity suit after the court ruled that "disclosure of evidence relevant to a correct determination of paternity was of greater importance than any injury which might inure to the relationship between social worker and his clients" (p. 734). Should this occur, social workers must make a difficult decision about the extent to which the disclosure of confidential information is justifiable, that is, the extent to which the information is essential to prevent basic harm to the parties involved. In addition to considering the possible impact of their decision on clients and people involved in clients' lives, it is legitimate for social workers to consider as well the possible impact of their decision on their own careers.

CASE 4.4

Jeff G. was a social worker at the Harborplace Youth Guidance Center. The center provides counseling and related services to troubled children, adolescents, and their families.

One of Jeff G.'s clients was a sixteen-year-old high school student, Allan S. Allan S. had been referred to Jeff G. by the school guidance counselor because Allan's grades had been dropping steadily, he had missed many school days, and, according to one of Allan's teachers, he seemed "out of it."

After several counseling sessions, Allan admitted to Jeff G. that he was having a serious problem with cocaine. Allan admitted that he had been addicted to cocaine for several months, after being introduced to the drug at a friend's party.

Jeff G. received a telephone call from Allan's parents. They asked Jeff G. about his impressions of their son's problems. They wanted to know whether Jeff G. had discovered the reasons for Allan's school difficulties.

Social workers who provide services to minors often face this predicament, where parents or guardians request information about the youths being served. In addition, social workers who serve minors often face situations where they need to make decisions about whether to disclose certain confidential information shared by minors to parents or guardians, even when the parents and guardians have not asked for it. This information often has to do with minors' drug use, sexual activity, pregnancies, and delinquent behavior.

In this case the social worker, Jeff G., has to weigh Allan S.'s right to confidentiality against Allan's parents' right to know about their son's drug use. Although we can understand why Allan would not want his parents to know about his drug use, we can also understand how Allan's parents would want to know, and might feel entitled to know, about their son's drug problem. If Allan were an adult the case would be much simpler. His status as a minor, however, complicates the situation. If Jeff G. withholds the information from Allan's parents he may enhance the quality of his therapeutic relationship with Allan. In contrast, if Jeff G. shares the confidential information with Allan's parents he runs the risk of alienating his client, disrupting the therapeutic relationship, and contributing to a strained relationship between Allan and his parents. A possible positive outcome, however, is that Allan's parents would respond constructively and support their son's efforts to address his problem.

From a deontological perspective, Jeff G. may have an obligation to respect Allan's right to confidentiality. An act utilitarian also might argue that disclosure of the confidential information would not be justifiable, on the grounds that more harm than good would result (in the form of jeopardizing the therapeutic relationship, for example). A rule utilitarian might claim that the breach of confidentiality would set an unfortunate and harmful precedent with regard to social workers' trustworthiness. Of course, a rule utilitarian with a different perspective might be concerned about long-term harm that might result when secrets are harbored between parents and their children.

A widely embraced guideline for social workers is that information shared with them in confidence by minors can be kept confidential as long as its disclosure is not necessary to protect the minors from harming themselves or others. Many social workers also believe that minors who disclose that they have been involved in a serious delinquent act forfeit their right to confidentiality, although information shared by minors about their involvement in not-so-serious offenses may not need to be disclosed. As Wilson (1978) concludes, "In reality, many professional helping persons who learn of minor infractions of the law by children and adolescents choose not to report the violations because the damage to the relationship and the helping process would be too great" (p. 123). This conclusion is also consistent with the ethical guideline that harm caused by the disclosure of confidential information may be outweighed by the need to prevent basic harms to individuals.

In light of these guidelines, the social worker should disclose details about his client's drug use only if he believes his client's drug use is continuing and that his client may seriously harm himself or others as a result. However, if the social worker believes that his client is addressing his drug problem and receiving appropriate treatment, disclosure would not be justifiable.

• SELF-DETERMINATION AND PATERNALISM

Social workers are usually drawn to the profession because of their sincere desire to assist people who are experiencing serious problems in living, such as mental illness, poverty, domestic violence, physical impairment, and so on. In general, social workers embrace the profession's long-standing commitment to the principle of client self-determination, which ordinarily entails "the rights and needs of clients to be free to make their own choices and decisions" (Barker 1991:210). As the NASW Code of Ethics (1994) asserts, "The social worker should make every effort to foster maximum self-determination on the part of clients" (principle II.G).

Social work's literature contains an impressive number of scholarly discussions of the concept of self-determination (McDermott 1975). Far less common are discussions of instances when social workers believe it may not be appropriate to respect clients' right to self-determination. Often these are instances when social workers are inclined to interfere with clients' right to self-determination "for their own good." These are cases involving *professional paternalism.*

CASE 4.5

Marcia R. was a social worker at Owings Mills General Hospital. She was assigned primarily to the hospital's medical-surgery unit, where she worked with cancer patients and their families. One of the patients was a sixty-eight-year-old man, Michael H., who was admitted for exploratory surgery of his abdomen. Michael H. was a frail man who was described by his attending physician as "emotionally labile."

One afternoon Marcia R. was approached by Michael H.'s daughter, Ellen S. Ellen S. told Marcia R. that her father's physician had just informed her that the lab report from the exploratory surgery indicated that her father had terminal cancer. Ellen S. said that she and the family were "in shock. We never imagined he was this sick. We just can't tell him his life will be over soon. He can't handle it." Ellen S. told Marcia R. that she and the rest of the family had decided that they did not want the hospital staff to tell her father about the terminal nature of his cancer once he recovered from anesthesia. Ellen S. said she wanted Marcia R. to help her explain this to the attending physician involved in her father's care.

On the surface it appears that Ellen S. and her family are concerned primarily about their father. That is, they want to withhold from him information about his terminal cancer because of their belief that he would not be able to cope with the news. In contrast, the social worker, Marcia R., and other medical staff may believe that the patient, Michael H., has the right to be informed about his medical status and that staff have an obligation to disclose this information to him.

A deontologist might argue that withholding information from Michael H. would constitute a form of deception that, from this perspective, is unethical. A deontologist would likely endorse the medical staff's obligation to tell the truth, that anything short of that would violate the patient's rights. An act utilitarian, however, might be able to justify withholding the truth, if it can be shown that the emotional suffering Michael H. would likely experience upon hearing the truth would cause more harm than would be caused by the benevolent deception involved in withholding information about his diagnosis from him.

This kind of dilemma is not unique in social work. It occurs whenever social workers must decide whether to be *paternalistic*, that is, to interfere with clients' rights for their own good. Paternalism can occur in three different forms. The first, as is evident in this case, occurs when a social worker believes that it is justifiable to withhold information from clients for their own good. This can involve any kind of information that is relevant to clients' lives but that, their social workers believe, would be harmful for them to have, such as certain diagnostic information, information about their psychiatric status, mental health prognosis, and so on.

The second form of paternalism involves actual lying to clients for their own good, in contrast to merely withholding information from them. This occurs when social workers deliberately give clients false information about some aspect of their lives, perhaps in response to clients' questions. For example, a social worker would be paternalistic if she told an abandoned child that his father really loves him when in fact that does not appear to be the case.

The third form of paternalism involves physical interference with clients, against their wishes, for their own good. Forcing individuals to receive medical treatment or reside in a shelter against their wishes are common forms of paternalism. Consider the following example (Hornblower 1987:29).

CASE 4.6

In the fall of 1987, Joyce Brown, a forty-year-old former stenographer who had been living on New York City streets, was taken against her wishes to Bellevue Hospital. Ms. Brown, also known as Billie Boggs, had lived on Manhattan sidewalks for one year. With proceeds from panhandling, she lived on about seven dollars a day to buy food. Ms.

Brown typically relieved herself in the gutter. City workers described her as dirty and incoherent and noted her tendency to tear up paper money and burn it.

The debate concerning the obligation to protect people from harm— using deception or coercion—is an ancient one. It focuses on the tension between practitioners who believe in clients' right to set and pursue their own goals, take risks, and possibly make mistakes and those who believe that at least some degree of deception and coercion may be necessary to protect clients from harm. At the heart of this tension is the enduring social work value of client self-determination (Reamer 1983b). As Biestek (1975) has observed,

> The principle of client self-determination is the practical recognition of the right and need of clients to freedom in making their own choices and decisions in the casework process. Caseworkers have a corresponding duty to respect that right, recognize that need, stimulate and help to activate that potential for self-direction by helping the client to see and use the available and appropriate resources of the community and of his own personality. The client's right to self-determination, however, is limited by the client's capacity for positive and constructive decision making, by the framework of civil and moral law, and by the functions of the agency. (P. 19)

The concept of paternalism has been debated since Aristotle's time, although the term itself is of more recent origin. Aristotle argued in his *Politics,* written in the fourth century B.C., that some degree of paternalism is appropriate in a society in which certain elite individuals are clearly more informed and wiser than others.

The best-known classic statement on paternalism is John Stuart Mill's 1859 essay *On Liberty.* Mill is widely regarded as one of history's most ardent opponents of paternalism, especially in the form of government interference in the lives of private citizens. In *On Liberty* Mill presents his oft-cited view that the "sole end for which mankind are warranted, individually or collectively, in interfering with the liberty of action of any of their number, is self-protection. That the only purpose for which power can be rightfully exercised over any member of a civilized community, against his will, is to prevent harm to others. His own good, either physical or moral, is not a sufficient warrant. . . . Over himself, over his own body and mind, the individual is sovereign" (Mill 1973:484).

Contemporary debate about the nature and limits of paternalism was especially intense during the 1960s, largely because of the widespread focus on civil rights and civil liberties issues. Controversy about paternalistic treatment of the mentally ill, prisoners, welfare recipients, and children stimulated a great deal of philosophical speculation about the limits of coercion.

It is not surprising, then, that perhaps the best-known modern-day essay on paternalism was written in the 1960s. In his 1968 essay "Paternalism," Gerald Dworkin, a moral philosopher, defines paternalism as "interference with a person's liberty of action justified by reasons referring exclusively to the welfare, good, happiness, needs, interests, or values of the person being coerced" (Wasserstrom 1971:108). Examples include laws that justify civil commitment to prevent people from harming themselves, requiring members of certain religious groups to receive compulsory treatment for their own good, prohibiting suicide, and requiring motorcyclists to wear safety helmets.

The philosopher Rosemary Carter (1977) offers a broader definition of paternalism, including interference with individuals' emotional states as well as their physical activity. She defines a paternalistic action as "one in which the protection or promotion of a subject's welfare is the primary reason for attempted or successful coercive interference with an action or state of that person" (p. 133). Allen Buchanan (1978), also a moral philosopher, offers an even broader definition that includes interference with individuals' right to accurate and truthful information relevant to their lives. For Buchanan, paternalism is "interference with a person's freedom of action or freedom of information, or the deliberate dissemination of misinformation, where the alleged justification of interference or misinforming is that it is for the good of the person who is interfered with or misinformed" (p. 372). All these definitions include reference to the use of coercion or interference that is justified by concern for the good of the individual who is being coerced or interfered with.

What makes paternalism such a difficult problem for social workers is that most practitioners are attracted to the profession because of a strong and sincere desire to help people through some kind of meaningful intervention into their lives. There may be, in fact, a variety of instances when coercive intervention into clients' lives is necessary, at least temporarily, to prevent some tragic outcome (recognizing that one must also keep in mind the ethical guideline that a client's right to self-determination, which may involve some degree of self-harm, can take precedence over his or her own right to basic well-being). Paternalism is a problem, however, when interference with clients goes beyond what is absolutely necessary or is used as camouflage for actions that are really motivated by individual or agency self-interest. In the case involving Michael H. and Marcia R., for instance, it is possible that the family's reluctance to inform Michael H. of his grim diagnosis was motivated in part, perhaps to a large extent, by family members' own discomfort with the topics of death and dying, in addition to whatever genuine concern family members had about Michael H.'s ability to cope with the unfortunate news. In the Joyce Brown case, it is possible that efforts by social service professionals to hospitalize Ms. Brown were motivated as much by their wish to contain the "public nuisance" created by Ms. Brown's behavior as by their genuine wish to protect her from harming herself. Unfortunately, arguments that clients need to be lied to, deceived, or interfered with for their own good are sometimes couched in the language of paternalism when they are really rooted in self-interested motives—the problem of "pseudopaternalism."

In general, then, clients should not be interfered with paternalistically, unless there is substantial and compelling evidence that they pose a serious threat of harm to themselves. Hence, patients have the right to know about their diagnoses, and homeless people have the right to reject shelter, as long as there is evidence that they are making informed decisions voluntarily, with a clear understanding of the consequences. Paternalism may be justifiable if clients are not mentally competent or if in some other way they would harm themselves seriously.

• DIVIDED LOYALTIES

Social workers who are not in private or independent practice sometimes find themselves torn between their clients' and their employers' interests. This can occur when social workers believe that an administrator's decision or agency practice undermines clients. These situations present social workers with the problem of divided loyalties, when practitioners must choose whether their employers' interests or their clients' interests will take precedence.

CASE 4.7

Alma B. was a social worker at the Gwynn Oak Nursing Home. All the nursing home's residents are elderly or seriously disabled. Alma B.'s position included a variety of responsibilities, including individual casework, counseling, and facilitating "reminiscence groups."

Alma B. has spent considerable time with one particular resident, Richard D. A seventy-seven-year-old, Richard D. has lived at Gwynn Oak for the last three years. He moved to Gwynn Oak following a massive heart attack that left him seriously disabled.

During a recent conversation Richard D. told Alma B. that he was involved in a sexual relationship with another Gwynn Oak resident, Barbara L., a seventy-one-year-old woman who has been at the nursing home for the last year. Richard D. told Alma B. that he knows residents are not permitted to have sexual contact with one another, but he explained that he and Barbara L. have become very close friends and "it's no one's business but our own what we do with each other." Richard D. concluded the conversation with Alma B. by saying, "I know I can trust you with this."

On one hand, it may be tempting to conclude that as long as the two nursing home residents are consenting adults the nursing home has no business interfering with their sexual activity. On the other hand, Alma B. is now in a position where she knows that her client is defying the home's well-known policy. In fact, Alma B. believes that the home's policy is unreasonable. At the same time, she feels as if she is colluding with a client who has decided to openly defy the home's policy.

From a deontological point of view, one could argue that the social worker has an inherent obligation to uphold the nursing home's well-known policy, no matter how unjust she believes the policy to be. Of course, a deontologist who has a different vantage point could argue that the social worker has an inherent obligation to respect her client's right to self-determination.

An act utilitarian would not be very concerned about an inherent obligation to respect the nursing home's policy prohibiting sexual contact. Instead, an act utilitarian would more likely be concerned about the consequences for the parties involved in this particular case. This could very well lead to the conclusion that more good than harm would result from the sexual relationship between the two residents. It is difficult to know how a rule utilitarian would view this case. One line of reasoning could be that the long-term consequences of sexual relationships among residents would be harmful because of the interpersonal complications that might ensue as a result. Another line of reasoning, however, could be that permitting consenting adults to determine for themselves what kinds of relationships they want to enter into would produce the greatest happiness for the residents.

At first blush it appears that the NASW Code of Ethics is not very helpful in this case. On one hand, the code contains principles that would seem to support a social worker who decides to respect her clients' wish to engage in a consenting sexual relationship: "The social worker's primary responsibility is to clients" (principle II.F); "The social worker should make every effort to foster maximum self-determination on the part of clients" (principle II.G); and "The social worker should respect the privacy of clients and hold in confidence all information obtained in the course of professional service" (principle II.H). On the other hand, there are other principles that suggest that the social worker in this case would be obligated to uphold agency policy prohibiting sexual contact among residents. For example, the principle "The social worker should share with others confidences revealed by clients, without their consent, only for compelling professional reasons" (principle II.H.1) could be interpreted by some to mean that the social worker has an obligation to disclose to nursing home administrators the residents' violation of nursing home policy. In addition, the principle "The social worker should adhere to commitments made to the employing organization" (principle IV.L) suggests that the social worker should not knowingly defy agency policy.

The ethical guideline that social workers ordinarily have an obligation to obey rules and regulations to which they have voluntarily and freely consented suggests that Alma B. should not participate in a deliberate attempt to defy nursing home policy. Violation of rules and regulations may be permissible in some instances, particularly when such violation is essential to prevent serious harm or injury, but the standard that must be met to justify such violation is a high one. Violation of policies, rules, and regulations in order to save a life or prevent serious injury may be warranted; violation to prevent less severe harm, however, is much more difficult to justify.

Instead, social workers who have divided loyalties and believe that agency policies, rules, or regulations are unjust have a responsibility to challenge them and seek necessary change. Several overriding principles in the NASW Code of Ethics support this conclusion: "The social worker should act to prevent practices that are inhumane or discriminatory against any person or group of persons" (principle I.C.2); "The social worker should work to improve the employing agency's policies and procedures, and the efficiency and effectiveness of its services" (principle IV.L.1); "The social worker should act to ensure that all persons have access to the resources, services, and opportunities which they require" (principle VI.P.2); and "The social worker should act to expand choice and opportunity for all persons, with special regard for disadvantaged or oppressed groups and persons" (principle VI.P.3).

In this case the social worker has to decide whether to enforce an agency policy about which she had some question and reservations. In other instances, however, social workers face the situation in reverse, when they feel caught between an agency policy with which they agree and clients who are requesting exceptions to the policy.

CASE 4.8

Peggy P. was a social worker at Pawtucket General Hospital. She was assigned to the neonatal unit. In the unit was a three-day-old infant, Baby R., who was born severely impaired. Baby R. was born missing most of his brain, was blind and unable to hear, and had severe heart damage.

Baby R.'s parents, who had no health care coverage, were overwhelmed with grief about their baby's medical condition. The hospital's doctors had explained to the parents that their child would never lead a normal life and would probably die within a year, even with aggressive medical care. The doctors also explained that the baby would have to undergo several complicated operations on his heart to save his life.

The doctors told the parents that, in their judgment, it would be a mistake to take extraordinary measures to save the baby's life. They explained that the surgical procedures were complex and remarkably expensive. The doctors were also unsure whether their efforts would improve the quality of or prolong the baby's life.

This social worker, Peggy P., agreed with the doctors that it did not make sense to pursue aggressive medical procedures in this case. The cost would be astronomical and the likely benefits minimal.

Peggy P. met with Baby R.'s parents to discuss their reactions to the options described by the doctors. Baby R.'s parents said they wanted to insist that the hospital staff do everything possible to save and improve their child's life. They explained that they felt "bonded" with the baby and believed he had a right to as much health care as any other baby.

This kind of case forces social workers to confront the limits of their beliefs about their duties to clients, particularly when clients' wishes are contrary to agency policy with which social workers agree. In this particular case, the parents are understandably concerned about their baby's welfare. All of us can understand their wish to do whatever is necessary to enhance the infant's life.

At the same time, this case shows in stark relief the complexity of contemporary debate about the limits of health care. In this instance it is possible that extraordinary amounts of public funds would be spent to care for a severely impaired infant whose life chances would be, under the best of circumstances, terribly limited. The physicians' recommendation in this case seems reasonable. Although it may appear that their recommendation is based on a coldhearted cost-benefit calculus, it is also evident that their conclusion may be based on concern about the baby and the need to preserve limited health care funds for other cases in which medical intervention is more likely to be effective.

A deontologist in this case might argue that there is an obligation to save Baby R.'s life, or any life for that matter. Of course, a deontologist with a different perspective might believe that the most important obligation in a case such as this is to prevent harm and pain and therefore that it would be justifiable to discontinue aggressive care and let Baby R. die of "natural causes." An act utilitarian might argue that withholding extraordinary care is the right thing to do so that this money could be used to help other patients who stand a better chance of survival and improvement in the quality of their lives. It is hard to know how a rule utilitarian would argue. Perhaps a rule utilitarian would be concerned about the precedent set when extraordinary amounts of money are spent on a case with such weak prospects. The consequence may be that in the future health care funds will be spent very inefficiently and perhaps wasted. Another rule utilitarian, however, might be concerned that failure to intervene aggressively in this case may set a damaging and harmful standard with regard to the value of life itself. That is, from this point of view it might be dangerous to set a precedent where lines are drawn between "worthy" and "unworthy" lives. In the long run, a proponent of this view might claim, aggressive medical care ought to be provided in every instance in order to avoid such value judgments.

The NASW Code of Ethics contains principles that may suggest contradictory courses of action. For example, the principle that states that "the social worker should make every effort to foster maximum self-determination on the part of clients" (principle II.G) suggests that Peggy P. should advocate on Baby R.'s parents' behalf, in spite of her doubts about the wisdom of their decision. However, the code also states that "the social worker should promote the general welfare of society" (principle VI.P), which suggests that social workers should also take into consideration the implications of their decisions for others who may need assistance.

In a case of this sort it is legitimate for social workers to share their opinions with clients, in an effort not so much to persuade them as to inform them of the social workers' own biases. Social workers are not obligated to endorse clients' views blindly, particularly if social workers do not agree with them. Social workers should have confidence in their clients' ability to accept or reject social workers' views. Clients also have the right to know about practitioners' biases that may influence their work in any given case.

At the same time, social workers have an obligation to advocate on their clients' behalf and to make their clients' wishes known to others as clearly and forthrightly as possible. Clients can decide for themselves whether they are comfortable having social workers who disagree with them serve as their advocates. Clients in this sort of predicament may decide that they prefer to have another social worker with different views, or no social worker at all, advocate on their behalf. This is a legitimate position to take.

This case also illustrates an instance in which social workers may want to avail themselves of an agency-based or institutional ethics committee (see chapter 3 and Reamer 1987b). An ethics committee may provide a useful forum for disciplined evaluation of the case by a thoughtful panel of interested professionals trained to think ethically, particularly with regard to the divided loyalties issue faced by the social worker and the difficult ethical questions concerning the conflict between the parents' wishes and the views of hospital medical staff. Cases of this sort often contain complex legal issues (in this instance regarding the hospital's legal obligation to patients and related liability risks); an ethics committee can provide an opportunity to think through these issues as well.

• PROFESSIONAL BOUNDARIES

Social workers are trained to maintain clear boundaries in their relationships with clients. Clear boundaries are important so that practitioners and clients understand the nature and purpose of their relationship with each other. In clinical practice especially, social workers must avoid conveying mixed messages about their role in clients' lives. Confusion about the worker-client relationship can interfere significantly with the pair's therapeutic goals and process. Clients who view social workers as someone other than their source of professional help —for example, as their friend or business associate—may have difficulty developing a therapeutic alliance and making maximum use of the worker-client relationship.

CASE 4.9

Marilyn J. was a social worker in private practice. Ruth S. had been her client for five months. Ruth S., an obstetric nurse at a local hospital, sought counseling to address issues that had surfaced related to sexual abuse she had experienced as a child.

Marilyn J. was also struggling in her own life. She and her husband had been trying to conceive for seven years. Marilyn J. and her husband had been through a wide range of infertility tests and medical procedures, all without success. The couple were distraught about their infertility and equally upset about all the difficulty they were having in their attempt to adopt a baby.

During one of the counseling sessions, Ruth S. talked about how happy she was that she was able to refer an unmarried birth mother at the hospital to one of Ruth S.'s close friends who was interested in adopting a newborn. Ruth S. explained that her friend had undergone "terribly painful and intrusive infertility tests and procedures." Ruth S. spoke at length about how fulfilling it was for her to be able to "get my friend a baby."

Marilyn J. was feeling so desperate about finding a baby to adopt that she began to think seriously about asking her client, Ruth S., whether she might be able to help her and her husband.

It is essential that social workers maintain clear and unambiguous boundaries in their relationship with clients. Effective practice depends on a clear delineation of professional roles. Worker-client relationships that are based on confused boundaries can be very destructive.

In this particular case the social worker, Marilyn J., was tempted to resolve an important problem in her own life by taking advantage of her client's professional position. It is not hard to understand Marilyn J.'s temptation, given the intense frustration she has experienced. This case thus provides a good example of an instance where social workers must reconcile their own needs with those of their clients.

Ruth S. (the client), Marilyn J. (the social worker), and Marilyn J.'s husband are the parties who would be most directly affected by the outcome of this situation. Marilyn J. and her husband would stand to benefit if Ruth S. were able to use her position at the hospital to locate an adoptable baby. Ruth S. might benefit in one respect because of the satisfaction she might experience as a result of helping her social worker.

Clearly, however, the parties involved in this case can also be harmed by what is generally known as a dual relationship (Brodsky 1986). Marilyn J.'s reputation and professional standing could be harmed should it come to light that she located a baby through the direct efforts of her client. This activity would be viewed by most as unethical. More important, Ruth S. could be harmed as a result of the confused relationship she might then have with her social worker. At the point that Marilyn J. becomes dependent upon her client, it would be very difficult for Marilyn J. and Ruth S. to sustain an appropriate therapeutic relationship. Traditional assumptions about the appropriate role for clients, who seek help, and social workers, who are in a position to help, would be undermined, ultimately interfering with Ruth S.'s right to effective service.

From a strictly act utilitarian perspective, one might argue that it would be justifiable for Marilyn J. to locate a baby with Ruth S.'s assistance. The pleasure Marilyn J. and her husband would experience would, perhaps, outweigh whatever damage there might be to the social worker's and client's therapeutic relationship. From a rule utilitarian perspective, however, one might argue that Marilyn J.'s dependence on her client to locate a baby would be ethically wrong because, *in the long run*, social worker–client relationships and the profession itself would be damaged if such a practice were generalized to all other cases in which social workers might benefit from their clients' access to resources or positions of authority. That is, although Marilyn J.'s use of Ruth S.'s access to adoptable infants may be justifiable in this one instance, as an act utilitarian might claim, the general practice cannot be defended on ethical grounds. This would be consistent with the ethical guideline that states that an individual's right to well-being (in this case, the client's right) takes precedence over another individual's right to self-determination or freedom (Marilyn J.'s wish to use her client's position to locate an adoptable baby).

The NASW Code of Ethics contains several relevant principles, all of which imply that it would be wrong for Marilyn J. to approach her client about adopting an infant. One principle, "The social worker's primary responsibility is to clients" (II.F), states clearly that social workers must consider their clients' interests first and foremost. This sentiment is reinforced by several other principles, including: "The social worker should be alert to and resist the influences and pressures that interfere with the exercise of professional discretion and impartial judgment required for the performance of professional functions" (I.D.1); "The social worker should not exploit professional relationships for personal gain" (I.D.2); "The social worker should not exploit relationships with clients for personal advantage" (II.F.2); and "The social worker should not condone or engage in any dual or multiple relationships with clients or former clients in which there is a risk of exploitation or of potential harm to the client. The social worker is responsible for setting clear, appropriate, and culturally sensitive boundaries" (II.F.4).

It is difficult to find a principle in the NASW Code of Ethics that would support the social worker's decision to approach her client about adopting a baby. The only principle that is even remotely related concerns the social worker's obligation to "make every effort to foster maximum self-determination on the part of clients" (II.G). Perhaps Marilyn J. would argue that it would be fine for her client to help her locate an adoptable baby as long as the client was clear about the possible implications of this activity on the therapeutic relationship and was willing to assume the risks involved. Such a conclusion, however, would be stretching beyond reason what is ordinarily meant by the social worker's obligation to foster clients' self-determination. Justifying such a dual relationship by resorting to the ethical principle concerning social workers' obligation to promote client self-determination seems self-serving. As Brodsky (1986) states with respect to dual relationships engaged in by psychologists,

> Dual relationships involve more than one purpose of relating. A therapy relationship is meant to be exclusive and unidimensional. The therapist is the expert, the patient the consumer of that expertise. Once a patient accepts an individual as a therapist, that individual cannot, without undue influence, relate to that patient in any other role. Relating to the patient as an employer, business partner, lover, spouse, relative, professor, or student would contaminate the therapeutic goal. The contami-

nation is much more intense in a psychotherapy relationship than it would be in the relationship between a client and a professional in any other field—for example, between a client and an internist, a dentist, a lawyer, or an accountant. (P. 155)

A distressing percentage of dual relationships engaged in by social workers involves intimate and sexual contact with clients (Reamer 1994b). These relationships often begin in the context of psychotherapy, as illustrated by the following case:

CASE 4.10

George D. was a social worker in a community mental health center. He had worked as a caseworker and casework supervisor for nine years.

Joanne R. was one of George D.'s clients. She sought counseling because she "was feeling depressed" and "full of self-hatred." During the course of their professional relationship Joanne R. talked to George D. at length about problems in her marriage, particularly with respect to her sexual relationship with her husband.

After about four months of therapy, Joanne R. informed George D. that she was having sexual fantasies about him. She said she felt as if she needed to address the issue in therapy. She and George D. spent two sessions focusing on this issue.

During the next session Joanne R. told George D. that she was still feeling attracted to him. George D. responded by saying that he too felt an attraction and that they should continue exploring this issue. George D. said he was unsure about whether their professional relationship should continue, in light of this development, and suggested that the two of them schedule some additional time to address this. George D. told Joanne R. that he would not charge her for this additional time since some of his "own issues" were involved. Joanne R. pleaded with George D. to continue counseling her; she said that she didn't feel comfortable addressing her issues with anyone else.

It may be that the social worker in this case fully intends to deal responsibly with the confused boundaries that are emerging. Nonetheless, this case is riddled with ethical red flags that the social worker needs to address, particularly related to whether the professional relationship ought to continue.

In the short run, the social worker's client, Joanne R., may be harmed if the mutual attraction between her and George D. interferes with her efforts to address the issues concerning which she originally sought therapy. The boundary problems in this case could certainly affect George D.'s ability to be objective and insightful and Joanne R.'s ability to confront the issues in her life. On the other hand, although it might be a minority opinion, one might argue that there is no better person for Joanne R. to consult about the issues in her life than the individual with whom she is developing some emotional involvement.

It is difficult to know what ethical value would be most important to a deontologist's assessment of this case. If it is something like "do no harm," perhaps a case could be made that George D. should withdraw from the professional relationship because of the possibility that Joanne R. would be hurt. At the same time, one can imagine a deontologist focusing on social workers' primary obligation to their clients and on clients' right to self-determination, which may mean that it would be irresponsible for George D. to withdraw his services against his client's wishes.

An act utilitarian would be much more interested in forecasting the likely consequences of the available courses of action. If there were evidence that maintaining the therapeutic relationship would enable Joanne R. to resolve her issues, an act utilitarian might conclude that it would be justifiable for George D. to continue to provide professional services to Joanne R. However, if there were evidence that maintaining the professional relationship would ultimately be more harmful than helpful (considering the effect of the relationship on the client and the social worker, including the social worker's own professional reputation and mental health), an act utilitarian would conclude that George D. should terminate the relationship. A rule utilitarian would probably be concerned about the consequences that would result from setting a precedent where a social worker continues to provide therapy to a client with whom a complicated emotional relationship is developing. One can imagine damage to the profession's integrity and to clients were such a practice to become widespread.

The NASW Code of Ethics contains several relevant principles, all of which suggest that it would be wrong for George D. to continue to provide professional services to Joanne R. or to discontinue their professional relationship and then pursue a personal relationship: "The social worker should act in accordance with the highest standards of professional integrity and impartiality" (principle I.D); "The social worker should be alert to and resist the influences and pressures that interfere with the exercise of professional discretion and impartial judgment required for the performance of professional functions" (principle I.D.1); "The social worker should not exploit professional relationships for personal gain" (principle I.D.2); "The social worker should not exploit relationships with clients for personal advantage" (principle II.F.2); and "The social worker should not condone or engage in any dual or multiple relationships with clients or former clients in which there is a risk of exploitation or of potential harm to the client. The social worker is responsible for setting clear, appropriate, and culturally sensitive boundaries" (principle II.F.4). It appears clear, then, that the arguments against continuation of the therapeutic relationship are compelling, assuming that George D. would continue the relationship with Joanne R. at least in part to meet his own needs, in addition to or instead of those of his client. This conclusion is consistent with the ethical guideline that an individual's right to basic well-being (in this case the client, Joanne R.) takes precedence over another individual's right to self-determination (George D.'s wish to continue the relationship). That Joanne R. might be willing to engage in what amounts to a self-destructive relationship (consistent with the ethical guideline that clients may have the right to assume risk and to engage in self-destructive activities) is not compelling here, given that George D.'s actions, were he to continue the relationship, would likely be in violation of the profession's ethical standards.

Should George D. decide to terminate the relationship, with or without Joanne R.'s consent and cooperation, he would need to do so in a manner consistent with social work ethics. This would include providing a clear explanation to his client and an opportunity for his client to deal with pertinent issues related to the termination. The social worker should also help the client locate another therapist to help her deal with the issues in her life, including the ramifications of the termination of the therapeutic relationship with George D. Several principles in the NASW Code of Ethics make it clear that there are ethical standards governing proper termination of a therapeutic relationship: "The social worker should terminate service to clients, and professional relationships with them, when such service and relationships are no longer required or *no longer serve the clients' needs or interests*" (principle II.F.9; emphasis added); "The social worker should withdraw services precipitously only under unusual circumstances, giving careful consideration to all factors in the situation and taking care to minimize possible adverse effects" (principle II.F.10); and "The social worker who anticipates the termination or interruption of service to clients should notify clients promptly and seek the transfer, referral, or continuation of service in relation to the clients' needs and preferences" (principle II.F.11).

• PROFESSIONAL AND PERSONAL VALUES

Some of the most difficult ethical dilemmas that social workers face occur when their personal values conflict with the profession's values. This can occur when a formally enacted policy, such as an NASW policy or an informal but long-standing policy of the profession, is contrary to social workers' deep-seated beliefs.

CASE 4.11

Brent C. was a social worker at the Burrilville Family Service Center. His caseload consisted primarily of adolescents enrolled in the local school district. The school district had a contract with the agency to provide counseling when a referral is made by a school social worker or counselor.

Courtney R., age sixteen, was recently referred to Brent C. for counseling. According to the school counselor who made the referral, Courtney R. has been "sullen and depressed."

Brent C. and Courtney R. spent several sessions exploring various issues in Courtney R.'s life. They talked about her relationship with her parents, three siblings, and boyfriend and about the difficulty Courtney R. has been having in school.

During the fourth session Courtney R. told Brent C. she had something important to tell him. After Brent C. reminded Courtney R. of confidentiality limits, Courtney told Brent C. that she was pregnant. Courtney R. explained that the pregnancy was a surprise to her, that she and her boyfriend had always been "real careful."

Courtney R. told Brent C. that she was apparently six weeks pregnant and that she was seriously considering obtaining an abortion. Courtney R. asked Brent C. to help her think through this decision.

It happens that Brent C. is adamantly opposed to abortion, on religious grounds. He was raised to believe that abortion is morally wrong and that he must not do anything to encourage or facilitate abortion.

This case raises a number of complicated ethical issues. The most prominent issue concerns Brent C.'s obligation to his client, Courtney R., who has asked Brent C. to help her think through her decision about whether to have an abortion. For religious reasons, Brent C. believes he cannot be neutral on the issue and merely help his client decide whether abortion is appropriate for her. His personal values are such that neutrality on this issue would be tantamount to encouraging an abortion.

Brent C. must also consider his relationship with his employer, which acknowledges clients' right to make up their own minds concerning the morality of abortion. Thus Brent C. must also reconcile his own personal beliefs with agency policy.

One option is for Brent C. to disclose his personal beliefs to Courtney R. and to let her make up her own mind about whether she wants to continue seeing Brent C. A second option is for Brent C. actively to discourage Courtney R. from seeking an abortion. Yet another option is for Brent C. to withhold his own views on the issue and do his best, albeit indirectly, to discourage Courtney C. from seeking an abortion and to encourage her to explore alternatives (for example, parenting the baby herself or pursuing an adoption). Of course, Brent C. could also withdraw from the case and refer Courtney R. to another worker.

An act utilitarian who opposes abortion might argue that it would be appropriate for Brent C. to actively discourage the abortion. A deontologist might embrace a similar view, arguing that there is an inherent obligation to save a fetus from an abortion. An act utilitarian who is pro-choice, however, might argue that more good than harm would likely result if Courtney R. is encouraged to consider abortion, since there could be serious "costs" if an unplanned and unwanted child is born (for example, medical bills and welfare expenses paid for by the public, or the effects on the child that might result from being raised by a teenage single parent). A rule utilitarian also might argue that Brent C. should not impose his own personal beliefs on his client, because if that practice were generalized the consequences for the profession could be disastrous in the long run (that is, this precedent might suggest to prospective clients that social workers should be avoided because they impose their own values and beliefs on their clients).

The NASW Code of Ethics does not address the issue of abortion directly. The one principle that seems relevant is the principle that highlights social workers' obligation to foster clients' right to self-determination (principle II.G). There is also a principle that suggests that Brent C. should respect his employer's policy, assuming that, at the time of his employment, Brent C. agreed to uphold agency policy: "The social worker should adhere to commitments made to the employing organization" (principle IV.L).

It is well known that, as an organization, NASW has traditionally respected clients' decisions about whether to seek a legal abortion. NASW is not "pro-abortion"; rather, the association is "pro-choice." That is, NASW policy respects clients' right to obtain information and services from social workers that will enable them to make their own decision (National Association of Social Workers 1994b:3).

In light of this policy and the agency's similar policy, Brent C. would be obliged to provide Courtney R. with the information and services she needs to make her decision about an abortion. If Brent C. feels that he cannot participate in any way in Courtney R.'s decision—short of discouraging abortion—he would be obligated to withdraw from the case and refer Courtney R. to a colleague who is in a position to provide her with that assistance. According to NASW's *Encyclopedia of Social Work*,

> Clearly, the arguments for and against "free choice" are numerous and complex. Each social worker who is involved as a professional in issues related to abortion will need to think through carefully his or her beliefs and values about this subject and such associated ones as nonmarital

coitus, contraception, adolescent sexuality, unwanted pregnancies, forced marriages, and adoption. Social workers who find that they cannot take an objective, informed approach to these topics should probably abstain from both direct and indirect professional practice dealing with problem pregnancies unless they are employed by agencies with clearly stated "pro-life" or "pro-choice" policies with which they personally agree.
(Chilman 1987:5)

In the present case the social worker felt uncomfortable discussing the abortion option with his client because of his religious beliefs. In other instances, however, a social worker faces this predicament in reverse, that is, when practitioners believe they have an obligation to discuss topics or issues with clients in a way that agency policy prohibits. The following case illustrates this dilemma:

CASE 4.12

Martha S. was employed by Catholic Human Services. She was hired by the agency shortly after receiving her B.S.W. degree. Martha S. was eager to be hired by the agency so that she could work in the agency's new program for battered women. Martha has had a long-standing interest in women's issues and hopes someday to create her own agency to serve vulnerable and oppressed women.

Dawn E., a twenty-eight-year-old mother of four children, recently became a client in the agency's program for battered women. During their first interview she told Martha S. that her husband had been abusive for the last six months. Martha S. and Dawn E. met weekly to discuss Dawn E.'s feelings about her marriage and its future.

During their fifth meeting, Dawn E. informed Martha S. that she was about one month pregnant. Dawn E. told Martha S. that she is sure she became pregnant when her husband sexually assaulted her five weeks earlier. She told Martha S. that she could not imagine having another child, particularly one conceived under these circumstances. Dawn E. asked Martha S. how she would go about arranging an abortion. Martha S. was caught off guard by the question. When she joined the agency Martha knew that Catholic Human Services had a policy that prohibits staff from discussing abortion-related issues. Although Martha S. is "pro-choice," she agreed to this policy because she did not expect abortion issues to come up in her job. In spite of this, Martha S. felt strongly that Dawn E. has a right to information about the abortion option and locally available services. Martha S. was torn about whether to provide Dawn E. with this information.

In contrast to the preceding case, this case requires the social worker to decide whether to deliberately violate a well-known agency policy prohibiting discussion of a certain topic. From a deontological point of view, one could argue that it would be wrong for Martha S. to violate a clearly enunciated agency policy prohibiting discussion of abortion-related issues. Deontologists typically argue that laws, rules, and regulations ought to be obeyed. An act utilitarian might disagree, however, arguing that in light of Dawn E.'s particular circumstances (i.e., she has four children and a fragile marriage, and the pregnancy is the result of a sexual assault), it would be justifiable for Martha S. to provide Dawn E. with the information she has requested. Martha S. would not be violating any law; rather, she would simply be disobeying an agency policy. From this point of view, more good than harm would result if Martha S. were to provide the abortion-related information to Dawn E.

A rule utilitarian might argue, however, that it would be wrong for Martha S. to defy agency policy. From this perspective, more harm than good might result if Martha S. sets this precedent and if, as a result, social workers defy agency policies whenever they believe that it is in clients' or someone else's best interests to do so. A rule utilitarian would be concerned about the damaging consequences and possible chaos that might result.

According to the ethical guidelines presented in chapter 3, "The obligation to obey laws, rules, and regulations to which one has voluntarily and freely consented ordinarily overrides one's right to engage voluntarily and freely in a manner which conflicts with these laws, rules, and regulations." A strict interpretation of this guideline suggests that Martha S. should not violate Catholic Human Services' policy prohibiting discussion of abortion-related issues. This would also be consistent with the principle contained in the NASW Code of Ethics that states that "the social worker should adhere to commitments made to the employing organization" (principle IV.L). After all, one might argue, Martha S. knew about the agency's clearly stated policy when she accepted employment there; therefore it would be wrong for her to defy the agency's policy in this particular case.

However, another guideline presented in chapter 3 states that "individuals' rights to well-being may override laws, rules, regulations, and arrangements of voluntary associations in cases of conflict." That is, it may be justifiable to violate laws, rules, and regulations if doing so is necessary to protect someone's right to basic well-being. Violating a traffic rule or eligibility criteria may seem justifiable if doing so is necessary to save someone's life.

Is there a sufficient threat to Dawn E.'s basic well-being to justify Martha S.'s deliberate violation of agency policy? It appears not, in spite of the fact that Martha S.'s "pro-choice" position is consistent with NASW policy and the majority of social workers' views on the abortion issue. Martha S. is free to disagree with her agency's policy on the issue; however, it would be wrong for her to accept employment that requires compliance with the agency's policy and then deliberately act in a manner inconsistent with this policy. If Martha S. disagrees with the agency's policy, she has a responsibility to challenge it and seek alterations to it. As the NASW Code of Ethics states, "The social worker should work to improve the employing agency's policies and procedures" (principle IV.L.1). If Martha S. is unsuccessful in her attempts to change her agency's policy, and if she believes that compliance with agency policy would compromise her own legitimate values, she may have to consider whether to continue her employment there.

Given that Dawn E. has a right to abortion-related information, it would be appropriate for Martha S. to explain that because of agency policy she is not able to discuss abortion-related issues. She should then inform Dawn E. that she can obtain the information she seeks from other agencies and provide her with agency names and telephone numbers. Martha S. has an obligation to provide clients with appropriate referrals in instances when she is not in a position to serve them. This is consistent with the NASW Code of Ethics principle that states that "the social worker should provide clients with accurate and complete information regarding the extent and nature of the services available to them" (principle II.F.6).

My discussion in this chapter focused on ethical dilemmas related to direct practice. I now turn to ethical dilemmas related to indirect practice in social work.

• • •

As I discussed in the preceding chapter, many ethical dilemmas in social work are related to the delivery of services to individuals, families, and groups, or what is generally known as direct practice. In addition, social workers also encounter a wide variety of ethical dilemmas related to what I shall call *indirect* practice. Indirect practice includes such activities as community organization, social policy and planning, and social work administration. In this chapter I shall focus on a number of ethical dilemmas that are prominent in indirect social work practice, including the allocation of limited resources; government and private sector responsibility for social welfare; compliance with regulations and laws; labor-management disputes; the use of deception in social work; and whistle blowing. As in the preceding chapter, I shall apply the decision-making framework introduced in chapter 3 in my analysis of these ethical dilemmas.

• THE ALLOCATION OF LIMITED RESOURCES

Social workers frequently find themselves without sufficient resources to administer adequately the policies and programs for which they are responsible. Meager funding, budget cuts, and increased demand for social services often require social workers to make difficult decisions about how to allocate scarce or limited resources.

CASE 5.1

Natalie K. was the executive director of the Camden Yards Drug Treatment Center. The center provides counseling and supportive services for individuals who have substance abuse problems. For years the center has depended on state contracts and fees paid by insurance companies and self-pay clients.

Natalie K. was recently informed by the director of the state's substance abuse division that state funding for the next fiscal year was to be cut by 25 percent. State revenues had been down because of a sluggish economy and, as a result, funding for most state programs had to be reduced.

Natalie K. knew that it would be impossible for her staff to continue serving as many clients. During the past year the center's staff provided services to approximately 500 clients. Ordinarily the agency had no waiting list, or had a very short one. Natalie K. estimated that with the funding cuts her staff would be able to serve only approximately 375 clients.

Natalie K. assembled her administrative staff and presented them with the bad news. She told the staff that together they would have to decide how to determine which clients would be served, because the agency would not be able to accommodate the usual demand for its services.

In many social service settings decisions about allocating scarce resources are made without full consideration of relevant ethical issues. Criteria for allocating resources may be determined by an administrator's personal biases, political pressure, or agency tradition. In fact, however, these decisions are profoundly ethical ones in that they raise complex issues of fairness and justice. As I shall discuss presently, in this case scarce substance abuse services could be allocated in a variety of ways, each of which has ethical implications.

Debate about criteria for allocating scarce resources concerns what philosophers call distributive justice. Distributive justice involves the use of ethical concepts and criteria to determine how scarce resources should be divided among people, communities, groups, organizations, and so on. The distribution of scarce resources in social work has generally been guided by four criteria: equality, need, compensation, and contribution. Sometimes these criteria are considered independently of one another, and sometimes they are considered in combination.

The idea of equality is among the most popular criteria for allocating scarce resources. On the surface, the concept of equality seems straightforward. Individuals who are eligible for services or resources (such as money, housing, health care, or a social worker's time) simply have an equal right to them. As I shall point out, however, in actuality the concept of equality is quite complicated.

One way to define equality is in terms of equal shares. That is, when there are insufficient resources, all eligible people (or groups, communities, organizations, etc.) would receive an equal share of what is available. This way of looking at equality emphasizes the *outcome* of the distribution; each eligible recipient should receive an equal share.

This approach may be feasible in some instances, such as when those standing in a line at a soup kitchen receive equal portions of the available food. This outcome may not be very satisfying, but it may be fair. Each person would receive at least some food, although perhaps not enough. Similarly, low-income communities might divide up available community development funds into equal portions, so that each community receives a portion. In the present case, Natalie K. could, in principle, divide staff members' available time in order to provide each eligible prospective client with at least some service.

In many instances, however, this approach would not work. Suppose the director of an emergency shelter for the homeless discovers that there are only four beds available for seven people who have requested them. Clearly one cannot divide up the four beds to accommodate seven people. The homeless individuals cannot receive a fraction of a bed. Similarly, scarce public housing units cannot be broken into smaller portions to accommodate excess demand for them.

Another way to think about equality is to emphasize the *procedures* used to allocate resources rather than the actual outcome. Under this arrangement services and resources are not necessarily distributed equally; instead, potential recipients have equal opportunity to compete for them. Thus those who arrive first, under the principle of "first come, first served," would receive a bed in the shelter or food from the soup kitchen. The 375 individuals who are first to request services from Natalie K.'s program would be the recipients. Here the emphasis is on the *process* involved in allocating scarce resources rather than on the outcome.

Another interpretation of the principle of equality involves the use of random selection, particularly when scarce resources cannot be distributed equally among eligible recipients. Here, for example, applicants for scarce public housing units or community development funds might have their names selected randomly to determine who will receive available resources. Like the principle of "first come, first served," this use of a lottery or random selection procedures provides what is generally known as *equality of opportunity*.

In contrast to the principle of equality, in other instances scarce resources are allocated based on potential recipients' need. That is, those responsible for the resource's distribution make some determination about which individuals, communities, or organizations are most in need, and the neediest receive the available resources. Instead of dividing resources into equal portions or allowing individuals to compete for them, either in the form of a lottery or according to "first come, first served," individuals are ranked according to their level or severity of need, however need is defined. Thus those individuals requesting food or shelter, and those communities requesting community development funds, might be ranked based on their respective level of need, and the resources would be allocated accordingly. Those eligible for services at the Camden Yards Drug Treatment Center could, in principle, be ranked based on their level of individual need, with those most in need being provided with counseling and supportive services.

Some people argue that social workers cannot simply consider the criteria of equality and need. Affirmative action principles should also be considered, with preferential consideration given to individuals, groups, organizations, and communities that have been discriminated against. That is, people, communities, and organizations that have been treated unjustly would be compensated and given priority. Hence, residents of communities with a large minority or oppressed population might be favored over communities with relatively few minorities and oppressed people when community development funds are allocated. Minorities and oppressed people in need of food, clothing, shelter, or other social services might take precedence over nonminorities and people who have not been oppressed.

Finally, social workers also allocate scarce resources based on the criterion of contribution. According to one interpretation of this principle, scarce resources should be distributed in proportion to the contribution potential that recipients have made or might make. For example, one way to implement this approach is to allocate scarce resources to those who can pay for them or contribute to coverage of related costs. Thus those who can contribute to coverage of the costs involved in providing shelter, health care, or substance abuse services should be given priority. Of course, this approach can be self-defeating in social work because so often the profession deals with clients who do not have the ability to pay for services.

Another approach to allocation based on contribution involves the nonmonetary contribution of potential recipients. That is, some have argued that some people, communities, and organizations are more worthy than others because of their ability to contribute to society's quality of life. From this point of view, which is anathema to most social workers, scarce health care or substance abuse services would be allocated to people who are considered more "valuable," for example, talented professionals, civic leaders, and athletes.

Social workers must think carefully about the criteria they use to allocate scarce resources. In some instances the principle of equality, in one of its several forms, might seem more compelling and just than the principle of need or compensation. In other situations the principle of need might seem most appropriate. The main point is that social workers must be aware of the various possible criteria and distributive mechanisms, the ethical nature of their decisions, and must be willing to justify their choices in any given case. Deontological and teleological or utilitarian theories can also be applied to distributive justice cases. In the present case involving Natalie K.'s need to allocate limited resources at the drug treatment center, we can imagine a deontologist focusing primarily on the executive director's inherent obligation to provide equal opportunity to those eligible for the center's services. Of course, there are several ways to interpret the concept of equal opportunity in a case such as this, including the principle of "first come, first served" and the mechanism of a lottery or random selection. However, another deontologist with different values might argue that Natalie K. has an inherent obligation to focus on the relative severity of potential clients' needs and should rank them accordingly.

An act utilitarian would not be concerned about the executive director's inherent obligation but instead would focus on the distributive mechanism that would produce the greatest good for the individuals involved in this one case. From this point of view, Natalie K. should try to anticipate which approach would benefit the largest number of people. In this respect, principles such as equality and affirmative action would be unimportant. What would matter more is the ultimate outcome, which might be achieved by identifying those who are most needy and who are most likely to respond well and be affected by the agency's services. Although this would be difficult to do, this approach entails a fundamentally different way of conceptualizing how to allocate the agency's limited resources.

A rule utilitarian would also be concerned about the consequences of different distributive mechanisms but primarily with regard to the long-term results of whatever precedent is set in this case. Let us suppose, for example, that Natalie K. decides to incorporate affirmative action principles in her effort to allocate her program's resources. A rule utilitarian would speculate about the long-term implications of this approach—in terms of community reaction, addressing the community's substance abuse problem, and so on—if it were generalized to other programs that must allocate scarce resources. A rule utilitarian might favor the use of affirmative action principles, for example, if he or she believes that widespread use of such principles would ultimately produce the greatest good.

The NASW Code of Ethics does not include principles directly related to the problem of scarce resources. Although there are several principles that refer to social workers' obligation to promote the general welfare of society (principle VI.P), prevent discrimination (principle VI.P.1), ensure that all persons have access to the resources, services, and opportunities that they require (principle VI.P.2), and act to expand choice and opportunity for all persons (principle VI.P.3), there are no specific guidelines in the code that would help Natalie K. determine the most appropriate mechanism for allocating her agency's limited resources. In the final analysis, Natalie K. should be guided by her beliefs about what constitutes the fairest and most just distributive approach, after carefully considering the strengths and limitations of the various options. Ultimately, she should strive to enhance potential recipients' basic rights to self-determination and well-being.

In addition, as the NASW Code of Ethics suggests, Natalie K. should also engage in social action and advocacy designed to increase overall funding for these important services: "The social worker should advocate changes in policy and legislation to improve social conditions and to promote social justice" (principle VI.P.6). This might entail legislative lobbying, community organizing, and other social action activities.

Cases involving distributive justice typically entail difficult decisions about what criteria and mechanisms should be used to allocate limited resources. In this respect, these cases tend to focus on the *process* that should be used to allocate limited resources. In some cases, however, there is an additional complication, one that involves debate concerning the morality of the program itself.

CASE 5.2

Shelly G. was the executive director of the Metropolitan United Federation, the local organization responsible for soliciting donations and raising funds to be distributed to social service agencies. As part of her responsibilities Shelly G. oversees the annual allocation of the organization's funds to member agencies. Ordinarily the Metropolitan United Federation distributes money to a wide variety of social service agencies, including programs for the elderly, children, substance abusers, homeless, disabled, mentally ill, and so on. Funding decisions are based on recommendations submitted to the organization's board of directors by several allocations panels that review proposals prepared by agencies requesting funds.

This year Shelly G. and the organization's board of directors found themselves embroiled in a difficult controversy. An allocations panel had approved funding for the local Planned Parenting agency. Planned Parenting provides a wide range of services, including sex education throughout the community, abortion counseling, and abortion.

Two members of the board of directors were appalled by the decision. They argued that the United Federation should not be funding an organization that supports abortion-related services. These two members contacted local antiabortion groups, which subsequently threatened to mount negative publicity and to discourage potential donors from contributing to the next United Federation campaign. Shelly G. called a special meeting of her executive committee to discuss this predicament. She was worried that the United Federation would be significantly harmed by the controversy.

Unlike the previous case (case 5.1), this case raises complicated ethical issues related to the resources being distributed, in addition to issues related to the process involved in allocating limited resources. The abortion issue is very controversial and understandably stirs up considerable emotion and strong opinions.

It would be unrealistic, of course, for social workers to expect that they will be able to settle debate about the morality of abortion. It is far more realistic to assume that the abortion controversy will continue indefinitely and that social workers involved in abortion-related debate will have to determine for themselves the nature of their ethical obligation.

Like the public in general the social work profession is divided on the abortion issue. Although most social workers are "pro-choice," meaning that they respect women's right to make their own informed choice about abortion, there is a significant minority within the profession that opposes abortion under all or most circumstances. Certainly some social workers would take the deontological view that abortion is inherently wrong and that practitioners should not in any way condone, encourage, or participate in abortion-related activities. This would mean that the Metropolitan United Federation should not provide funds to Planned Parenting, since this organization provides abortion services and abortion counseling. However, this traditional deontological view conflicts with another deontological perspective, which argues that social workers have an inherent obligation to respect clients' right to self-determination (in this case, clients' right to make their own choice about abortion). From this point of view, it would be appropriate for the United Federation to provide funding for Planned Parenting.

An act utilitarian would approach this case very differently. If there is evidence that the controversy surrounding possible funding of Planned Parenting would ultimately reduce contributions to the United Federation—because of all the negative publicity and the support that would be withdrawn from contributors who oppose abortion—an act utilitarian would probably argue that more harm than good would result if the United Federation provides the funding. That is, an act utilitarian would not be concerned about the morality of abortion itself; rather, a proponent of this view would be concerned about the net benefits and costs involved in the different courses of action. If supporting Planned Parenting would enable the United Federation to raise more funds to support important programs and services, an act utilitarian would endorse funding of the agency. However, if such funding would have an adverse effect on contributions overall, an act utilitarian would argue against supporting Planned Parenting.

A rule utilitarian, in contrast, would focus on the long-term consequences that would result from the precedent set if the United Federation were to fund Planned Parenting. A rule utilitarian would probably raise questions about the long-term consequences that might result if the United Federation allows political pressure and local controversy to determine its funding decisions. From this perspective, one could argue that the United Federation would be establishing a dangerous precedent and therefore ought to fund Planned Parenting if the allocations panel and board of directors believe that it is a worthy program. Of course, another rule utilitarian who opposes abortion might argue that the United Federation would be establishing a dangerous precedent by using private donations to fund abortion-related services. From this point of view, such funding might be seen as a serious threat to the moral fabric of the society as a whole.

The NASW Code of Ethics does not address the abortion controversy directly. Indirectly, however, several principles in the code can be cited in support of women's right to be informed about and to choose legalized abortion: "The social worker should provide clients with accurate and complete information regarding the extent and nature of the services available to them" (principle II.F.6); "The social worker should apprise clients of their risks, rights, opportunities, and obligations associated with social service to them" (principle II.F.7); "The social worker should make every effort to foster maximum self-determination on the part of clients" (principle II.G); and "The social worker should act to ensure that all persons have access to the resources, services, and opportunities which they require" (principle VI.P.2).

Although there is controversy within the profession, the prevailing ethical norms and values in social work generally support women's right to be informed about and choose legalized abortion. It is unfortunate that controversy related to the issue might result in some decline in contributions to the United Federation—a consequence that would be of considerable concern to an act utilitarian. This, however, can be addressed by thinking creatively about the ways in which donors contribute to the United Federation campaign. A reasonable option, one that is being exercised by a number of federated agencies, is to encourage donors to designate the agencies to which they would like their contributions allocated. Thus donors who are uncomfortable with the mission of and services provided by agencies such as Planned Parenting would be able to avoid supporting them by simply designating other agencies to which their money would be allocated. In this way, the United Federation would be able to fund organizations it believes warrant support and would allow donors who do not want to support certain agencies to have their contributions directed elsewhere. This is an example of how some, although certainly not all, ethical dilemmas can be addressed through creative problem solving. This solution is also consistent with the ethical guideline that an individual's right to basic well-being (in this case a woman's right to decide about her own health care and the future of a pregnancy) takes precedence over another individual's right to freedom and self-determination (that is, the freedom of those opposed to abortion services to interfere with those who want to be informed about abortion and to have the option to choose legalized abortion).

• GOVERNMENT AND PRIVATE-SECTOR RESPONSIBILITY FOR SOCIAL WELFARE

As a profession, social work has always had close ties with government. Many of the social service programs and much of the funding on which the profession depends are government sponsored, whether at the federal, state, or local levels.

The relationship between social work and government has evolved over time; during some periods there has been an active partnership (for example, during the Progressive and New Deal eras and the War on Poverty years), whereas at other times there has been an uneasy tension (for example, during presidential administrations when government-sponsored programs were cut back significantly and viewed with suspicion and hostility). In every instance the nature of the relationship between social work and government has raised ethical issues, primarily with respect to the nature of government's duty to citizens.

CASE 5.3

Aaron K. was the assistant director for program services in the state Department of Mental Health. One of his primary duties was to establish, fund, and monitor community-based facilities for mentally ill individuals. In light of the emphasis on deinstitutionalization in mental health care, Aaron K.'s responsibilities had increased substantially over the years.

Aaron K. was attempting to establish a new group home in a section of the state that has not had any community-based facilities. The proposed home would accommodate seven residents who otherwise would be cared for in one of the state's psychiatric hospitals. Following procedures used in his successful effort to establish group homes elsewhere in the state, Aaron K. consulted with local community leaders and officials, architects, and community representatives. He and his staff identified an appropriate site and began renovation of a large private residence that had been foreclosed by the bank that held the property's mortgage.

Shortly after construction crews began appearing at the house Aaron K. received a telephone call from a lawyer who told Aaron K. that she had been retained by "a group of concerned community residents" who were upset about the state's plan to establish a group home in their neighborhood. The lawyer told Aaron K. that the group was not pleased with the way the state "decided to dump this residence in the community's backyard" and that her clients were planning to go to court to stop further work on the house. The lawyer invited Aaron K. to attend a meeting to discuss the possibility of locating the group home elsewhere.

This case provides a good example of tension between the private sector and a government agency's attempt to assist a vulnerable population. For decades, and especially since the deinstitutionalization movement began in earnest in the United States in the 1960s, government agencies have encountered resistance when they have attempted to establish community-based facilities. Attempts to create affordable housing in communities have also encountered significant opposition, raising ethical questions about the role of government in communities' lives. This is sometimes referred to as the "NIMBY" ("not in my backyard") phenomenon.

Such issues raise fundamental questions about the proper role of government in citizens' lives. These questions have been addressed at least since Greco-Roman times. Although there is evidence of some debate about the role of government in earlier cultures (for example, the laws of Hammurabi of Babylon, c. 1750 B.C., and the sixth-century B.C. writings of Confucius), much of the intense debate began in ancient Greece ("Political Philosophy" 1988).

In the *Republic*, for example, Plato explored the nature of political life and the role of government in the lives of private citizens. Aristotle's *Politics* provides another classic example from this era of an analysis of the nature of governmental involvement in a society. Other philosophers and scholars, such as Machiavelli, Thomas Hobbes, John Locke, John Stuart Mill, Jean-Jacques Rousseau, Alexis de Tocqueville, and Karl Marx, also wrote prominent essays and books on the subject. Their arguments have ranged from dissertations about the evils of governmental intrusion in private citizens' lives to the compelling obligation that government has actively to organize, structure, and engineer social life (Reamer 1993).

Opinions about the appropriate extent of government involvement in private lives are often classified into three categories: conservative, liberal, and radical. People who are considered conservative believe that government involvement can be very harmful because it interferes with individuals' rights to privacy and with market forces. Conservatives often argue that economic markets are very efficient and that any interference with them through government regulation results in inefficiencies, excessive costs, and unnecessary intrusion into people's lives. Conservatives also tend to believe that government involvement promotes dependence and discourages independence among citizens. Hence, conservatives might argue that the state department of mental health should not interfere with a local community's wish not to have a group home in its vicinity. From a conservative perspective, if economic incentives are not sufficient to interest a community in a group home (for example, in the form of profits that might be derived from administering the group home or in the form of increased local spending and revenue), government should not dictate to local residents what sorts of programs and neighbors they ought to have. Market forces alone should determine whether such programs emerge in any given community. Government-sponsored programs that are created without local consent constitute an unwarranted form of coercion and invasion of privacy.

In contrast, the liberal perspective holds that some degree of government involvement may be necessary to meet the needs of vulnerable citizens. From this point of view, market forces may not be sufficient to create programs for vulnerable people, particularly if the general public is not enthusiastic about having certain client groups in their midst (for example, the poor, mentally disabled, or ex-offenders). Liberals often argue that government officials and agencies must create social programs proactively in order to fill in gaps left by the products of market forces. If private enterprise and market forces do not create community-based programs for the mentally ill, it is government's job to do so.

The radical perspective is less clear cut. Many radicals tend to agree with conservatives that government intrusion can be excessive and ought to be limited whenever possible. But many radicals also argue that government, in the form of the legislative and executive branches of federal, state, and local governments, often does not go far enough in its efforts to correct imperfections of free enterprise and to promote social justice. Many radicals are critical of capitalist forms of government that encourage profit-seeking private enterprise that often fails to meet the needs of vulnerable citizens.

From the perspective of moral philosophy—as opposed to the conservative, liberal, and radical ideologies associated with political philosophy—deontologists might make several very different arguments.

From one deontological perspective, it would be inherently wrong for a government agency to coerce a neighborhood's residents and force them to accept a residential program against their wishes. Citizens have an intrinsic right to privacy and to noninterference (consistent with a conservative view). However, from a different deontological perspective one might argue that mentally ill individuals have an inherent right to live in the least restrictive settings possible, which may mean that neighborhoods must accommodate community-based programs designed for this population (consistent with a liberal and radical view).

In contrast, an act utilitarian would not be concerned about the inherent rights of community residents or of mentally ill individuals. An act utilitarian would be more concerned about whether any particular community-based location would produce more good than harm, factoring in the therapeutic benefit of the program, ill will on the part of community residents, the effect of the residential facility on adjacent property values, and so on. A rule utilitarian, however, would be concerned about the effect of the precedent set by requiring a community to accept a residential program against its wishes. A rule utilitarian might argue that government coercion in this form would be detrimental in the long run, because of the wedge it might drive between private citizens and their government and between private citizens and people with special needs (in this case those who are mentally ill). Of course, a rule utilitarian with a different perspective might argue that government involvement in such a community-based program would help create a new standard with regard to every community's responsibility to absorb its fair share of individuals with special needs and that in the long run this would benefit society.

The NASW Code of Ethics does not contain principles that bear directly on the issue of government involvement in private communities. The code contains only general principles about social workers' obligation to promote the general welfare of society (principle VI.P), to prevent and eliminate discrimination against any person or group on the basis of various attributes, including mental disability (principle VI.P.1), to ensure that all persons have access to the resources and services they need (principle VI.P.2), and to act to expand choice and opportunity for oppressed groups and persons (principle VI.P.3).

The weight of social work values and ethical principles suggests that it is appropriate for government agencies to be able to require local communities to accommodate their fair share of individuals with special needs, including those who have some form of mental illness. This is consistent with the ethical guideline that individuals' right to basic well-being (in this case the rights of those who are mentally ill to safe, secure, and nurturing residential settings) takes precedence over other individuals' right to freedom and self-determination (the freedom of community residents to prevent the development of a group residence for a special needs population).

This case is important because it illustrates once again that it is a mistake to focus exclusively or even primarily on the outcome of an ethical decision. It may be, for example, that ethical theories, principles, and codes of ethics would lead reasonable people to conclude that government agencies have a duty and a right to establish community-based residences against the wishes of neighbors. But it would be a mistake to conclude that on this basis alone government officials should move to create such programs. Rather, social workers involved in these sorts of activities should be mindful of the *process* involved in formulating and implementing such policies and programs, particularly the ethical dimensions of such process. That is, social workers must recognize the right of local residents who may be affected by such policies and programs to participate in their development, their right to voice their opinions, and their right to engage in dialogue about the merits and demerits of these proposals. Including individuals likely to be affected by such policies and programs can often enhance support and minimize the adverse effects of opposition. This approach is also consistent with ethical principles in social work that seek to promote citizen self-determination as much as possible, recognizing, of course, that there are limits to this right, and to encourage full disclosure and debate related to controversial policies and programs.

Another prominent controversy related to government involvement in social welfare concerns government's obligation to provide financial assistance and supportive services to needy individuals, primarily the poor. For centuries there have been vigorous debates about government's duty to aid poor people with funds raised through taxation and, conversely, the right that poor people have to government assistance in the form of welfare.

CASE 5.4

Susan R. was director of the state Department of Social Services. She was appointed to the position shortly after the current governor was elected to office two years ago.

The governor informed Susan R. and all other state agency directors that because of the current financial crisis each department would be expected to reduce its budget by 10 percent for the next fiscal year. The governor ordered each department director to submit a proposed revised budget to her within thirty days.

Susan R. met with her senior staff to discuss ways to cut 10 percent from the departmental budget. She told her staff that cuts would have to be made from most of the department's programs, including general public assistance, medical assistance, vocational rehabilitation, and child care. Susan R. explained that to comply with the governor's mandate the department would have to reduce the number of people eligible for emergency public assistance from 153,000 to 110,000. That is, approximately 43,000 people, primarily single people who are unable to work and require emergency welfare assistance and health care, would not receive state-subsidized aid. Susan R. acknowledged that this was a bitter proposal; however, she claimed that there was no other source of funds large enough to meet the governor's required budget cuts.

Like the preceding case (case 5.3), this case raises ethical questions about the nature of government obligation, in particular its duty to assist vulnerable people. This case also raises questions that I addressed earlier concerning the allocation of limited resources. However, this case also raises an additional ethical issue that is critically important for the social work profession: to what extent does government have an obligation to raise revenue, through the mechanism of taxation, to provide for the basic needs of its citizens?

Debate about the duty of government to aid the poor is centuries old. As I discussed earlier, there has been enduring tension between those who believe that government has a fundamental obligation to use its powers and authority to mandate and finance programs to aid those in need and those who oppose government involvement in private lives. Many critics argue that government should not interfere with the compelling forces of the marketplace and that, in the end, the impressively efficient dynamics of free enterprise—in the form of economic incentives and disincentives—should determine who gets help and who does not.

Perhaps the best historical example of this debate in social welfare surrounded enactment and implementation of the English Poor Law Reform Bill of 1834. The Royal Poor Law Commission for Inquiring into the Administration and Practical Operation of the Poor Laws was influenced by people who believed that the famous Elizabethan Poor Law of 1601, which was designed to aid the destitute, was flawed because poverty was the natural state of the wage-earning classes. From this point of view, the original poor law was a mistake, an artificial creation of government that taxed the middle and upper classes in order to provide care for the those in need (Trattner 1979:42–47).

A significant result of the commission's report was an end to public assistance to able-bodied people, except in public institutions. The commission's report characterized poverty as a condition that resulted from individuals' moral inferiority. Hence, assistance for the poor was designed to increase "fear of insecurity, rather than to check its causes or even to alleviate its problems. At best, it would prevent starvation or death from exposure, but it would do so as economically and unpleasantly as possible" (Trattner 1979:47).

Despite this significant chapter in social welfare history, government's involvement in public welfare has grown dramatically over the years. One of the major reasons for this growth was the public's declining confidence, following the Great Depression of the 1870s, in the ability of free enterprise to ensure an adequate standard of living. The ideas of prominent British thinkers such as John Maynard Keynes and Sir William Beveridge helped shape what would eventually become an ambitious and comprehensive plan for government to pursue "an attack upon want" while doing its best to discourage the poor's dependence on the state (Beveridge 1942:6–7).

We might expect a deontologist to argue that the budget cuts in this case are inherently unethical, because government has an obligation to assist those who are most vulnerable. People who are disabled and who, for whatever reasons, are unable to care for themselves have a right to public assistance. Of course, a deontologist with a different political bent might argue that government has an inherent obligation to avoid intrusion in private lives and hence would support even larger budget cuts.

In contrast, an act utilitarian would be concerned about the consequences of the budget cuts. From this perspective, the budget cuts would be justifiable if they enable the state to balance its budget, pave the way for economic health (for example, through an enhanced bond rating that would result from a balanced budget), and eventually to provide important government-sponsored services in the future. Of course, an act utilitarian with a different outlook might argue that the benefit cuts are unethical because they will ultimately cause more harm than good. This would occur because many individuals whose benefits would be cut would end up requiring far more services and assistance as a result, for example, in the form of hospitalization, incarceration, and case management needed to address problems created by the budget cuts. That is, individuals whose benefits are cut may end up stealing in order to eat, breaking into business establishments for a place to sleep, manifesting psychotic symptoms because they do not have the money for medication, and so on. The consequence may be that these individuals' problems end up being much more costly than the amount of money involved in providing them with the benefits that are scheduled to be cut.

It is difficult to know how rule utilitarians would view this case. Because of their concern about the consequences of precedents established by individual cases, rule utilitarians might be concerned about the impact the cuts might have on the society at large, particularly with respect to the precedent set by the removal of much-needed benefits for vulnerable people. At the same time, rule utilitarians might be concerned about negative consequences that could result from the government's failure to balance its budget. A pattern of unbalanced budgets could have a disastrous impact on a state's economy, its bond ratings, and its ability to borrow money, encourage business develop-ment, generate tax revenue, and so on.

The NASW Code of Ethics includes only vague principles related to this case. Several principles pertain to social workers' obligation to society and to engage in community service: "The social worker should assist the profession in making social services available to the general public" (principle V.N); "The social worker should support the formulation, development, enactment, and implementation of social policies of concern to the profession" (principle V.N.2); "The social worker should promote the general welfare of society" (principle VI.P); "The social worker should act to ensure that all persons have access to the resources, services, and opportunities which they require" (princi-ple VI.P.2); and "The social worker should act to expand choice and opportunity for all persons, with special regard for disadvantaged or oppressed groups and persons" (principle VI.P.3). Considered as a group, these principles strongly suggest that it would be unethical to cut benefits provided to people in need. This conclusion is also con-sistent with the ethical guideline that the obligation to prevent basic harms takes precedence when values or duties conflict.

It is not enough, however, for social workers to decide whether the benefit cuts in this one case are unethical. Social workers also have an ethical obligation to advocate on clients' behalf and to try to enhance the public and private funds made available to assist vulnerable peo-ple. Social workers should not merely accept budgets as they are passed by state and federal legislatures and then participate in debates about how to divide up the budgetary pie. Social workers also have a responsibility to try to enlarge the pie. As the NASW Code of Ethics states, "The social worker should advocate changes in policy and leg-islation to improve social conditions and to promote social justice" (principle VI.P.6).

• COMPLIANCE WITH REGULATIONS AND LAWS

Social work administrators and community organizers sometimes encounter regulations and laws that seem unjust. In these instances, social workers face difficult decisions about their obligation to adhere to or obey these regulations and laws.

CASE 5.5

Alvin B. was the executive director of the Refugee Resettlement Center. The agency provides a wide range of social services to individuals who immigrate to the United States, including housing referrals, financial and job counseling, language tutoring, and concrete help with federal immigration officials.

As a result of the agency's work, it is not unusual for the staff to receive requests for services from people who are in the United States illegally. For a number of years the center's staff have taken the position that they should not notify immigration officials of illegal immigrants. Staff members have argued that the agency's mission is to assist immigrants regardless of their legal status in the United States.

At a recent staff meeting, however, Alvin B. suggested that staff revisit the issue. He told the staff that he was concerned about the agency's policy, particularly if staff had information that, in their judgment, public officials ought to have (for example, concerning the committing of a serious crime, or child abuse and neglect).

Social workers generally agree that they are obliged to obey regulations and laws. After all, without regulations and laws life would be intolerably chaotic. As I discussed earlier, however, circumstances sometimes arise that lead social workers to conclude that there are exceptions to this general expectation. In work with individual clients, for example, social workers may argue that violation of an agency rule or policy may be justifiable if it is necessary to save someone from serious injury. Does the same reasoning apply in social work administration and community organization? Is it ethically permissible for agency administrators deliberately to violate statutes or regulations to prevent some form of harm?

Similar issues arise with respect to the morality of civil disobedience. Throughout history there have been instances when social workers and others have felt it necessary to violate laws and regulations to protest some injustice or to achieve some higher-order good. Examples include disrupting work in welfare offices to protest inadequate benefits or unjust regulations, demonstrating illegally at legislative hearings to draw attention to the plight of the poor, violating segregation laws in order to fight racial discrimination, and sabotaging military records in an effort to challenge unjust wars. In the face of gross injustice, many social workers agree with the philosopher John Rawls (1975): "We are not required to acquiesce in the crushing of fundamental liberties by democratic majorities which have shown themselves blind to the principles of justice upon which justification of the constitution depends" (p. 352).

Some social workers embrace a different view, that laws and regulations that are legally enacted must be obeyed. Although social workers and others are entitled to challenge laws and regulations, and might even be encouraged to do so, they have an inherent obligation to obey existing ones. The philosopher Richard Wasserstrom (1975) summarizes this view: "Given what we know of the possibilities of human error and the actualities of human frailty, and given the tendency of democratic societies to make illegal only those actions which would, even in the absence of law, be unjustified, we can confidently conclude that the consequences will on the whole and in the long run be best if no one ever takes it upon himself to 'second-guess' the laws and to conclude that in his case his disobedience is justified" (p. 383).

What, for example, should the staff of the Refugee Resettlement Center do if they suspect that an illegal immigrant has neglected or abused a child? Should the agency have a policy that requires staff to comply with the mandatory reporting law, which would then alert officials to the immigrants' illegal status and likely lead to deportation, or should staff protect the client's identity and seek to address their concerns about possible abuse and neglect internally?

According to the deontological school of thought, as reflected previously in Wasserstrom's quotation, the agency must comply with laws and regulations that mandate reporting of suspected child abuse and neglect. In addition, staff would be expected to comply with federal or local regulations concerning disclosure of the identity of illegal immigrants.

An act utilitarian might reach a similar conclusion. That is, an act utilitarian might agree that the greater good would result if all individuals, including illegal immigrants, who are suspected of engaging in abuse or neglect (or any serious crime, for that matter) are reported to the appropriate public officials. An act utilitarian might also argue that

United States citizens should not be obligated to provide subsidies and services to illegal immigrants and therefore that it would be ethical for staff of the Refugee Resettlement Center to disclose their identity so they can be deported.

A rule utilitarian might also be concerned about the long-term consequences of an agency policy that would, in effect, conceal important information about possible child abusers and about the identity of illegal immigrants. A rule utilitarian might claim that the net result of this precedent could be widespread harm to abused or neglected children and a growing burden on United States citizens created by increasing numbers of illegal aliens.

It is not hard to imagine, however, that a rule utilitarian with a different outlook might argue that the long-term effectiveness of agencies such as the Refugee Resettlement Center would be undermined if word got out that the agency violates clients' confidentiality and discloses their identity to public officials.

Interestingly, the NASW Code of Ethics does not include any principles concerning social workers' obligation to obey laws or regulations. The code does, however, include several relevant principles concerning social workers' obligation to prevent discriminatory practices (principles I.C.2 and VI.P.1); serve clients with devotion and loyalty (principle II.F.1); foster maximum self-determination on the part of clients (principle II.G.1); ensure that all persons have access to the resources, services, and opportunities that they require (principle VI.P.2); and expand choice and opportunities for all persons, with special regard for disadvantaged or oppressed groups and persons (principle VI.P.3).

Considered as a group, these principles suggest that social workers have an obligation to assist all oppressed and vulnerable individuals, regardless of their immigration status. In this respect, it would be appropriate for the Refugee Resettlement Center to have a policy that prohibits disclosure of illegal immigrants' identity to public officials.

This conclusion does not take into account, however, instances in which disclosure of an illegal immigrant's identity may be necessary in order to obey the law and protect another individual, such as an abused child, from serious harm. Under these circumstances, it would be appropriate for social workers to take the steps necessary to protect those third parties, which may include obeying a law that requires disclosure of the identity of suspected perpetrators. It may be unfortunate that a consequence of this action might be deportation or some other harm to one's client, but this may be necessary to protect a third party. This is analogous to situations in which social workers are obligated to violate clients' prima facie right to confidentiality in order to protect third parties from harm, such as abused children, or spouses or partners who may be harmed by an angry, vindictive client. This conclusion is consistent with the principle in the NASW Code of Ethics that states that "the social worker should share with others confidences revealed by clients, without their consent, only for compelling professional reasons" (principle II.H.1). It is also consistent with the ethical guideline that asserts that rules against basic harms to the necessary preconditions of human action (such as life itself, health, food, shelter, mental equilibrium) take precedence over rules against harms such as lying or revealing confidential information.

• LABOR-MANAGEMENT DISPUTES

A significant number of social workers assume management positions during their careers, typically in the form of department directors and agency administrators. Social work administrators sometimes find themselves in the midst of a difficult ethical dilemma when there is labor-management conflict between line staff, including other social workers, and administrative superiors or an agency's board of directors.

CASE 5.6

Downcity General Hospital is a five-hundred-bed facility that primarily serves a low-income community. Because of funding problems, the hospital's board of directors announced that staff in the hospital's union, to which line social workers belong, would receive only a 2 percent salary increase for the next fiscal year. In addition, staff would be expected to make a larger contribution to their own health care plans.

After considerable debate and deliberation, union members voted to strike. They established a picket line and union members signed up for two-hour shifts.

Following the vote, hospital social workers met to discuss how they would handle the problems that patients were likely to encounter as a result of the strike. The group quickly discovered that they were divided about their participation in the strike. Several social workers argued that they had to support the union and take drastic measures to provide hospital staff, including themselves, with adequate salaries and benefits. Other social workers argued, however, that the social work staff had an obligation to provide services to patients and their families and that it would be unethical to withhold needed services.

It is not unusual for social workers to find themselves caught in the middle of labor-management disputes. These situations pose a very difficult ethical dilemma. As Bertha Reynolds (1956:237) observed decades ago, "In the history of unionization in social work it is impossible to separate the two notions of protecting one's own condition as a worker and safeguarding the right to treat clients ethically." Thus if social workers participate in a strike or related job action, there is the possibility that their clients will be deprived of critically important services. Some social workers believe that it would be unconscionable to abandon clients in order to pursue their own employment-related interests. From this perspective, social workers may have legitimate employment concerns and complaints, but strikes that result in the withdrawal or termination of services to vulnerable clients are unacceptable.

Some argue, however, that if social workers cross picket lines and provide services to clients, there is the possibility that their actions will undermine the unions' efforts to address significant and legitimate employment issues related to wages, benefits, and so on. Some social workers believe that because of the profession's altruistic mission they are particularly vulnerable to exploitation by management. Hence many practitioners believe that social workers must be willing to strike and engage in vigorous job action in order to avoid exploitation (Reamer 1988). One popular argument, espoused by a former prominent AFL-CIO official (Gotbaum 1978), is that the threat of a strike actually enhances labor-management relations:

> We need the possibility of a strike. Take what I call the Red China experience. When the Red Chinese did not have the atom bomb, they were

the most militant and irresponsible of sovereign states. They wanted Russia to invade the United States; they were flexing their nonexistent muscles. But as soon as they got the bomb, the Chinese became much more responsible, because they could also create havoc. The same thing happens with workers. (P. 158)

As a group, social workers have been ambivalent about striking and job action. In one survey, social workers were evenly divided as to whether they should have joined a walkout at a large metropolitan state hospital in Pennsylvania (Bohr, Brenner, and Kaplan 1971). Rehr (1960) reported a similar split among social workers concerning a strike by nonprofessional workers at a large New York City hospital; half the staff remained on the job while the other half decided not to cross the picket line. Although physicians and nurses were instructed by their respective professional organizations to continue providing patient care, the New York City chapter of NASW concluded that employees had a right to determine for themselves whether or not to report to work. Interestingly, staff at the same hospital were similarly divided during a second strike twenty-five years later (Fisher 1987).

Lightman (1983) also reports significant differences of opinion among social workers, based on his survey of Canadian practitioners. Lightman found that many social workers (53 percent) disagreed with the statement "Social workers provide an essential service [that] should not be interrupted by a strike." Only 29 percent of the sample agreed with the statement (18 percent were uncertain). As Lightman concludes, "Such a conflictual and power-based approach toward decision making sits uncomfortably with many social workers who prefer to believe that good faith and reasoned interchange can resolve any work-related problem. At the same time, conflict and power do not fit easily with many traditional social work values" (p. 143).

A social worker with a deontological perspective might argue that members of the profession have an inherent obligation to assist people in need. That is, the principal mission of social work is to help, and self-interested motives related to practitioners' employment should not interfere with social workers' fundamental duty to provide services to vulnerable people. Although social workers might claim that they also have a duty to themselves, in the form of meeting their own needs, a strict deontological perspective would likely emphasize the profession's time-honored mission to help people in need.

This view would contrast sharply with an act utilitarian perspective. An act utilitarian would try to weigh the relative costs and benefits of a strike. From this vantage point, a strike would be justifiable if there were evidence that it would cause more good than harm, perhaps in the form of employees who are more content and consequently in the form of higher-quality services delivered to clients. Although hospital patients might suffer in the short run as a result of being deprived of services during the strike, in the long run patients as a group may benefit. Lightman (1983), for example, found that although only 50 percent of his sample of social workers would consider striking to enhance fringe benefits, 86 percent would consider striking to enhance quality of services for clients. Even NASW (1969), through its Ad Hoc Committee on Advocacy, has acknowledged the possibility that a strike or job action may be necessary to improve the quality of care for clients, even though clients may be harmed in the short run: "To what extent does one risk injury to his clients' interests in the short run on behalf of institutional changes in the long run? . . . One cannot arbitrarily write off any action that may temporarily cause his clients hardship if he believes the ultimate benefits of his action will outweigh any initial harm" (p. 19). In addition, in its Personnel Standards, NASW (1975) explicitly opposes "laws or policies that prohibit strikes by employees." These are views that are patently consistent with an act utilitarian perspective.

A rule utilitarian, in contrast, would emphasize the implications of the precedent that would be set by a labor strike. From this point of view, a strike may not be justifiable if the precedent would encourage labor strikes on a wide scale. Although clients might benefit, a rule utilitarian might be concerned about the damaging consequences and strife that could result from a large number of labor strikes. Of course, a rule utilitarian with a different view might conclude, consistent with an act utilitarian interpretation, that the threat of wide-scale strikes might ultimately enhance labor-management relations and thus ensure ongoing delivery of needed services to clients.

The NASW Code of Ethics does not contain principles that directly address the subject of labor strikes. Several of the code's principles are relevant, however, and most imply that social workers have a duty to serve their clients and that it would be unethical for practitioners suddenly to terminate services: "The social worker should regard as primary the service obligation of the social work profession" (principle I.C); "The social worker's primary responsibility is to clients" (principle II.F); and "The social worker should provide appropriate professional services in public emergencies" (principle VI.P.5). In addition, the code suggests that social workers have an obligation to abide by commitments they have made to their employers to provide services to clients: "The social worker should adhere to commitments made to the employing organization" (principle IV.L).

Having said this, however, I should point out at least one principle in the NASW code that acknowledges that special and compelling circumstances can arise in practice that warrant the termination of services to clients: "The social worker should withdraw services precipitously only under unusual circumstances, giving careful consideration to all factors in the situation and taking care to minimize possible adverse effects" (principle II.F.10). Although this principle does not state explicitly that social workers are permitted to strike, it implies that "giving careful consideration to all factors" could include the circumstances that often lead to labor strikes.

The code also states that social workers who decide to terminate services to clients must do so responsibly and with keen sensitivity to clients' ongoing needs: "The social worker who anticipates the termination or interruption of service to clients should notify clients promptly and seek the transfer, referral or continuation of service in relation to the clients' needs and preferences" (principle II.F.11). Hence, the norms in social work suggest that strikes should be avoided if at all possible, but when they are absolutely necessary—in order to address egregious working conditions or flagrant problems with the quality of care, as opposed to less serious employment-related issues—social workers have an obligation to ensure the continued delivery of services to clients in need. This is consistent with the ethical guidelines presented earlier, which assert that 1) the obligation to adhere to rules and regulations (such as employment policies) to which one has voluntarily and freely consented *ordinarily* overrides one's right to engage in a manner that conflicts with these rules and regulations (for example, in the form of a labor strike), and 2) individuals' rights to basic well-being may override the obligation to adhere to rules and regulations in cases of conflict (which would justify a labor strike in extreme circumstances, when individuals' basic well-being is at stake).

• THE USE OF DECEPTION

Social workers, like all professionals, understand the need for truth and honesty in their work. Candid communication is essential in relationships between professionals and clients and among professionals. On occasion, however, social work administrators, planners, researchers, and community organizers are tempted to believe that some degree of deception and dishonesty is necessary and justifiable. Whether deception and dishonesty are, in fact, ever justifiable is, of course, an important matter to debate.

CASE 5.7

Willard E. was the director of social work at the East Bay Children's Psychiatric Hospital. The hospital provides inpatient and outpatient services for children with severe emotional problems and behavior disorders.

The hospital was scheduled to be visited by an accreditation team. For many years the hospital has been accredited by a national organization, which conducts intensive site visits as part of its periodic review. The site visitors typically interview staff, inspect physical facilities, review hospital policies and procedures, and evaluate a sample of patient records. The quality of patient records is assessed according to a number of specific criteria, including the thoroughness of documentation related to patients' psychosocial history, admission, treatment plans, services received, and discharge.

Willard E. had some concern about the quality of his staff's entries in patients' records. He was particularly concerned about record-keeping problems that occurred under his predecessor's administration. At a staff meeting Willard E. instructed each member of his social work staff to review all records from the past year for which he or she had been responsible. All staff were told to review each record for its completeness and to identify any missing information (for example, a missing admission summary or discharge note). They were also told to fill in any missing information without indicating that the information had been added at a later date. Willard E. told his staff that they should do their best to "reconstruct each case as much as possible in order to fill in any gaps. If you don't remember exactly what happened, do your best to be accurate. I do not want the department to look bad. Do your best to clean up the records so we don't have a problem with the accreditation team."

As I discussed earlier, most social workers understand that under extreme circumstances—in order to protect someone from serious harm or to save a life, for example—some degree of deception may be necessary and justifiable. Lying to an abusive and threatening spouse concerning the whereabouts of his estranged wife may seem legitimate in order to protect her from likely injury.

In many instances, however, deception is clearly inappropriate or at the very least questionable (for example, when it is motivated by a social worker's self-interest, as opposed to concern about clients). Falsifying progress reports submitted to insurance companies or to funding agencies in order to increase profits is clearly wrong, as are deliberate attempts to deceive employees about their job security. Of course, in between cases of clearly justifiable deception and clearly inappropriate deception are ambiguous cases in which practitioners are likely to disagree. These cases typically involve "benevolent deception," or deception that is considered necessary to assist people in need.

Commentary and debate about the ethics of deception have an impressive history. Immanuel Kant, the eighteenth-century German philosopher, and Saint Augustine, the early Christian church father and philosopher from the fourth century, are well known for their forceful and oft-cited arguments claiming that deception is never permissible, regardless of the possible consequences. This is the classic deontological view of the matter. For Augustine, a deceptive individual is fundamentally defiled and tainted by the deception, regardless of whatever good might result. For Kant, deception is inherently wrong because "it is a perversion of one's uniquely human capacities irrespective of any consequences of the lie, and thus lying is not only intrinsically bad but wrong" (Fried 1978:60). On this basis, then, it would be inherently wrong for Willard E. or any member of his social work staff to engage in any form of deception with respect to the hospital records. Any record that is altered at a later date should clearly indicate that it has been amended; any attempt to conceal the alteration is wrong.

Obviously, this deontological perspective on the legitimacy of deception runs counter to the traditional act utilitarian view. An act utilitarian would be concerned only about the possible consequences of the deception. As Jeremy Bentham, an English philosopher who was one of the originators of the utilitarian school of thought in the eighteenth century, argued, deception is not necessarily unethical or intrinsically bad: "Falsehood, take it by itself, consider it as not being accompanied by any other material circumstances, nor therefore productive of any material effects, can never, upon the principle of utility, constitute any offense at all" (Bentham 1973 [originally published in 1789]:205). From this perspective, then, deception to cover up flaws in the social work staff's records would be justifiable if there is evidence that the hospital's accreditation would be in jeopardy if the deception did not occur. What matters most is the hospital's accreditation and viability, so that it can serve children with severe problems. Deception would be justified if it enabled the hospital to carry out its mission. The calculus is relatively straightforward.

A rule utilitarian would examine the situation quite differently. Most likely, a rule utilitarian would be concerned about the long-term consequences if the deception practiced in this one case were to become a precedent and thus carried out on a widespread basis. In this respect, a rule utilitarian would probably agree with a deontologist. Although the proponents of these two views would base their conclusions on different arguments (the former emphasizing the harmful consequences of the precedent that would be set in this case and the latter emphasizing the inherently unethical nature of deception regardless of the consequences), both would probably claim that the deception was wrong.

The NASW Code of Ethics contains one principle that has direct bearing on the use of deception: "The social worker should not participate in, condone, or be associated with dishonesty, fraud, deceit, or misrepresentation" (I.A.2). It is important to note that this principle resembles deontological thinking much more than utilitarian thinking. That is, the principle in no way acknowledges that some degree of deceit may be justifiable for compelling reasons, such as to ensure a program's accreditation and future. Dishonesty, fraud, and deceit are wrong, period.

It seems clear that it would be wrong for Willard E. to encourage his staff to participate in an attempt to deceive accreditation site visitors. Although the hospital may be criticized for gaps in its records, such criticism is not likely to jeopardize its accreditation. It would be far more appropriate for the hospital's administrators to acknowledge the problem that occurred, primarily under a prior administrator, and to present the accreditation team with a well constructed, thorough plan to address the shortcoming.

• WHISTLE BLOWING

One of the unfortunate features of social work is that practitioners sometimes encounter wrongdoing in the profession. On occasion, social workers encounter colleagues who are engaging in unethical conduct. Among the most difficult ethical decisions social workers face is whether or not to "blow the whistle" on a colleague and to report the misconduct to supervisors or other authorities.

CASE 5.8

Mark G. was a casework supervisor at the Wickenden Family Service Agency. He had worked at the agency as a caseworker for six years before being promoted a year ago by the agency's executive director, with whom Mark G. had a close professional relationship.

One day one of the agency's caseworkers, whom Mark G. supervised, asked to speak with him. The caseworker told Mark G. that he had some "disturbing news" to share with him. According to the caseworker, one of his new clients had just reported in a therapy session that she knew the agency's executive director. According to the client, several months earlier the executive director had paid her for sex in a hotel room and had shared cocaine with her. All together, the client said, she and the executive director have had "five or six dates." The client said she had "no idea he ran the agency. He told me he was an accountant. I was stunned when I saw him in the hallway here. He just looked the other way."

Mark G. was torn about how to handle the situation, particularly since he regarded the executive director as a friend.

Understandably, social workers are often reluctant to report colleagues who are engaged in wrongdoing. Colleagues' careers can be ruined as a result, and individuals who blow the whistle can be ostracized throughout an agency and professional community.

At the same time, most social workers understand why it may be necessary in some instances to blow the whistle. Clients' well being and entire programs may be at risk because of a colleague's misconduct or impaired condition. In these situations social workers have to weigh the competing reasons for and against whistle blowing. As Barry (1986) observed with regard to whistle blowing in agency settings,

> Truthfulness, noninjury, and fairness are the ordinary categories of obligations that employees have to third parties, but we can still ask: How are workers to reconcile obligations to employers or organizations and others? Should the employee ensure the welfare of the organization by reporting the fellow worker using drugs, or should she be loyal to the fellow worker and say nothing? Should the secretary carry out her boss's instructions, or should she tell his wife the truth? Should the accountant say nothing about the building code violations, or should she inform authorities? In each case the employee experiences divided loyalties. Resolving such conflict calls for a careful weighing of the obligations to the employer or firm, on the one hand, and of those to the third party, on the other. The process is never easy. (P. 239)

Very often the circumstances surrounding a colleague's alleged misconduct are ambiguous. The evidence of wrongdoing may be questionable, the impact of the misconduct may not be clear, and the likelihood of correcting the problem may be slim. Decisions to blow the whistle must be approached deliberately and cautiously. Before deciding to blow the whistle, social workers must carefully consider the severity of the harm and misconduct involved; the quality of the evidence of wrongdoing (one should avoid blowing the whistle without clear and convincing evidence); the possible impact on the colleague and agency; the whistle blower's motives (that is, whether the whistle blowing is motivated primarily by a wish for revenge); and the viability of alternative, intermediate courses of action (whether other, less drastic means might address the problem—for example, directly confronting the alleged wrongdoer). As Fleishman and Payne (1980) argue, "There may be other ways to do right . . . than by blowing a whistle on a friend. A direct personal confrontation may serve both public interest and personal loyalty, if the corrupt practice can be ended and adequate restitution made" (p. 43).

Some cases involving misconduct are so serious, however, that there is no alternative but to blow the whistle. From a deontological perspective, some forms of misconduct are inherently wrong and must be disclosed, regardless of the consequences to the individuals or agencies involved. Of course, an act utilitarian would want to examine the consequences of blowing the whistle and would encourage such action only if there were evidence that it would produce more good than harm. If it appeared that Mark G.'s blowing the whistle on his executive director would cause substantial damage to the director's career and to the agency, an act utilitarian might conclude that it is not justifiable.

An act utilitarian would also argue that it is legitimate and appropriate for the worker contemplating blowing the whistle to consider the possible impact on her or his own career. As Peters and Branch (1972) have noted, "If an employee becomes a damaged good, tainted by a reputation as an organizational squealer, he may find so many doors locked that a drop in station or a change in profession will be required" (p. 280).

A rule utilitarian might also be concerned about the long-term consequences that would result from the precedent set by whistle blowing in this case. From this perspective, whistle blowing might not be justified if it would lead to widespread whistle blowing, since this might undermine employees' trust in their colleagues, increase work-environment suspicion, and in general weaken morale in agencies. Of course, a rule utilitarian with a different point of view might argue that it is essential to blow the whistle, because this action may raise ethical standards throughout the social work field if it encourages other professionals to disclose wrongdoing.

The NASW Code of Ethics is clear that social workers have an obligation to confront wrongdoing, although it does not explicitly endorse whistle blowing: "The social worker should take action through appropriate channels against unethical conduct by any other member of the profession" (principle V.M.2). Although this principle does not spell out what "appropriate channels" entails, clearly whistle blowing is one possibility. Milder forms of misconduct can perhaps be addressed by negotiating directly with the alleged wrongdoer.

In the preceding case, it appears that Mark G. would have to take aggressive steps to confront the executive director's alleged wrongdoing. If the evidence that Mark G. is able to collect strongly suggests misconduct, he would have an obligation to share that information with individuals who are in a position to address the problem—for example, the chairperson or executive committee of the agency's board of directors. This assumes, of course, that Mark G. has shared the information and evidence with his executive director and given him an opportunity to respond. Mark G. should also do his best to minimize possible harm to the agency and its staff by being discreet about with whom he shares the evidence of wrongdoing.

The prospect of whistle blowing is disconcerting for most social workers who encounter misconduct in the profession. As I shall discuss in the next chapter, unethical behavior and the whistle blowing that sometimes accompanies it can cause significant problems for clients, practitioners, and third parties. Social workers have an obligation to confront misconduct responsibly. As Fleishman and Payne (1980) conclude with regard to whistle blowing in the political arena, "The moral problems caused by other people's sins are an old story. When one discovers the corruption of a friend or political ally, personal or political loyalties may conflict with legal duty or devotion to the public interest. The high value of loyalty in politics may make the conflict a wrenching one, but on principled grounds the sacrifice of law or public interest to loyalty in such a case can hardly be justified" (p. 43).

⑥ PROFESSIONAL MALPRACTICE AND MISCONDUCT

THE ENFORCEMENT OF SOCIAL WORK ETHICS

• • •

Thus far I have examined the nature of social work values, the process of ethical decision making, and various ethical dilemmas in social work practice. As I have shown, many of the ethical issues that practitioners encounter raise difficult philosophical questions—for example, whether social workers are always obligated to be truthful and to respect clients' right to self-determination, how limited resources should be allocated, and when social workers should blow the whistle on ethical wrongdoing.

Many of these ethical issues do not raise legal questions or issues that would warrant discipline by a regulatory body, such as a state licensing board, or a professional body, such as the National Association of Social Workers. Whether a particular social worker ought to be entirely truthful in response to a client's question about his or her prognosis, how scarce resources at an emergency shelter should be distributed, and a decision by a caseworker whether to blow the whistle on a lazy colleague may not involve legal questions or questions of misconduct. Instead, these ethical dilemmas are more likely to involve ethical issues in their most innocent form, that is, ethical issues requiring thoughtful deliberation and application of sound ethical principles. These are the issues about which reasonable practitioners may disagree.

Unfortunately, however, many ethical issues in social work are not so innocent. They raise questions about ethical misconduct and wrongdoing of a sort that may constitute violations of the law, professional codes of ethics, and publicly enacted regulations. These are cases that may result in lawsuits, ethics complaints, or criminal charges filed against social workers.

In this chapter I shall discuss various examples of unethical behavior or professional misconduct. Some of these cases involve genuine mistakes practitioners may make that lead to allegations of unethical behavior or professional misconduct. Examples include social workers who simply forget to obtain clients' consent before sharing confidential records with third parties, practice social work after neglecting to renew their licenses, and inadvertently bill insurance companies for services that were not rendered. These are cases in which social workers do not intend to harm or defraud anyone; rather, these are cases in which social workers unintentionally make mistakes that injure someone or some organization. The injury is sufficiently serious that the injured party charges the social worker with some form of unethical behavior or professional misconduct.

In contrast, other cases are related to the ethical dilemmas I discussed in chapters 4 and 5. In these cases, social workers face very difficult ethical decisions and do their best to handle them responsibly. These social workers may be remarkably conscientious in the way they go about making the ethical decision. They may review relevant literature, consult with colleagues who have expertise on the subject, document their decision making, and so on. What may happen in spite of this thoroughness and diligence, however, is that some individual or organization may allege that the social worker mishandled the case and acted unethically. Some party may file a lawsuit or ethics complaint alleging that the social worker violated prevailing ethical standards in the profession and that consequently injury resulted. An example is the case in which a social worker has to decide whether to disclose confidential information about a client who is HIV-positive in order to protect the client's lover, who is not aware of her lover's HIV-positive status, from harm. The social worker has to choose between the client's right to confidentiality and the social worker's obligation to protect a third party from harm. It is not hard to imagine that a social worker in this predicament might be sued no matter what course of action she takes. If she respects her client's right to confidentiality and subsequently the client's lover becomes infected, the social worker might be sued or have an ethics complaint filed against her by the client's lover alleging that the social worker failed to protect her from serious harm. Conversely, if the social worker discloses the confidential information, without her client's permission, in order to protect the client's lover from harm, the social worker might be sued or have an ethics complaint filed against her by her client alleging that the social worker violated the client's right to confidentiality. Thus in some of these cases, even the most conscientious, thoughtful, and prudent social worker can have charges filed against him or her alleging ethical misconduct or unprofessional behavior.

In addition, some cases involve allegations that a social worker engaged in gross professional misconduct and knowingly harmed a client or some other party. These are not the cases in which social workers inadvertently make harmful mistakes, or make difficult ethical decisions in a responsible manner but in a way that triggers an ethics complaint or lawsuit. Rather, these are cases in which there are allegations that social workers willfully violated individuals' rights. Examples include cases where social workers become sexually involved with clients, extort money from clients, and commit fraud against insurance companies. In addition to ethics complaints and lawsuits, these cases may also result in criminal charges.

• THE ADJUDICATION OF SOCIAL WORKERS

There are three prominent ways in which social workers are held accountable for professional misconduct. These include ethics complaints filed against members of the National Association of Social Workers, ethics complaints filed with state licensing or regulatory boards, and lawsuits filed against social workers who have malpractice and liability coverage. In some instances, social workers are also subjected to review by other professional organizations to which they belong, such as the American Board of Examiners in Clinical Social Work, the National Federation of Societies for Clinical Social Work, and the American Association for Marriage and Family Therapy. In addition, criminal charges may be filed against social workers, although this is relatively rare.

Members of NASW may be named in ethics complaints alleging violation of specific principles in the association's code of ethics.

Examples are "The social worker should maintain high standards of personal conduct in the capacity or identity as social worker" (principle I.A).; "The social worker should act in accordance with the highest standards of professional integrity and impartiality" (principle I.D); and "The social worker should not exploit professional relationships for personal gain" (principle I.D.2).

In general, there has been a steady increase in the number of ethics complaints filed against social workers. These complaints cite a wide variety of the code's principles, including those related to confidentiality, sexual misconduct, social workers' relationships with colleagues, and conduct as a social worker (Berliner 1989).

Ethics complaints filed against NASW members are processed initially by chapter Committees on Inquiry (COIs). Based on a peer review model, these committees made up of NASW members initially review each complaint and may accept or reject it for further hearing. If a complaint is accepted, the chapter COI conducts a hearing during which the complainant (the person filing the complaint), the respondent (the person against whom the complaint is filed), and witnesses have an opportunity to testify. After hearing all parties and discussing the testimony, the COI presents a report to elected chapter officers summarizing its findings and presenting its recommendations. Recommendations may include sanctions or various forms of corrective action, such as suspension from the NASW, mandated supervision or consultation, censure in the form of a letter, or instructions to send the complainant a letter of apology. In some cases the sanction may be publicized through local and national NASW newsletters or public newspapers. The parties involved in the complaint may appeal the chapter officials' decision, first to the National Committee on Inquiry and then, if necessary, to the executive committee of the NASW national board of directors.

Many states also have licensing or regulatory boards that process ethics complaints filed against social workers. Ordinarily, these boards appoint a panel of colleagues to review the complaint and if necessary to conduct a hearing (Barker and Branson 1993).

In addition, growing numbers of social workers have been named in lawsuits alleging some form of ethical misconduct or malpractice. This trend is clearly reflected in liability claims filed against social workers insured through the NASW Insurance Trust, the largest insurer of social workers in the United States (Reamer 1994b).

Claims filed against social workers insured by the NASW Insurance Trust can be divided into two broad groups. The first includes claims that allege that social workers carried out their duties improperly or in a fashion inconsistent with the profession's standards (often called acts of commission or of misfeasance or malfeasance). Examples include improper treatment of a client (for example, using a treatment technique for which one has not received proper training), sexual misconduct, breach of client confidentiality, wrongful removal of a child from a home, assault and battery, improper peer review, and improper termination of services.

The second broad category includes claims that allege that social workers failed to perform a duty that they are ordinarily expected to perform, according to the profession's standards (acts of omission or nonfeasance). Examples include failure to obtain a client's informed consent before releasing confidential information, failure to prevent a client's suicide, failure to be available when needed, failure to protect third parties from harm, failure to supervise a client properly, and failure to refer a client for consultation or treatment by a specialist.

Of course, not all claims filed against social workers are substantiated. Some claims are frivolous, and others lack the evidence necessary to demonstrate malpractice and negligence. However, many claims are substantiated, ultimately costing social workers considerable expense and emotional anguish (although insurance coverage helps to ease the financial burden).

Social workers must know what kinds of professional misconduct or unethical behavior constitute malpractice. Malpractice is a form of negligence that occurs when a social worker, or any other professional, acts in a manner inconsistent with the profession's *standard of care*—the way an ordinary, reasonable, and prudent professional would act under the same or similar circumstances (Reamer 1994c).

Lawsuits and liability claims that allege malpractice are civil suits, in contrast to criminal proceedings. Ordinarily civil suits are based on tort or contract law, with plaintiffs (the individuals bringing the suit) seeking some sort of compensation for injuries they claim to have incurred (Hogan 1979). These injuries may be economic (for example, lost wages or medical expenses), physical (for instance, as a result of an assault by a person the social worker was supposed to have been supervising), or emotional (for example, depression that may result from a social worker's sexual contact with a client).

As in criminal trials, defendants in lawsuits are presumed to be innocent until proved otherwise. In ordinary civil suits, defendants will be found liable for their actions based on the standard of *preponderance of the evidence*, as opposed to the stricter standard of *beyond a reasonable doubt* used in criminal trials. In some civil cases—for example, those involving contract disputes—the court may expect *clear and convincing evidence*, a standard of proof that is greater than preponderance of the evidence but less than for beyond a reasonable doubt (Gifis 1991).

In general, malpractice occurs when there is evidence that 1) at the time of the alleged malpractice, a legal duty existed between the practitioner and the client (for example, a social worker has a duty to keep information shared by a client confidential); 2) the practitioner was derelict in that duty, either through an action that occurred or through an omission (confidential information about a client's alcohol use was divulged to the client's employer without the client's permission); 3) the client suffered some harm or injury (the client alleges that he was fired from his job because the social worker inappropriately divulged confidential information to the client's employer); and 4) the harm or injury was directly and proximately caused by the social worker's dereliction of duty (the client's dismissal was the direct result of the social worker's unauthorized disclosure of confidential information).

There are six broad categories of cases that involve malpractice, ethical misconduct, or unprofessional behavior: confidentiality and privacy; delivery of services; supervision of clients and staff; consultation, referral, and records; deception and fraud; and termination of service.

• CONFIDENTIALITY AND PRIVACY

Earlier I discussed ethical dilemmas related to confidentiality. In those cases social workers had to decide how to handle the disclosure of confidential information to protect third parties, to protect or benefit clients in response to a court order, and to parents or guardians concerning minor children. My discussion focused on the process of ethical decision making rather than the possibility of misconduct involved in the inappropriate disclosure of confidential information.

Social workers can be charged with misconduct if they violate clients' right to confidentiality. Relevant principles from the NASW code of ethics include "The social worker should respect the privacy of clients and hold in confidence all information obtained in the course of professional service" (principle II.H); "The social worker should share with others confidences revealed by clients, without their consent, only for compelling professional reasons" (principle II.H.1); and "The social worker should inform clients fully about the limits of confidentiality in a given situation, the purposes for which information is obtained, and how it may be used" (principle II.H.2).

A social worker who decides to breach a client's confidentiality in order to protect a third party from harm may have an ethics complaint filed against him or her by the social worker's client. The client might claim that the social worker violated his or her right to privacy and that the client was injured as a result. The client may also file a civil suit for damages. Of course, the social worker might also be charged with misconduct by an injured third party if the practitioner decides to respect the client's right to confidentiality and hence does not warn or take steps to protect the third party. This is what happened to the psychologist and other university staff in the famous *Tarasoff* case discussed earlier. As Lewis (1986) has observed, "*Tarasoff* and its progeny established that persons harmed by individuals undergoing therapy may sue that patient's psychotherapist for negligent failure to protect them from the patients' dangerous propensities. Case law also makes it clear that mental health professionals have a duty to maintain the confidential nature of their relationships to those to whom they are rendering treatment. A breach of either duty may result in civil liability" (p. 606).

The *Tarasoff* case and various other "duty to protect" cases that have been litigated since then have helped to clarify the delicate balance between social workers' obligation to respect clients' right to confidentiality and their simultaneous duty to protect third parties from harm. Although some of the court decisions in these cases are contradictory and inconsistent with one another, in general four conditions should be met to justify disclosure of confidential information to protect third parties from harm: 1) The social worker should have evidence that the client poses a threat of *violence* to a third party. Although court decisions have not provided precise definitions of *violence*, the term ordinarily implies the use of force—such as with a gun, knife, or other deadly weapon—to inflict injury. 2) The social worker should have evidence that the violent act is *foreseeable*. The social worker should be able to present evidence that suggests significant risk that the violent act will occur. Although courts recognize that social workers and other human service professionals cannot always predict violence accurately, social workers should expect to have to demonstrate that they had good reasons for believing that their client was likely to act violently. 3) The social worker should have evidence that the violent act is *imminent*. The social worker should be able to present evidence that the act was impending or likely to occur relatively soon. *Imminence* may be defined differently by different social workers; some social workers think imminence implies a violent incident within minutes, whereas others think in terms of hours or days. In light of this difference of professional opinion, it is important for social workers to be able to explain their definition and interpretation of imminence should they have to defend their decision regarding the disclosure of confidential information. 4) Many, although not all, court decisions imply that a practitioner must be able to identify the probable victim. A number of courts have ruled that practitioners should have very specific information about the parties involved, including the potential victim's identity, in order to justify disclosure of confidential information against the client's wishes. Schutz (1982) summarizes current thinking on the subject of "duty to protect":

> Generally, it is suggested that the authorities and/or the intended victim should be warned. Warning the authorities makes the most sense when the intended victims are the patient's children, since a warning to the victim is ordinarily useless, and the child protective agency often has broader powers than the police—who might say that they cannot detain the patient (particularly after a failed commitment) because he has not done anything yet. If one decides to warn the victim—who is naturally shocked and terrified by the news that someone intends to kill him—and if nothing occurs, one could be liable for the infliction of emotional dis-

tress by a negligent diagnosis. One way to reduce this risk might be to include as a part of the warning a statement of professional opinion about the nature and likelihood of the threat; to recommend that the victim contact the police, an attorney, and a mental health professional for assistance to detain (or try to commit) the patient; to inform the victim of his legal rights; and to offer assistance with the stress of such a situation.

(P. 64)

Social workers can take several additional steps to protect themselves and to help reduce the chances of civil suits and ethics complaints. These include consulting an attorney who is familiar with statutes and case law related to "duty to protect" cases; seeking the client's consent for the social worker to warn the potential victim; and considering asking the client to warn the victim (unless the social worker believes this contact would only increase the risk); disclosing only the minimum amount necessary to protect the potential victim; encouraging the client to surrender any weapons he or she may have; and if clinically warranted referring the client to a psychiatrist for an evaluation (Austin, Moline, and Williams 1990; Reamer 1994b).

In the final analysis, social workers must use their professional judgment in their decisions about protecting clients' right to confidentiality and protecting third parties from harm. Explicit criteria that can be applied to all situations simply do not exist. As Lewis (1986) concludes, "It must, however, be recognized that psychotherapy is an imperfect science. A precise formula for determining when the duty to maintain confidentiality should yield to the duty to warn is therefore beyond reach" (pp. 614–15).

It is very important for social workers to inform clients at the beginning of their relationship about the limits of confidentiality. Clients have the right to know what information they share with a social worker might have to be disclosed to others against clients' wishes (for example, evidence of child abuse or neglect, or of a client's threat to harm a third party). Social workers who are involved in group treatment, or who provide counseling services to couples and families, must be particularly aware of confidentiality issues. Social workers disagree about the extent to which members of groups, couples, and families have a right to expect that information they share in therapy will not be disclosed to others. Although social workers can encourage others involved in treatment to respect a particular individual's wish for privacy, there is considerable debate about the limits of confidentiality in these contexts. Some social workers believe, for example, that those involved in couples or family counseling should not have the right to convey secrets to the practitioner that will not be shared with others involved in the treatment (for example, family members, spouse, or partner). Other social workers, however, believe that secrets can be appropriate and in some cases can actually enhance the effectiveness of treatment (for example, when the disclosure of a man's extramarital affair would only undermine the substantial progress being made by him and his wife).

"Duty to protect" cases, when social workers may make deliberate decisions intentionally to violate clients' right to confidentiality, are among the more dramatic ways in which social workers can be charged with unethical behavior or misconduct as a result of the way in which they handled confidential information. Far more common, however, are cases in which confidential information about clients is disclosed unintentionally, thus leading to lawsuits or ethics complaints. Very often these cases involve social workers who are simply absent-minded, careless, or sloppy. Examples include social workers who talk about clients in agency waiting rooms, elevators, hallways, or restaurants while in the presence of others; leave confidential documents on top of their desks or in a photocopy machine for others to see; do not dispose of confidential information properly; and so on. In these cases the social workers involved mean no harm. They simply make mistakes, ones that may be costly.

Social workers can take a number of steps to prevent these mistakes or at least minimize the likelihood that they will occur. Social workers should be sure to train all agency staff members, including all professional staff and nonprofessional staff (for example, secretaries, clerical workers, custodians, cooks) concerning the concept of confidentiality, the need to protect confidentiality, and common ways that confidentiality can be violated. Training should cover the need to protect confidential information contained in written records and documents from inappropriate access by third parties outside of the agency (for example, other human service professionals, insurance companies, clients' family members and guardians) and by other staff within the agency who have no need to know the confidential information. All agencies should have clear policies governing access to confidential information by third parties and clients themselves.

Staff should also be trained about inappropriate release of confidential information through verbal communication. Social workers and other staff members in social service agencies need to be careful about what they say in hallways and waiting rooms, on elevators, in restaurants and other public facilities, on answering machine messages, and over the telephone to other social service professionals, clients' family members and friends, and representatives of the news media.

In addition, social workers should prepare clear written explanations of their agency's confidentiality guidelines. These should be shared with every client (many agencies ask clients to sign a copy acknowledging that the guidelines were shared with them and that they understand the guidelines).

To understand the limits of privacy and confidentiality social workers must be familiar with the concept of *privileged communication*. The right of privileged communication means that a professional cannot disclose confidential information without the client's consent. Among professionals the attorney-client relationship was the first to be granted the right of privileged communication. Over time other groups of professionals, such as social workers, physicians, psychiatrists, psychologists, and clergy, sought legislation to provide them with this right (Wilson 1978).

Whereas confidentiality refers to the professional norm that information shared by or pertaining to clients should not be shared with third parties, the concept of privilege refers specifically to the disclosure of confidential information in court proceedings (Meyer, Landis, and Hays 1988). Many states now grant social workers' clients the right of privileged communication, which means that social workers cannot disclose privileged information in court without clients' consent. Social workers must understand, however, that privileged communication statutes do not guarantee that social workers will never be required to disclose information without clients' consent. In fact, despite a privileged communication statute, a court of law could formerly order a social worker to reveal this information if the judge believed that it was essential to a case being tried (Reamer 1994b). As discussed briefly in chapter 4, in New York state a social worker whose client was presumably protected by the right of privileged communication was ordered to testify in a paternity case after the court ruled that "disclosure of evidence relevant to a correct determination of paternity was of greater importance than any injury which might inure to the relationship between the social worker and his clients if such admission was disclosed" (*Humphrey v. Norden* 1974).

• DELIVERY OF SERVICES

A substantial portion of claims filed against social workers allege some kind of misconduct related to the delivery of services. These services take various forms—such as individual psychotherapy, family treatment and couples counseling, casework, group counseling, program administration, and research—and are delivered in a wide variety of settings, including public and private human service agencies.

Claims alleging improper delivery of services raise various issues, including problems with informed consent procedures, client assessment and intervention, undue influence, suicide, civil commitment proceedings, protective services, defamation of character, and sexual contact with clients.

The concept of informed consent has always been prominent in social work. Consistent with social workers' long-standing embrace of the principle of client self-determination (Bernstein 1960; Freedberg 1989; Keith-Lucas 1963; McDermott 1975; Perlman 1965; Reamer 1987a), informed consent procedures require social workers to obtain clients' permission before releasing confidential information to third parties; allowing clients to be photographed, videotaped, or audiotaped by the media; permitting clients to participate as subjects in a research project; and so on. Relevant principles from the NASW Code of Ethics include "The social worker should make every effort to foster maximum self-determination on the part of clients" (principle II.G); "The social worker should apprise clients of their risks, rights, opportunities, and obligations associated with social service to them" (principle II.F.7); and "The social worker should obtain informed consent of clients before taping, recording, or permitting third party observation of their activities" (principle II.H.5).

States and local jurisdictions have different interpretations and applications of informed consent standards. Nonetheless, there is considerable agreement about what constitutes valid consent by clients in light of prevailing legislation and case law. In general, for consent to be considered valid six standards must be met: 1) coercion and undue influence must not have played a role in the client's decision; 2) clients must be mentally capable of providing consent; 3) clients must consent to specific procedures or actions; 4) the consent forms and procedures must be valid; 5) clients must have the right to refuse or withdraw consent; and 6) clients' decisions must be based on adequate information (Cowles 1976; President's Commission 1982; Reamer 1994b; Rozovsky 1984). Social workers should be familiar with ways to prevent the use of coercion to obtain client consent; ways to assess clients' competence to give consent; information that should appear on consent forms (for example, a statement of purpose, possible risks and benefits, clients' right to withdraw or refuse to given consent, an expiration date); the need to have a conversation with clients about the content of the consent form; the need for interpreters in cases where clients do not read or understand English; exceptions to informed consent (for example, genuine emergencies); and common problems associated with consent forms (such as having clients sign a blank form that the social worker plans to complete sometime later, including jargon in the description of the purpose of the consent).

Allegations of improper client assessment and intervention concern a wide range of activities. Very often these claims of malpractice or misconduct allege that the social worker assessed a client's needs or provided services in a way that departed from the profession's standard of care. That is, the social worker failed to assess properly, failed to provide a needed service, or provided a service in a way that was inconsistent with professional standards and caused some kind of harm. Social workers may neglect to ask important questions during an assessment or may use some treatment technique for which they do not have proper training.

It is important to note that courts do not expect perfection in social workers' assessments and service delivery. Judges recognize the inexact nature of these phenomena. What they do expect, however, is conformity with social work's standard of care with regard to assessment and service delivery. Although a client may have been harmed somehow, the social worker may have acted reasonably and in a way that is widely accepted in the profession. An error in judgment is not by itself negligent (Schutz 1982). As a judge concluded in one prominent court case where family members alleged that hospital staff were negligent in assessing a patient's suicide risk, "Diagnosis is not an exact science. Diagnosis with absolute precision and certainty is not possible" (Austin, Moline, and Williams 1990:167).

Many claims related to assessment and service delivery involve suicide. For example, a client who failed in an attempt to commit suicide and was injured in the process, or family members of someone who committed suicide, may allege that a social worker did not properly assess the suicide risk or properly respond to a client's suicidal ideation and tendencies. As Meyer, Landis, and Hays (1988) observe, "While the law generally does not hold anyone responsible for the acts of another, there are exceptions. One of these is the responsibility of therapists to prevent suicide and other self-destructive behavior by their clients. The duty of therapists to exercise adequate care in diagnosing suicidality is well-established" (p. 38).

Some claims include allegations that practitioners used unconventional or nontraditional intervention techniques that proved harmful. As Austin, Moline, and Williams (1990) conclude,

> If you are using techniques that are not commonly practiced, you will need to have a clear rationale that other professionals in your field will accept and support. It is important to consult colleagues when you are using what are considered to be nontraditional approaches to treatment. This is primarily because it is not difficult to prove deviation from average care. Some examples of what may be considered nontraditional therapeutic techniques might include asking clients to undress, striking a client, or giving "far-out" homework assignments.   (Pp. 155–56)

Another problem area involves advice giving. Social workers must be careful to not give clients advice outside their areas of training and expertise. For example, a social worker who gives a client advice about the proper use of medication that a psychiatrist has prescribed could be charged with practicing medicine without a license.

Some claims allege that social workers used what is known as undue influence. *Undue influence* occurs when social workers use their authority improperly to pressure, persuade, or sway a client to engage in an activity that may not be in the client's best interest or that may pose a conflict of interest. Examples include convincing a dying client to include the social worker in her will and becoming involved with a client in a profitable business.

Social workers must also be aware of liability, negligence, and misconduct claims that can arise in relation to protective services, that is, efforts to protect abused and neglected children, elderly, and other vulnerable populations. Every state has a statute obligating mandated reporters, including social workers, to notify local protective service officials when they suspect abuse or neglect of a child. Some states have similar statutes concerned with the elderly.

Social workers need to be familiar with possible allegations that they failed to report suspected abuse or neglect; knowingly made false accusations of abuse and neglect ("bad faith" reporting); inadequately protected a child who was apparently abused or neglected (for example, by failing to investigate a complaint swiftly and thoroughly, failing to place an abused or neglected child in foster care, or returning an at-risk child to dangerous guardians); violated parental rights (for example, by conducting unnecessarily intrusive investigations); or placed children in dangerous or inadequate foster homes (Besharov 1985).

One of the most common allegations of misconduct against social workers involves sexual abuse of clients (Reamer 1994b). This is a very serious problem that is found in other helping professions as well, such as psychiatry and psychology. Various studies suggest that the vast majority of cases involving sexual contact between professionals and clients involve a male practitioner and a female client (Brodsky 1986; Pope 1988). In a typical study, Gartrell et al. (1986; cited in Meyer, Landis, and Hays 1988:23) report in their nationwide survey of psychiatrists that 6.4 percent of respondents acknowledged sexual contact with their own patients; 90 percent of the offenders were male. In a comprehensive review of a series of empirical studies focused specifically on sexual contact between therapists and clients, Pope (1988) concluded that the aggregate average of reported sexual contact is 8.3 percent by male therapists and 1.7 percent by female therapists. Pope reported that one study (Gechtman and Bouhoutsos 1985) found that 3.8 percent of male social workers admitted to sexual contact with clients. Based on her research on therapists who sexually abuse clients, Brodsky (1986:157–58) concluded that the typical therapist who is sued is male, middle-aged, involved in unsatisfactory relationships in his own life, and perhaps in the process of divorce proceedings. His clients are primarily female and over time he is sexually involved with more than one. The therapist shares details of his personal life with his client, suggesting to her that he needs her, and the therapist spends time during treatment sessions asking her for help with his problems. The therapist is a lonely man and isolated professionally, although he enjoys a good reputation in the professional community. He convinces his client that he is the most appropriate person for her to be sexually involved with.

Several principles in the NASW code of ethics are relevant, directly or indirectly, to sexual misconduct: "The social worker should maintain high standards of personal conduct in the capacity or identity as social worker" (principle I.A); "The private conduct of the social worker is a personal matter to the same degree as is any other person's, except when such conduct compromises the fulfillment of professional responsibilities" (principle I.A.1); "The social worker should act in accord with the highest standards of professional integrity and impartiality" (principle I.D); "The social worker should not exploit professional relationships for personal gain" (principle I.D.2); "The social worker should not exploit relationships with clients for personal advantage" (principle II.F.2); and "The social worker should under no circumstances engage in sexual activities with clients" (principle II.F.5). Further, the most recent principle added to the code of ethics concerning dual relationships is relevant: "The social worker should not condone or engage in any dual or multiple relationships with clients or former clients in which there is a risk of exploitation or of potential harm to the client. The social worker is responsible for setting clear, appropriate, and culturally sensitive boundaries" (principle II.F.4).

• SUPERVISION: CLIENTS AND STAFF

Social workers routinely supervise clients, especially in day-treatment and residential programs. On occasion social workers will be accused of misconduct related to this supervision. Social workers may be charged with, for example, failing properly to supervise residents of an intensive treatment unit of a psychiatric hospital. A resident may have jumped from a window in a suicide attempt, or one resident may have assaulted another, and the allegation may be that the social worker on duty failed to provide adequate supervision.

In addition, many social workers supervise staff. A clinical director in a community mental health center may supervise caseworkers, the director of a battered women's shelter may supervise counselors, and the district director of a public child welfare agency may supervise protective service workers. Typically, supervisors will provide case supervision and consultation, evaluate workers' performance, and offer training. Because of their oversight responsibilities, supervisors can be named in ethics complaints and lawsuits involving mistakes or unethical conduct engaged in by the people who work under them. These claims usually cite the legal concept of *respondeat superior*, which means "let the master respond," and the doctrine of "vicarious liability." That is, supervisors may be found liable for actions or inactions in which they were involved only vicariously, or indirectly. According to respondeat superior and vicarious liability, supervisors are responsible for the actions or inactions of the people they supervise and over which the supervisors had some degree of control. Of course, the staff member who made the mistake that led to the claim against the supervisor can also be found liable.

There are several specific issues that supervisors should be concerned about, including supervisors' failure to provide information necessary for supervisees to obtain clients' consent; to identify and respond to supervisees' errors in all phases of client contact, such as the inappropriate disclosure of confidential information; to protect third parties; to detect or stop a negligent treatment plan or treatment carried out longer than necessary; to determine that a specialist is needed for treatment of a particular client; to meet regularly with the supervisee; to review and approve the supervisee's records, decisions, and actions; and to provide adequate coverage in the supervisee's absence (Besharov 1985; Cohen and Mariano 1982; Hogan 1979).

Social workers in private practice face special issues. Independent practitioners do not always have easy access to regular supervision. It is important for independent social workers to contract for supervision with a colleague or participate in peer supervision or peer consultation groups. Otherwise, these solo private practitioners may be vulnerable to allegations that they failed to obtain proper supervision should some question be raised about the quality of their work.

Supervisors should be careful to document the nature of the supervision they have provided. They should have regularly scheduled appointments with supervisees, request detailed information about the cases or other work they are supervising, and if possible occasionally observe their supervisees' work. Supervisors should be careful not to sign off on insurance or other forms for cases they have not supervised.

One way for supervisors to minimize the likelihood of malpractice or negligence allegations is to provide comprehensive training to their subordinates. Such training should include a discussion and review of issues related to relevant practice skills, professional ethics and liability, and relevant federal, state, and local statutes. Possible topics include assessment tools, intervention techniques, evaluation methods, emergency assistance and suicide prevention, supervision of clients in residential programs, confidentiality and privileged communication, informed consent, improper treatment and service delivery, defamation of character, boundary issues in relationships with clients, consultation with and referral to specialists, fraud and deception, and termination of services.

• CONSULTATION, REFERRAL, AND RECORDS

There are many occasions when social workers need to or should obtain consultation from colleagues, including social workers and members of other professions, who have special expertise. Clinical social workers may encounter a case in which consultation is needed about a client's unique problem, such as an eating disorder or psychotic symptoms. If the client's presenting problem is outside the social worker's expertise, the social worker should seek consultation or make an appropriate referral. As the NASW Code of Ethics states, "The social worker should seek advice and counsel of colleagues and supervisors whenever such consultation is in the best interest of clients" (principle II.F.8).

Social workers can be vulnerable to ethics complaints and malpractice allegations if they fail to seek consultation when it is warranted. In addition, social workers can be vulnerable if they do not refer a client to a specialist for an assessment, evaluation, or treatment. For instance, if a client who is being treated for symptoms of depression complains to her social worker that she has chronic headaches, the social worker would be wise to refer the client to a physician who can rule out any organic problem, such as a brain tumor. As Meyer, Landis, and Hays (1988) conclude, if a practitioner proceeds on the assumption that there is no organic damage, he or she "could be held liable for negligently failing to refer the patient to a practitioner capable of treating his problem" (p. 50). Some social workers routinely encourage all clients to have a physical as part of their treatment (Barker and Branson 1993).

Social workers can also encounter ethics complaints or lawsuits when they fail to consult an *organization* for advice. For example, this could happen to a social worker who suspects that a particular child has been abused but decides not to consult with or report to the local child welfare authorities. This may occur when social workers believe they are better off handling the case themselves, they do not have confidence in the child protection agency staff, and they do not want to undermine their therapeutic relationship with their clients. The result may be that the social worker will be cited or sued for failing to consult with a specialist (in this case, the child welfare agency).

Clinical social workers who believe that their work with particular clients is ineffective or has hit a dead end should seek consultation from colleagues. As Schutz (1982) observes,

> When therapy reaches a prolonged impasse, the therapist ought to consider consulting another therapist and possibly transferring the patient. Apart from the clinical and ethical considerations, his failure to seek another opinion might have legal ramifications in the establishment of proximate cause in the event of a suit. While therapists are not guaran-

tors of cure or improvement, extensive treatment without results could legally be considered to have injured the patient; in specific, the injury would be the loss of money and time, and the preclusion of other treatments that might have been more successful. (P. 47)

In addition to case consultation, social workers also provide consultation to agencies and organizations related to program design, evaluation, and administration. It is important for social workers who provide this sort of consultation to have the expertise they claim to have. Otherwise, they risk being named in an ethics complaint or lawsuit if they provide incompetent assistance that somehow harms their client (which could be an individual, family, community, or agency).

Social workers must pay close attention to the procedures they use when they refer clients to another practitioner. They have a responsibility to refer clients to colleagues with strong reputations and to practitioners with appropriate credentials. Otherwise, the social worker may be cited for *negligent referral*. As Cohen (1979) notes, "If a referral is indicated, the professional has a duty to select an appropriate professional or institution for the patient. Barring any extraordinary circumstances, the professional making the referral will not incur any liability for the acts of the person or institution that he refers the patient to, provided that the person or institution is duly licensed and equipped to meet the patient's needs" (p. 239).

Social workers who consult with or refer clients to colleagues should provide careful documentation of the contact in the case record. It is extremely important for social workers to be able to demonstrate the assistance they received in cases, in the event that a client or some other party raises questions concerning the appropriateness of the practitioners' actions.

The same advice applies to record keeping in general. Careful and diligent recording enhances the quality of services provided to clients. Thorough records identify, describe, and assess clients' situations; define the purpose of service; document service goals, plans, activities, and progress; and evaluate the effectiveness of service (Kagle 1987, 1991; Wilson 1980). Recording also helps to maintain the continuity of care. Carefully recorded notes help social workers recall relevant detail from session to session and can enhance coordination of service and supervision among staff members within an agency. Recording also helps to ensure quality care if a client's primary social worker becomes unavailable because of illness, vacation, or departure from the agency. As Kagle (1987) asserts, "By keeping accurate, relevant, and timely records, social workers do more than just describe, explain, and support the services they provide. They also discharge their ethical and legal responsibility to be accountable" (p. 463).

• DECEPTION AND FRAUD

The vast majority of social workers are honest in their dealings with staff, other social service agencies, insurance companies, and so on. Unfortunately, however, some social workers engage in some form of deception and fraud in their dealings with these parties. As Schutz (1982) suggests,

> Fraud is the intentional or negligent, implied, or direct perversion of truth for the purpose of inducing another, who relies on such misrepresentation, to part with something valuable belonging to him or to surrender a legal right. If one misrepresents the risks or benefits of therapy for one's own benefit and not the patient's, so as to induce him to undergo treatment and pay the fee, this is fraud. Telling a patient that sexual intercourse is therapy may be seen as a perversion of the truth so as to get the patient to part with something of value. Hence, this would be seen as fraud. (P. 12)

Social workers may engage in deception and fraud for various reasons and with different motives. Some social workers—a small percentage, fortunately—are simply dishonest and attempt to take advantage of others for reasons of greed, malice, self-protection, or self-satisfaction. Social workers who become sexually involved with clients, extort money from clients, and bill clients' insurance companies for services that were never rendered are examples. After investigating the extent to which a national sample of clinical social workers deliberately misdiagnose clients, Kirk and Kutchins (1988) conclude that "such acts are legal and ethical transgressions involving deceit, fraud, or abuse. Charges made for services not provided, money collected for services to fictitious patients, or patients encouraged to remain in treatment longer than necessary are examples of intentional inaccuracy" (p. 226).

Kirk and Kutchins (1988) found that in many instances clinicians use a more serious clinical diagnosis than is warranted by the client's clinical symptoms. Nearly three-fourths of the sample (72 percent) reported being aware of cases in which more-serious-than-warranted diagnoses were used to qualify for reimbursement. About one-fourth of the sample reported that this practice occurs frequently. Most of the sample (86 percent) reported being aware of instances of listing diagnoses for individuals although the focus of treatment was on the family (many insurance companies do not reimburse for family treatment). Kirk and Kutchins (1988) conclude from these data that "deliberate misdiagnosis occurs frequently in the mental health professions" (p. 231). These authors acknowledge the possibility that misdiagnosis may occur to benefit clients—to enable them to receive services that they would not be able to afford otherwise—but they argue that social workers' self-interest is often the reason for misdiagnosis: "In particular, misdiagnosis is used so that the therapist's services will qualify for third-party reimbursement. Here the rationale is also nonclinical, but the argument that the therapist is acting only for the client's benefit is strained. The rationale that it is being done so that the client can obtain needed service is colored by the obvious self-interest of the therapist. Agencies, both public and private, also benefit when they obtain reimbursement as a result of such diagnostic practices" (p. 232).

Social workers who market or advertise their services also need to be careful to avoid deception and fraud. Practitioners must be sure to provide fair and accurate descriptions of their services, expertise, and credentials and to avoid exaggerated claims of effectiveness. As the NASW Code of Ethics states, "The social worker should not misrepresent professional qualifications, education, experience, or affiliations" (principle I.B.2); and "The social worker should make no misrepresentation in advertising as to qualifications, competence, service, or results to be achieved" (principle V.M.4). In addition, standard 9 of the NASW's *Standards for the Practice of Clinical Social Work* (1989) states the need for accuracy clearly:

Standard 9. Clinical social workers shall represent themselves to the public with accuracy.

Interpretation

The public needs to know how to find help from qualified clinical social workers. Both agencies and independent private practitioners should ensure that their therapeutic services are made known to the public. In this regard, it is important that telephone listings be maintained in both the classified and alphabetical sections of the telephone directory, describing the clinical social work services available.

Although advertising in various media was once thought to be questionable professional practice in the past, recent judicial decisions, Federal Trade Commission rulings, as well as current professional practices have made such advertising acceptable. The advertisement must be factual and should avoid false promises of cures.

Social workers must also avoid deception and fraud when applying for liability insurance, employment, a license, or some other form of certification. Social work administrators must be careful not to provide false accounts of grant or budget expenditures, or personnel evaluations. In addition, practitioners must not alter or falsify case records to create the impression that they provided services or supervision that were never actually provided. If a practitioner finds that accurate details were inadvertently omitted from a record, the information can be added, but the record should clearly indicate that the entry was made subsequently. The social worker should sign and date the addition to indicate that it was an amendment.

In some instances, social workers engage in deceit or fraud for what appear to be more altruistic reasons, that is, to be as helpful as they can be to their clients and employers. For example, clinical social workers may underdiagnose clients to avoid giving them unflattering labels that may stigmatize them or injure their self-esteem. In addition to documenting the extent of *over*diagnosis, as described earlier, Kirk and Kutchins (1988) found that social workers sometimes *under*diagnose, presumably to benefit clients. Some of the practices observed and reported by Kirk's and Kutchins's sample suggest that practitioners often misdiagnose in order to help clients, that is, to avoid labeling them. For example, most respondents (87 percent) indicated that a less serious diagnosis than clinically indicated was used frequently or occasionally to avoid labeling clients. Seventy-eight percent reported that frequently or occasionally only the least serious of several appropriate diagnoses was used on official records.

Social workers also must be careful to avoid deception and fraud when they write letters of reference for staff members or when they submit letters to employers or other parties, such as insurers or government agencies, on clients' behalf. On occasion social workers have exaggerated staff members' skills (or problems), or embellished their descriptions of clients' disabilities, in order to be helpful (or harmful). Practitioners incur considerable risk if they knowingly misrepresent staff members' or clients' qualities. Social workers should issue only statements about colleagues and clients that they know to be true or have good reason to believe are true.

Finally, social workers should avoid deception and fraud when they are involved in research or program evaluations. This can be a problem in agencies when continued funding from an outside source may depend on the extent to which research results demonstrate a program's effectiveness. Falsified results may mislead other professionals who try to replicate the agency's program and services, and place social workers involved in the deception in jeopardy. As the NASW Code of Ethics states, "The social worker should not participate in, condone, or be associated with dishonesty, fraud, deceit, or misrepresentation" (principle I.A.2).

• TERMINATION OF SERVICE

In addition to ethical problems related to confidentiality, the initiation and delivery of services, supervision, consultation and referral, and deception and fraud, social workers also need to be concerned about the ways in which they terminate services. Improper or unethical termination of services might occur when a social worker leaves an agency or a community suddenly without adequately preparing a client for the termination or without referring a client to a new service provider. In other instances a social worker might terminate services abruptly to a client in dire need of assistance because the client is unable to pay for the care. Social workers can also encounter problems when they are not available to clients or do not properly instruct them about how to handle emergencies that may arise.

Many ethical problems related to termination of services involve the concept of abandonment. *Abandonment* is a legal concept that refers to instances when a professional is not available to a client when needed. Once a social worker begins to provide service to a client, she or he incurs a legal responsibility to continue that service or to properly refer a client to another competent service provider. Of course, social workers are not obligated to serve every individual who requests assistance. A particular social worker might not have room to accept a new referral or may lack the unique expertise that a particular client's case may require.

Nonetheless, once a social worker begins service, it cannot be terminated abruptly. Rather, social workers are obligated to conform to the profession's standard of care regarding termination of service and referral to other providers in the event the client is still in need. As Schutz (1982) notes with respect to termination of psychotherapy services, "Once a patient makes a contact with a therapist and the therapist agrees to see him, he is that therapist's patient. The therapist then assumes the fiduciary duty not to abandon the patient. At the very least, therefore, he must refer the patient to another therapist if he elects to terminate the relationship" (p. 50).

Several principles in the NASW Code of Ethics are relevant to social workers' termination of services: "The social worker should terminate service to clients, and professional relationships with them, when such service and relationships are no longer required or no longer serve the clients' needs or interests" (principle II.F.9); "The social worker should withdraw services precipitously only under unusual circumstances, giving careful consideration to all factors in the situation and taking care to minimize possible adverse effects" (principle II.F.10); and "The social worker who anticipates the termination or interruption of service to clients should notify clients promptly and seek the transfer, referral, or continuation of service in relation to the clients' needs and preferences" (principle II.F.11).

Principle II.F.9 suggests that social workers must not extend services to clients beyond the point where they are clinically or otherwise necessary. Unfortunately, some social workers have failed to terminate services when termination is in the client's best interest. For example, unscrupulous independent private practitioners—clearly a minority of private practitioners—have been known to encourage clients to remain in treatment longer than necessary in order to generate income that would be lost if clients terminated treatment. In the process, clients' lives may be inconvenienced, they may be misled about the nature of their problems, and third-party payers, primarily insurance companies, may be spending funds that do not need to be spent (which may lead to an increase in premiums for other policyholders). A similar phenomenon occurs when social workers in residential programs seek to extend residents' stay beyond what is clinically warranted in order to enhance revenue for the program.

A more common problem occurs when clients' services are terminated prematurely, before termination is clinically warranted. This may occur for several reasons. Clients themselves may request termination of service, perhaps because of the expense or inconvenience involved. In these cases termination of service may be against the advice of the social worker involved in the client's care. For example, clients in residential and nonresidential substance abuse treatment programs may decide on their own that they do not want to continue receiving services. They may leave residential programs against professional advice or may decide not to return for outpatient services.

In other instances, services may be terminated at the social worker's request or initiative, for instance, when social workers believe that a client is not making sufficient progress to warrant further treatment or is not able to pay for services. In some cases program administrators in a residential program may want to terminate a client whose insurance benefits have run out or in order to make a bed available for a client who will generate a higher reimbursement rate because of his or her particular insurance coverage. In a number of cases, social workers terminate services when they find clients to be uncooperative or too difficult to handle. Social workers may also terminate services prematurely because of poor clinical judgment; that is, social workers may believe that clients have made more progress than they have in fact made.

Premature termination of services can result in ethics complaints and lawsuits alleging that, as a result, clients were harmed or injured, or injured some third party because of their continuing disability. A client who attempts to commit suicide following premature termination from a psychiatric hospital may allege that the premature termination was the direct cause of the attempt. Family members who are physically injured by a client who was discharged prematurely from a substance abuse treatment program may claim that their injuries are the direct result of poor clinical judgment.

On occasion, services must be terminated earlier than a social worker or client would prefer for reasons that are quite legitimate. This may occur because a client does not make reasonable progress or is uncooperative, or because the social worker moves out of town or discovers that she or he does not have the particular skills or expertise needed to be helpful to the client. When this occurs, social workers must be careful to terminate services to clients properly. As Cohen (1979) observes with regard to the termination of counseling services,

> No doctor in private practice is legally compelled to accept any patient for treatment. The mental health professional may feel that he does not have the expertise to deal with a particular problem; he may not have the number of hours needed to provide adequate services; he may not see himself as able to establish a good enough rapport with the patient; the patient may not be able to pay the doctor's fee, etc. But while there are any number of perfectly acceptable reasons for refusing to treat a patient, there is *no* reason to justify abandonment of a patient once treatment begins. Before accepting a new patient, the mental health professional would be wise to schedule an initial consultation for the purpose of a mutual evaluation of suitability. If a doctor accepts a patient but some time later believes he can no longer be of value (because, for example, he has discovered factors operating that are beyond his competence to deal with), "following through" would mean advising this patient of the state of affairs and referring him to an appropriate mental health professional. (P. 273)

Adequate follow-through should include providing clients as much advance warning as possible, along with the names of several other professionals they might approach for help. Social workers should also follow up with clients who have been terminated to enhance the likelihood that they receive whatever services they may need.

Social workers can also face ethics complaints or lawsuits if they do not provide clients with adequate instructions for times when the social workers are not available as a result of vacations, illness, or emergencies. Social workers should provide clients with clear and detailed information, verbally and in writing, about what they ought to do in these situations, such as whom to call, where to seek help, and so on.

Social workers who expect to be unavailable for a period of time—perhaps because of vacation or medical care—should be especially careful to arrange for competent coverage. The colleagues who are to provide the coverage should be given information about the clients sufficient to enable them to provide adequate care should the need arise. Of course, social workers should obtain clients' consent to the release of this information about their cases.

• THE IMPAIRED SOCIAL WORKER

As I observed earlier, many ethics complaints and lawsuits result from genuine mistakes made by social workers who are otherwise competent. In other instances, ethics complaints and lawsuits follow competent social workers' well-meaning attempts to make the right ethical judgment, for example, with respect to disclosing confidential information about a client to protect a third party. In many cases, however, ethics complaints and lawsuits are filed because of mistakes, judgment errors, or misconduct engaged in by social workers who are, in some way, impaired.[*]

In recent years the subject of impaired professionals has received increased attention. In 1972, for example, the Council on Mental Health of the American Medical Association issued a statement that said that physicians have an ethical responsibility to recognize and report impairment among colleagues. In 1976 a group of attorneys recovering from alcoholism formed Lawyers Concerned for Lawyers to address chemical dependence in the profession, and in 1980 a group of recovering psychologists began a similar group, Psychologists Helping Psychologists (Kilburg, Nathan, and Thoreson 1986; Knutsen 1977; Laliotis and Grayson 1985; McCrady 1989).

Social work's first national acknowledgment of the problem of impaired practitioners came in 1979, when NASW issued a public policy statement concerning alcoholism and alcohol-related problems (NASW 1987). By 1980 a nationwide support group for chemically

---

[*]Portions of this discussion are adapted from Reamer 1992b.

dependent practitioners, Social Workers Helping Social Workers, had formed. In 1982 NASW formed the Occupational Social Work Task Force, which was to develop a strategy to deal with impaired NASW members. In 1984 the NASW Delegate Assembly issued a resolution on impairment, and in 1987 NASW published the *Impaired Social Worker Program Resource Book* to help members of the profession design programs for impaired social workers. The introduction to the resource book states:

> Social workers, like other professionals, have within their ranks those who, because of substance abuse, chemical dependency, mental illness or stress, are unable to function effectively in their jobs. These are the impaired social workers. . . . The problem of impairment is compounded by the fact that the professionals who suffer from the effect of mental illness, stress or substance abuse are like anyone else; they are often the worst judges of their behavior, the last to recognize their problems and the least motivated to seek help. Not only are they able to hide or avoid confronting their behavior, they are often abetted by colleagues who find it difficult to accept that a professional could let his or her problem get out of hand.

Organized efforts to address impaired workers began in the late 1930s and early 1940s after Alcoholics Anonymous emerged and in response to the need that arose during World War II to sustain a sound work force. These early occupational alcoholism programs eventually led, in the early 1970s, to the emergence of employee assistance programs (EAPs), designed to address a broad range of problems experienced by workers.

More recently, strategies for dealing with professionals whose work is affected by problems such as substance abuse, mental illness, and emotional stress have become more prevalent. Professional associations and informal groups of practitioners are meeting to discuss the problem of impaired colleagues and to organize efforts to address the problem (Bissell and Haberman 1984; Prochaska and Norcross 1983).

Both the seriousness of impairment among social workers and the forms it takes vary. Impairment may involve failure to provide competent care or violation of the profession's ethical standards. It may also take such forms as providing flawed or inferior psychotherapy to a client, sexual involvement with a client, or failure to carry out professional duties as a result of substance abuse or mental illness. Lamb et al. (1987) provide a comprehensive definition of impairment among professionals:

> Interference in professional functioning that is reflected in one or more of the following ways: (a) an inability and/or unwillingness to acquire and integrate professional standards into one's repertoire of professional behavior; (b) an inability to acquire professional skills in order to reach an acceptable level of competency; and (c) an inability to control personal stress, psychological dysfunction, and/or excessive emotional reactions that interfere with professional functioning. (P. 598)

Impairment among professionals is the result of various causes. Stress related to employment, illness or death of family members, marital or relationship problems, financial problems, midlife crises, personal physical or mental illness, legal problems, and substance abuse may lead to impairment (Guy, Poelstra, and Stark 1989; Thoreson, Miller, and Krauskopf 1989). Stress induced by professional education and training can also lead to impairment, because of the close clinical supervision and scrutiny students receive, the disruption in students' personal lives caused by the demands of schoolwork and field placements, and the pressures of students' academic programs (Lamb et al. 1987).

According to Wood et al. (1985), psychotherapists encounter special sources of stress that may lead to impairment because their therapeutic role often extends into the nonwork areas of their lives (such as relationships with family members and friends), there is a lack of reciprocity in relationships with clients (therapists are "always giving"), therapeutic progress is often slow and erratic, and therapeutic work with clients may stir up therapists' own personal issues. As Kilburg, Kaslow, and VandenBos (1988) observe,

> [The] stresses of daily life—family responsibilities, death of family members and friends, other severe losses, illnesses, financial difficulties, crimes of all kinds—quite naturally place mental health professionals, like other people, under pressure. However, by virtue of their training and place in society, such professionals face unique stresses. And although they have been trained extensively in how to deal with the emotional and behavioral crises of others, few are trained in how to deal with the stresses they themselves will face. . . . Mental health professionals are expected by everyone, including themselves, to be paragons.

The fact that they may be unable to fill that role makes them a prime target for disillusionment, distress, and burnout. When this reaction occurs, the individual's ability to function as a professional may become impaired. (P. 723)

Unfortunately, many social workers are reluctant to seek help for personal problems. Also, many social workers are reluctant to confront colleagues about their impairment. Social workers may be hesitant to acknowledge impairment within the profession because they fear how colleagues would react to confrontation and how this might affect future collegial relationships (Bernard and Jara 1986; Guy, Poelstra, and Stark 1989; McCrady 1989; Wood et al. 1985). As VandenBos and Duthie (1986) have said,

The fact that more than half of us have not confronted distressed colleagues even when we have recognized and acknowledged (at least to ourselves) the existence of their problems is, in part, a reflection of the difficulty in achieving a balance between concerned intervention and intrusiveness. As professionals, we value our own right to practice without interference, as long as we function within the boundaries of our professional expertise, meet professional standards for the provision of services, and behave in an ethical manner. We generally consider such expectations when we consider approaching a distressed colleague. Deciding when and how our concern about the well-being of a colleague (and our ethical obligation) supersedes his or her right to personal privacy and professional autonomy is a ticklish manner. (P. 212)

Some social workers may find it difficult to seek help for their own problems because of their belief that they have infinite power and invulnerability, they should be able to work out their problems themselves, an acceptable therapist is not available, it is more appropriate for them to seek help from family members or friends, confidential information might be disclosed, proper treatment would require too much effort and cost, they have a spouse who is unwilling to participate in treatment, and therapy would not be effective (Deutsch 1985; Thoreson et al. 1983).

It is important for social workers to design ways to prevent impairment and respond to impaired colleagues. They must be knowledgeable about the indicators and causes of impairment, so that they can recognize problems that colleagues may be experiencing. Social workers must also be willing to confront impaired colleagues, offer assistance and consultation, and, if necessary as a last resort, refer the colleague to a supervisor or local regulatory or disciplinary body (such as a committee on inquiry of NASW or a local licensing or registration board).

To the profession's credit, in 1992 the president of NASW created the Code of Ethics Review Task Force (chaired by the author) that proposed adding new principles to the code on the subject of impairment. The approved additions, which became effective in 1994, are as follows:

- The social worker should not allow his or her own personal problems, psychosocial distress, substance abuse, or mental health difficulties to interfere with professional judgment and performance or jeopardize the best interests of those to whom the social worker has a professional responsibility (principle I.A.3).
- The social worker whose personal problems, psychosocial distress, substance abuse, or mental health difficulties interfere with professional judgment and performance should immediately seek consultation and take appropriate remedial action by seeking professional help, making adjustments in work load, terminating practice, or taking any other steps necessary to protect clients and others (principle I.A.4).
- The social worker who has direct knowledge of a social work colleague's impairment due to personal problems, psychosocial distress, substance abuse, or mental health difficulties should consult with that colleague and assist the colleague in taking remedial action (principle III.J.13).

Although some cases of impairment must be dealt with through formal adjudication and disciplinary procedures, many cases can be handled primarily by arranging therapeutic or rehabilitative services for distressed practitioners. For example, state chapters of NASW can enter into agreements with local employee assistance programs, to which impaired members can be referred (NASW 1987).

As social workers increase the attention they pay to the problem of impairment, they must be careful to avoid assigning all responsibility to the practitioners themselves. Although psychotherapy and individually focused rehabilitative efforts are appropriate, social workers must also address the environmental stresses and structural factors that can cause impairment. Distress experienced by social workers is often the result of the unique challenges in the profession for which resources are inadequate. Caring social workers who are overwhelmed by chronic problems of poverty, substance abuse, child abuse and neglect, hunger and homelessness, and mental illness are prime candidates for high degrees of stress and burnout. Insufficient funding, unpredictable political support, and public skepticism of social workers' efforts often lead to low morale and high stress (Jayaratne and Chess 1984; Johnson and Stone 1986; Koeske and Koeske 1989). Thus in addition to responding to the individual problems of impaired colleagues, social workers must confront the environmental and structural problems that can cause the impairment in the first place. This comprehensive effort to confront the problem of impaired practitioners can also help to reduce unethical behavior and professional misconduct in social work.

In this chapter I discussed the ways in which some social workers —clearly a minority of the profession—engage in malpractice or ethical misconduct. I reviewed various mechanisms available for sanctioning and disciplining social workers found in violation of ethical standards and discussed the problem of impaired practitioners.

AFTERWORD: A FUTURE AGENDA

• • •

The subject of social work values and ethics is clearly diverse. It includes topics as different as the core values of the profession and malpractice suits. Analysis of these issues incorporates diverse bodies of knowledge ranging from moral philosophy to legal theories of negligence. To understand contemporary issues of professional values and ethics adequately, today's social workers must grasp an impressive array of concepts, many of which were unknown to earlier generations of practitioners.

In these pages I have examined a complex mix of issues. I have explored the nature of social work values and their relevance to the profession's priorities. I have reviewed various typologies for classifying social work's values, and I have reviewed several intense debates about shifts in the profession's value base and mission.

I have also focused on the phenomena of ethical dilemmas and ethical decision making in social work. I have shown how social workers' values influence their ethical decisions, and I have looked at the complicated ingredients involved in ethical decisions related to both direct and indirect practice. Finally, I have addressed the nagging problem of ethical misconduct and various ways in which social workers can prevent ethics complaints and lawsuits. In light of this wide range of issues, what do social workers need to keep in mind as the profession evolves?

First, social workers need to continue to examine the nature of the profession's values and the ways in which they shape the profession's priorities. This is a never-ending process. We can never assume that social work's values are fixed in stone. Although some of the profession's values have endured over the decades, others have receded and emerged as a function of broader societal trends and trends within the profession itself. It is impossible for today's social workers to anticipate what values-related issues might appear in future years and decades, just as social workers in the early twentieth century could not possibly have anticipated some of the values issues that today's social workers face. We can expect only that changes in society's technology, cultural norms, demographic characteristics, and political landscape will create novel value issues that, at this point in our history, are unimaginable. For all we know, tomorrow's social workers will be involved in ethical decisions about the cloning of human beings or the confidentiality of information on computer chips that help impaired brains function. Who knows?

But what we do know is that social workers will need to be vigilant in their continued examination of what it means to be a social worker, the values on which the profession is built, and the ways in which social workers should alter the profession's values. Clearly, the most pressing debate for the profession concerns the extent to which social work will retain its fundamental commitment to society's most vulnerable and oppressed members. Some practitioners believe that the dramatic growth of clinical social work and private practice has threatened the profession's historic and enduring concern with the poor and least advantaged. Others believe that the growth of clinical social work has strengthened and revitalized the profession, enhanced its standing, and invigorated its sense of purpose. It is essential that social workers continue to debate the merits of this trend, particularly with respect to its implications for what we have come to believe are the profession's core values related to public social service on behalf of low-income and oppressed populations. This debate will not be settled easily, if at all. Nonetheless, the process of debate is itself important, because it serves to engage social workers in ongoing examination of their principal priorities and raison d'être.

The same point applies to the subject of ethical dilemmas and ethical decision making. There will always be ethical dilemmas related to direct practice—involving individuals, families, and groups—and indirect practice—involving social work administration, community work, and social welfare policy. However, the nature of these dilemmas will change over time, reflecting the changing nature of these areas of social work practice. New issues related to confidentiality and privacy are likely to emerge as technological advances enable storage and transmission of greater amounts of personal information for increasing numbers of purposes in both the public and private sectors. New ethical dilemmas related to clients' right to self-determination and professional paternalism are likely to appear as social workers become more involved in increasingly complex decisions about the termination of life and the use of extraordinarily controversial health care technology. As the demand for global resources heats up, social workers will have new opportunities to be involved in ethical decisions about their allocation. And of course social workers will forever be involved in controversy about the extent to which government and the private sector should be responsible for people in need.

Although new challenges will emerge with regard to professional values and ethical dilemmas, social workers have begun to develop a respectable track record in their efforts to grapple with these issues in a systematic, intellectually rigorous way. Especially since the late 1970s and early 1980s, social workers have been learning and writing about these phenomena.

The same, however, cannot be said with regard to the subjects of ethical misconduct, professional malpractice, and impaired practitioners. With regard to these subjects, social work's track record is much weaker. The profession's literature contains relatively little scholarship on these topics, and until very recently social work conferences and education programs had not devoted much attention to them. This is beginning to change, but the profession still has a long way to go if it is to address these problems adequately.

What can social workers do to strengthen the field's focus on these various and diverse issues of values and ethics? First, training and education programs can enhance focus on these subjects. Social work education programs (both undergraduate and graduate) and social work agencies can incorporate these topics into their curricula and training agendas more deliberately. Students and practitioners should be systematically exposed to debates about social work values and their influence on the profession's mission; the kinds of ethical dilemmas in social work and strategies for ethical decision making;

and the problems of professional misconduct and malpractice. More specifically, students and practitioners should be taught about the history of social work values, shifts in the profession's value base over the years, and contemporary debate about the profession's future; the relevance of ethical theory, codes of ethics, and various decision making models when practitioners are faced with difficult ethical dilemmas; the ways in which social workers can prevent ethics complaints and lawsuits related to confidentiality, service delivery, supervision, consultation and referral, deception and fraud, and termination of services; and the causes of, and possible responses to, impairment among social workers.

In addition, conference planners should make a deliberate attempt to place professional values and ethics high on the list of priorities. Professional conferences sponsored by professional associations and agencies are the principal source of continuing education for many social workers, and these regularly scheduled events provide a valuable opportunity continually to remind practitioners of the central importance of professional values and ethics.

Finally, social workers must contribute to the growing fund of scholarship on professional values and ethics. Until the mid-1970s, relatively little literature existed on these subjects, although there certainly were a number of important publications prior to this period. However, even with the significant increase in scholarship on social work values and ethics, much remains to be written. A scholarly tradition is just beginning to develop in this area. More empirical research and theoretical development need to occur, in order to enhance social workers' grasp of topics such as the criteria and procedures that social workers use to make ethical decisions, practitioners' beliefs about what is ethically acceptable and unacceptable in a variety of circumstances, the nature of ethical dilemmas encountered by social workers working in various practice settings and positions, and the effectiveness of education and training on values and ethics.

None of this is to suggest that enhancing practitioners' attention to these issues will enable social workers to settle all the vexing debates and controversies that have simmered for years. More likely, increased education, training, and scholarship will stir up even more debate and controversy and broach even more questions. This, however, is not a problem, for the nature of values and ethics is such that unresolved questions are an essential feature. Increased controversy and constructive debate among social workers who are well informed about values, ethical dilemmas, ethical decision making, and professional misconduct will enhance the likelihood that decisions and policies will be carefully thought through rather than made haphazardly.

By now it is evident that a great many questions related to values and ethics are of the sort that will always generate at least some degree—often a great deal—of disagreement. Skeptics sometimes ask whether, in light of this fact, there is much point to the kind of analysis, debate, and intellectual dissection I have engaged in here. After all, why go through this painstaking exercise when, in the end, even reasonable people are likely to disagree?

The answer to this question is that social workers have an obligation to carry out these thoughtful analyses and engage in the complex debates. The principal obligation is to social workers' clients, who ultimately stand to be affected most by the outcome of these deliberations. Social workers have a duty to analyze as thoroughly as possible the implications of the decisions they make about what kinds of clients they will serve, using what intervention methods, and towards what goals. These are essentially questions based on values and ethics.

In this respect, is social workers' approach to values and ethical issues any different from their approach to controversies related to social work practice? Although some practice decisions are relatively straightforward and noncontroversial, many are not. Think about how often agency-based social workers gather around a conference room table to consult one another on a complicated case, map out a complicated community organizing strategy, or design a challenging new program. How often in these instances does consensus quickly or easily emerge about how the client's treatment ought to be approached, how community members ought to be organized, or how the new program ought to be designed? Very often, once presented with the facts (or at least what appear to be the facts), staff will disagree about the assessment and most appropriate course of action. Even the most experienced and insightful practitioners will disagree when presented with hard and complicated case scenarios. Social workers have come to accept this fact of professional life, recognizing that consensus is difficult to achieve in the face of complex problems.

No one argues, however, that social workers should not engage in protracted discussion of these practice-based issues simply because participants are likely to disagree, at least to some extent, once the conversations unfold. Instead, practitioners have come to recognize that the *process* of analysis, discussion, and debate is a key ingredient in sound social work practice. This activity often produces new insights and understandings that would otherwise be missed. Social workers have come to believe that the services they offer clients are likely to be enhanced by thoughtful exploration of these issues, even when, in the final analysis, social workers may disagree.

In this respect, social work's approach to values and ethical issues is no different. The process is often what counts the most, as social workers try in earnest to uncover subtle aspects of the ethical issues they face, apply various points of view to them, and in the end make the wisest decision possible. Although there are some "givens" in social work values and ethics, just as there are in direct and indirect practice, we must accept the fact that some questions and dilemmas will never be resolved. Although there is virtual consensus in the field about some matters—for example, that social workers should not steal from their clients or have sexual contact with them—there are many ethical issues that will probably always remain unresolved and controversial —such as the limits of clients' right to engage in self-destructive behavior and the most appropriate ways to allocate scarce resources.

The bottom line is that social work is by definition a profession with a moral mission, and this obligates its members continually to examine the values and ethical dimensions of practice. Anything less would deprive social work's clients and the broader society of truly professional service.

APPENDIX:
CODE OF ETHICS OF THE NATIONAL ASSOCIATION
OF SOCIAL WORKERS AS ADOPTED BY
THE 1979 NASW DELEGATE ASSEMBLY AND REVISED
BY THE 1990 AND 1993 NASW DELEGATE ASSEMBLIES.
Reprinted with permission of the National Association of Social Workers

• • •

• **PREAMBLE**

This code is intended to serve as a guide to the everyday conduct of members of the social work profession and as a basis for the adjudication of issues in ethics when the conduct of social workers is alleged to deviate from the standards expressed or implied in this code. It represents standards of ethical behavior for social workers in professional relationships with those served, with colleagues, with employers, with other individuals and professions, and with the community and society as a whole. It also embodies standards of ethical behavior governing individual conduct to the extent that such conduct is associated with an individual's status as a social worker. This code is based on the fundamental values of the social work profession that include the worth, dignity, and uniqueness of all persons as well as their rights and opportunities. It is also based on the nature of social work, which fosters conditions that promote these values.

In subscribing to and abiding by this code, the social worker is expected to view ethical responsibility in as inclusive a context as each situation demands and within which ethical judgment is required. The social worker is expected to take into consideration all the principles in this code that have a bearing upon any situation in which ethical judgment is to be exercised and professional intervention or conduct is planned. The course of action that the social worker chooses is expected to be consistent with the spirit as well as the letter of this code.

In itself, this code does not represent a set of rules that will prescribe all the behaviors of social workers in all the complexities of professional life. Rather, it offers general principles to guide conduct, and the judicious appraisal of conduct, in situations that have ethical implications. It provides the basis for making judgments about ethical actions before and after they occur. Frequently, the particular situation determines the ethical principles that apply and the manner of their application. In such cases, not only the particular principles are taken into immediate consideration, but also the entire code and its spirit. Specific applications of ethical principles must be judged within the context in which they are being considered. Ethical behavior in a given situation must satisfy not only the judgment of the individual social worker but also that of an unbiased jury of professional peers.

This code should not be used as an instrument to deprive any social worker of the opportunity or freedom to practice with complete professional integrity; nor should any disciplinary action be taken on the basis of this code without maximum provision for safeguarding the rights of the social worker affected.

The ethical behavior of social workers results not from edict but from a personal commitment of the individual. This code is offered to affirm the will and zeal of all social workers to be ethical and to act ethically in all that they do as social workers.

The following codified ethical principles should guide social workers in the various roles and relationships and at the various levels of responsibility in which they function professionally. These principles also serve as a basis for the adjudication by the National Association of Social Workers of issues in ethics.

In subscribing to this code, social workers are required to cooperate in its implementation and abide by any disciplinary rulings based on it. They should also take adequate measures to discourage, prevent, expose, and correct the unethical conduct of colleagues. Finally, social workers should be equally ready to defend and assist colleagues unjustly charged with unethical conduct.

• THE NASW CODE OF ETHICS

I. The Social Worker's Conduct and Comportment as a Social Worker
A. Propriety—The social worker should maintain high standards of personal conduct in the capacity or identity as social worker.

1. The private conduct of the social worker is a personal matter to the same degree as is any other person's, except when such conduct compromises the fulfillment of professional responsibilities.

2. The social worker should not participate in, condone, or be associated with dishonesty, fraud, deceit, or misrepresentation.

3. The social worker should distinguish clearly between statements and actions made as a private individual and as a representative of the social work profession or an organization or group.

B. Competence and Professional Development—The social worker should strive to become and remain proficient in professional practice and the performance of professional functions.

1. The social worker should accept responsibility or employment only on the basis of existing competence or the intention to acquire the necessary competence.

2. The social worker should not misrepresent professional qualifications, education, experience, or affiliations.

3. The social worker should not allow his or her own personal problems, psychosocial distress, substance abuse, or mental health difficulties to interfere with professional judgment and performance or jeopardize the best interests of those for whom the social worker has a professional responsibility.

4. The social worker whose personal problems, psychosocial distress, substance abuse, or mental health difficulties interfere with professional judgment and performance should immediately seek consultation and take appropriate remedial action by seeking professional help, making adjustments in work load, terminating practice, or taking any other steps necessary to protect clients and others.

C. Service—The social worker should regard as primary the service obligation of the social work profession.

1. The social worker should retain ultimate responsibility for the quality and extent of the service that individual assumes, assigns, or performs.

2. The social worker should act to prevent practices that are inhumane or discriminatory against any person or group of persons.

D. Integrity—The social worker should act in accordance with the highest standards of professional integrity and impartiality.

1. The social worker should be alert to and resist the influences and

pressures that interfere with the exercise of professional discretion and impartial judgment required for the performance of professional functions.

2. The social worker should not exploit professional relationships for personal gain.

E. Scholarship and Research—The social worker engaged in study and research should be guided by the conventions of scholarly inquiry.

1. The social worker engaged in research should consider carefully its possible consequences for human beings.

2. The social worker engaged in research should ascertain that the consent of participants in the research is voluntary and informed, without any implied deprivation or penalty for refusal to participate, and with due regard for participants' privacy and dignity.

3. The social worker engaged in research should protect participants from unwarranted physical or mental discomfort, distress, harm, danger, or deprivation.

4. The social worker who engages in the evaluation of services or cases should discuss them only for the professional purposes and only with persons directly and professionally concerned with them.

5. Information obtained about participants in research should be treated as confidential.

6. The social worker should take credit only for work actually done in connection with scholarly and research endeavors and credit contributions made by others.

II. The Social Worker's Ethical Responsibility to Clients

F. Primacy of Clients' Interests—The social worker's primary responsibility is to clients.

1. The social worker should serve clients with devotion, loyalty, determination, and the maximum application of professional skill and competence.

2. The social worker should not exploit relationships with clients for personal advantage.

3. The social worker should not practice, condone, facilitate, or collaborate with any form of discrimination on the basis of race, color, sex, sexual orientation, age, religion, national origin, marital status, political belief, mental or physical handicap, or any other preference or personal characteristic, condition or status.

4. The social worker should not condone or engage in any dual or multiple relationships with clients or former clients in which there is a risk of exploitation of or potential harm to the client. The social worker is responsible for setting clear, appropriate, and culturally sensitive boundaries.

5. The social worker should under no circumstances engage in sexual activities with clients.

6. The social worker should provide clients with accurate and complete information regarding the extent and nature of the services available to them.

7. The social worker should apprise clients of their risks, rights, opportunities, and obligations associated with social service to them.

8. The social worker should seek advice and counsel of colleagues and supervisors whenever such consultation is in the best interest of clients.

9. The social worker should terminate service to clients, and professional relationships with them, when such service and relationships are no longer required or no longer serve the clients' needs or interests.

10. The social worker should withdraw services precipitously only under unusual circumstances, giving careful consideration to all factors in the situation and taking care to minimize possible adverse effects.

11. The social worker who anticipates the termination or interruption of service to clients should notify clients promptly and seek the transfer, referral, or continuation of service in relation to the clients' needs and preferences.

G. Rights and Prerogatives of Clients—The social worker should make every effort to foster maximum self-determination on the part of clients.

1. When the social worker must act on behalf of a client who has been adjudged legally incompetent, the social worker should safeguard the interests and rights of that client.

2. When another individual has been legally authorized to act in behalf of a client, the social worker should deal with that person always with the client's best interest in mind.

3. The social worker should not engage in any action that violates or diminishes the civil or legal rights of clients.

H. Confidentiality and Privacy—The social worker should respect the privacy of clients and hold in confidence all information obtained in the course of professional service.

1. The social worker should share with others confidences revealed by clients, without their consent, only for compelling professional reasons.

2. The social worker should inform clients fully about the limits of confidentiality in a given situation, the purposes for which information is obtained, and how it may be used.

3. The social worker should afford clients reasonable access to any official social work records concerning them.

4. When providing clients with access to records, the social worker should take due care to protect the confidences of others contained in those records.

5. The social worker should obtain informed consent of clients before taping, recording, or permitting third-party observation of their activities.

I. Fees—When setting fees, the social worker should ensure that they are fair, reasonable, considerate, and commensurate with the service performed and with due regard for the clients' ability to pay.

1. The social worker should not accept anything of value for making a referral.

III. The Social Worker's Ethical Responsibility to Colleagues

J. Respect, Fairness, and Courtesy—The social worker should treat colleagues with respect courtesy, fairness, and good faith.

1. The social worker should cooperate with colleagues to promote professional interests and concerns.

2. The social worker should respect confidences shared by colleagues in the course of their professional relationships and transactions.

3. The social worker should create and maintain conditions of practice that facilitate ethical and competent professional performance by colleagues.

4. The social worker should treat with respect, and represent accurately and fairly, the qualifications, views, and findings of colleagues and use appropriate channels to express judgments on these matters.

5. The social worker who replaces or is replaced by a colleague in a

professional practice should act with consideration for the interest, character, and reputation of that colleague.

6. The social worker should not exploit a dispute between a colleague and employers to obtain a position or otherwise advance the social worker's interest.

7. The social worker should seek arbitration or mediation when conflicts with colleagues require resolution for compelling professional reasons.

8. The social worker should extend to colleagues of other professions the same respect and cooperation that is extended to social work colleagues.

9. The social worker who serves as an employer, supervisor, or mentor to colleagues should make orderly and explicit arrangements regarding the conditions of their continuing professional relationship.

10. The social worker who has the responsibility for employing and evaluating the performance of other staff members, should fulfill such responsibility in a fair, considerate, and equitable manner, on the basis of clearly enunciated criteria.

11. The social worker who has the responsibility for evaluating the performance of employees, supervisees, or students should share evaluations with them.

12. The social worker should not use a professional position vested with power, such as that of employer, supervisor, teacher, or consultant, to his or her advantage or to exploit others.

13. The social worker who has direct knowledge of a social work colleague's impairment due to personal problems, psychosocial distress, substance abuse, or mental health difficulties should consult with that colleague and assist the colleague in taking remedial action.

K. Dealing with Colleagues' Clients—The social worker has the responsibility to relate to the clients of colleagues with full professional consideration.

1. The social worker should not assume professional responsibility for the clients of another agency or a colleague without appropriate communication with that agency or colleague.

2. The social worker who serves the clients of colleagues, during a temporary absence or emergency, should serve those clients with the same consideration as that afforded any client.

IV. The Social Worker's Ethical Responsibility to Employers and Employing Organizations

L. Commitments to Employing Organizations—The social worker should adhere to commitments made to the employing organization.

1. The social worker should work to improve the employing agency's policies and procedures, and the efficiency and effectiveness of its services.

2. The social worker should not accept employment or arrange student field placements in an organization that is currently under sanction by the NASW for violating personnel standards, or imposing limitations on or penalties for professional actions on behalf of clients.

3. The social worker should act to prevent and eliminate discrimination in the employing organization's work assignments and in its employment policies and practices.

4. The social worker should use with scrupulous regard, and only for the purpose for which they are intended, the resources of the employing organization.

V. The Social Worker's Ethical Responsibility to the Social Work Profession

M. Maintaining the Integrity of the Profession—The social worker should uphold and advance the values, ethics, knowledge, and mission of the profession.

1. The social worker should protect and enhance the dignity and integrity of the profession and should be responsible and vigorous in discussion and criticism of the profession.

2. The social worker should take action through appropriate channels against unethical conduct by any other member of the profession.

3. The social worker should act to prevent the unauthorized and unqualified practice of social work.

4. The social worker should make no misrepresentation in advertising as to qualifications, competence, service, or results to be achieved.

N. Community Service—The social worker should assist the profession in making social services available to the general public.

1. The social worker should contribute time and professional expertise to activities that promote respect for the utility, the integrity, and the competence of the social work profession.

2. The social worker should support the formulation, development,

enactment and implementation of social policies of concern to the profession.

O. Development of Knowledge—The social worker should take responsibility for identifying, developing, and fully utilizing knowledge for professional practice.

1. The social worker should base practice upon recognized knowledge relevant to social work.

2. The social worker should critically examine and keep current with emerging knowledge relevant to social work.

3. The social worker should contribute to the knowledge base of social work and share research knowledge and practice wisdom with colleagues.

VI. The Social Worker's Ethical Responsibility to Society

P. Promoting the General Welfare—The social worker should promote the general welfare of society.

1. The social worker should act to prevent and eliminate discrimination against any person or group on the basis of race, color, sex, sexual orientation, age, religion, national origin, marital status, political belief, mental or physical handicap, or any other preference or personal characteristic, condition, or status.

2. The social worker should act to ensure that all persons have access to the resources, services, and opportunities that they require.

3. The social worker should act to expand choice and opportunity for all persons, with special regard for disadvantaged or oppressed groups and persons.

4. The social worker should promote conditions that encourage respect for the diversity of cultures that constitutes American society.

5. The social worker should provide appropriate professional services in public emergencies.

6. The social worker should advocate changes in policy and legislation to improve social conditions and to promote social justice.

7. The social worker should encourage informed participation by the public in shaping social policies and institutions.

. . .

Abbott, A. A. 1988. *Professional Choices: Values at Work.* Silver Spring, Md.: National Association of Social Workers.

Alexander, P. M. 1987. "Why Social Workers Enter Private Practice: A Study of Motivations and Attitudes." *Journal of Independent Social Work* 1 (3): 7–18.

Allen, C. M., and M. A. Straus. 1980. "Resources, Power, and Husband-Wife Violence." In M. A. Straus and G. T. Hotaling, eds., *The Social Causes of Husband-Wife Violence,* pp. 188–208. Minneapolis: University of Minnesota Press.

Aptekar, H. 1964. "American Social Values and Their Influence on Social Welfare Programs and Professional Social Work." *Journal of Social Work Process* 14:19.

Austin, K. M., M. E. Moline, and G. T. Williams. 1990. *Confronting Malpractice: Legal and Ethical Dilemmas in Psychotherapy.* Newbury Park, Calif.: Sage.

Baer, B., and R. Federico, eds. 1979. *Educating the Baccalaureate Social Worker: A Curriculum Development Resource Guide,* vol. 2. Cambridge, Mass.: Ballinger.

Bagarozzi, D. A., and C. W. Giddings. 1983. "Conjugal Violence: A Critical Review of Current Research and Clinical Practices." *American Journal of Family Therapy* 11 (3): 3–15.

Barker, R. L. 1991a. "Point/Counterpoint: Should Training for Private Practice Be a Central Component of Social Work Education? Yes!" *Journal of Social Work Education* 27 (2): 108–11, 112–13.

———. 1991b. *The Social Work Dictionary.* 2d ed. Silver Spring, Md.: National Association of Social Workers.

Barker, R. L., and D. M. Branson. 1993. *Forensic Social Work.* Binghamton, N.Y.: Haworth Press.

Barry, V. 1986. *Moral Issues in Business.* 3d ed. Belmont, Calif.: Wadsworth.

Bartlett, H. M. 1970. *The Common Base of Social Work Practice.* New York: Columbia University Press.

Bass, D., and J. Rice. 1979. "Agency Responses to the Abused Wife." *Social Casework* 60:338–42.

Bentham, J. (1973). "An Introduction to the Principles of Morals and Legislation." In *The Utilitarians,* p. 205. New York: Anchor. (Originally published in 1789.)

Berlin, I. 1968. *Four Essays on Liberty.* Oxford: Oxford University Press.

Berliner, A. K. 1989. "Misconduct in Social Work Practice." *Social Work* 34:69–72.

Bernard, J., and C. Jara. 1986. "The Failure of Clinical Psychology Students to Apply Understood Ethical Principles." *Professional Psychology: Research and Practice* 17:316–21.

Bernstein, S. 1960. "Self-Determination: King or Citizen in the Realm of Values?" *Social Work* 5 (1): 3–8.

Besharov, D. J. 1985. *The Vulnerable Social Worker: Liability for Serving Children and Families.* Silver Spring, Md.: National Association of Social Workers.

Beveridge, Sir W. 1942. *Social Insurance and Allied Services.* New York: Macmillan.

Biestek, F. P. 1957. *The Casework Relationship.* Chicago: Loyola University Press.

——. 1975. "Client Self-Determination." In F. E. McDermott, ed., *Self-Determination in Social Work,* pp. 17–32. London: Routledge and Kegan Paul.

Biestek, F. P., and C. C. Geghrig. 1978. *Client Self-Determination in Social Work: A Fifty-Year History.* Chicago: Loyola University Press.

Billups, J. O. 1992. "The Moral Basis for a Radical Reconstruction of Social Work." In P. N. Reid and P. R. Popple, eds., *The Moral Purposes of Social Work,* pp. 100–119. Chicago: Nelson-Hall.

Bisno, H. 1956. "How Social Will Social Work Be?" *Social Work* 1:12–18.

Bissell, L., and P. W. Haberman. 1984. *Alcoholism in the Professions.* New York: Oxford University Press.

Blythe, B. J., and T. Tripodi. 1989. *Measurement in Direct Practice.* Newbury Park: Sage.

Bograd, M. 1982. "Battered Women, Cultural Myths, and Clinical Interventions: A Feminist Analysis." *Women and Therapy* 1:69–77.

——. 1984. "Family System Approaches to Wife Battering: A Feminist Critique." *American Journal of Orthopsychiatry* 54:558–68.

Bohr, R. H., H. I. Brenner, and H. M. Kaplan. 1971. "Value Conflicts in a Hospital Walkout." *Social Work* 16 (4): 33–42.

Bolton, F. G., and S. R. Bolton. 1987. *Working with Violent Families: A Guide for Clinical and Legal Practitioners.* Newbury Park, Calif.: Sage.

Brodsky, A. M. 1986. "The Distressed Psychologist: Sexual Intimacies and Exploitation." In R. R. Kilburg, P. E. Nathan, and R. W. Thoreson, eds., *Professionals in Distress: Issues, Syndromes, and Solutions in Psychology,* p. 153. Washington, D. C.: American Psychological Association.

Brown, P. M. 1990. "Social Workers in Private Practice: What Are They Really Doing?" *Clinical Social Work* (Winter): 56–71.

Buchanan, A. 1978. "Medical Paternalism." *Philosophy and Public Affairs* 7:370–90.

Butler, A. C. 1990. "A Reevaluation of Social Work Students' Career Interests." *Journal of Social Work Education* 26 (1): 45–51.

Cabot, R. C. 1973. *Social Service and the Art of Healing.* Washington, D.C.: National Association of Social Workers. (Original work published in 1915.)

Callahan, D., and S. Bok, eds. 1980. *Ethics Teaching in Higher Education.* New York: Plenum.

Campbell, C. S. 1991. "Ethics and Militant AIDS Activism." In F. G. Reamer, ed., *AIDS and Ethics,* pp. 155–87. New York: Columbia University Press.

Canda, E. R. 1988. "Spirituality, Religious Diversity, and Social Work Practice." *Social Casework* 69:238–47.

Cantoni, L. 1981. "Clinical Issues in Domestic Violence." *Social Casework* 62:3–12.

Carlson, B. E. 1991. "Domestic Violence." In A. Gitterman, ed., *Handbook of Social Work Practice with Vulnerable Populations,* pp. 471–502. New York: Columbia University Press.

Carter, R. 1977. "Justifying Paternalism." *Canadian Journal of Philosophy* 7:133–45.

Chilman, C. S. 1987. "Abortion." In *Encyclopedia of Social Work,* 18th ed., pp. 1–7. Silver Spring, Md.: National Association of Social Workers.

Cohen, C. B. 1988. "Ethics Committees." *Hastings Center Report* 18:11.

Cohen, R. J. 1979. *Malpractice: A Guide for Mental Health Professionals.* New York: Free Press.

Cohen, R. J., and W. E. Mariano. 1982. *Legal Guidebook in Mental Health.* New York: Free Press.

Compton, B. R., and B. Galaway, eds. 1989. *Social Work Processes.* 4th ed. Belmont, Calif.: Wadsworth.

Constable, R. 1983. "Values, Religion, and Social Work Practice." *Social Thought* 9 (4): 29–41.

Corey, G., M. Corey, and P. Callanan. 1988. *Issues and Ethics in the Helping Professions.* 3d ed. Pacific Grove, Calif.: Brooks/Cole.

Cowles, J. 1976. *Informed Consent.* New York: Coward, McCann, and Geoghegan.

Cranford, R. E., and E. Doudera, eds. 1984. *Institutional Ethics Committees and Health Care Decision Making.* Ann Arbor, Mich.: Health Administration Press.

Davis, A. 1967. *Spearheads for Reform.* New York: Oxford University Press.

Deutsch, C. 1985. "A Survey of Therapists' Personal Problems and Treatment." *Professional Psychology: Research and Practice* 16:305–15.

Donagan, A. 1977. *The Theory of Morality.* Chicago: University of Chicago Press.

Douglas, M. A. 1987. "The Battered Woman Syndrome." In D. J. Sonkin, ed., *Domestic Violence on Trial,* pp. 39–54. New York: Springer.

Dworkin, G. 1971. "Paternalism." In R. Wasserstrom, ed., *Morality and the Law,* pp. 107–26. Belmont, Calif.: Wadsworth.

Elliott, L. J. 1931. *Social Work Ethics.* New York: American Association of Social Workers.

Emmet, D. 1962. "Ethics and the Social Worker." *British Journal of Psychiatric Social Work* 6:165–72.

Ephross, P. H., and M. Reisch. 1982. "The Ideology of Some Social Work Texts." *Social Service Review* 56:273–91.

Felthouse, A. R. 1983. "Crisis Intervention in Interpartner Abuse." *Bulletin of the American Academy of Psychiatric Law* 11:249–60.

Fisher, D. 1987. "Problems for Social Work in a Strike Situation: Professional, Ethical, and Value Considerations." *Social Work* 32 (3): 252–54.

Fleishman, J. L., and B. L. Payne. 1980. *Ethical Dilemmas and the Education of Policymakers.* Hastings-on-Hudson, N.Y.: Hastings Center.

Fleming, J. 1979. *Stopping Wife Abuse.* New York: Anchor/Doubleday.

Frankel, C. 1959. "Social Philosophy and the Professional Education of Social Workers." *Social Service Review* 33:345–59.

——. 1969. "Social Values and Professional Values." *Journal of Education for Social Work* 5:29–35.

Frankena, W. K. 1973. *Ethics.* 2d ed. Englewood Cliffs, N.J.: Prentice Hall.

Freedberg, S. 1989. "Self-Determination: Historical Perspectives and Effects on Current Practice." *Social Work* 34 (1): 33–38.

Fried, C. 1978. *Right and Wrong.* Cambridge, Mass.: Harvard University Press.

Gartrell, N., J. Herman, S. Olarte, M. Feldstein, and R. Localio. 1986. "Psychiatrist-Patient Sexual Contact: Results of a National Survey." *American Journal of Psychiatry* 143 (9): 1126–31.

Gechtman, L., and J. Bouhoutsos. 1985. "Sexual Intimacy between Social Workers and Clients." Paper presented at the annual meeting of the Society for Clinical Social Workers, University City, Calif.

Gert, B. 1970. *The Moral Rules.* New York: Harper and Row.

Gewirth, A. 1978a. *Reason and Morality.* Chicago: University of Chicago Press.

——. 1978b. "Ethics." In *Encyclopedia Britannica*, 15th ed.

Gifis, S. H. 1991. *Law Dictionary.* 3d ed. Hauppauge, N.Y.: Barron's.

Gilbert, N., and H. Specht. 1974. "Social Work: The Incomplete Profession." *Social Work* 19:665–74.

Goldstein, H. 1983. "Starting Where the Client Is." *Social Casework* 64:264–75.

——. 1987. "The Neglected Moral Link in Social Work Practice." *Social Work* 32 (3): 181–86.

Goleman, D. 1985. "Social Workers Vault into a Leading Role in Psychotherapy." *New York Times* (April 30): C-1, C-9.

Goodstein, R. K., and A. W. Page. 1981. "Battered Wife Syndrome: Overview of Dynamics and Treatment." *American Journal of Psychiatry* 138:1036–44.

Gordon, W. E. 1962. "A Critique of the Working Definition." *Social Work* 7:32–39.

——. 1965. "Knowledge and Value: Their Distinction and Relationship in Clarifying Social Work Practice." *Social Work* 10 (3): 32–39.

Gorovitz, S., ed. 1971. *Mill: Utilitarianism.* Indianapolis: Bobbs-Merrill.

Gotbaum, V. 1978. "Public Service Strikes: Where Prevention Is Worse than the Cure." In R. T. DeGeorge and J. A. Pilcher, eds., *Ethics, Free Enterprise, and Public Policy*, p. 158. New York: Oxford University Press.

Grinnell, R. M., Jr., ed. 1993. *Social Work Research and Evaluation.* 4th ed. Itasca, Ill.: F. E. Peacock.

Grossman, M. 1973. "The Psychiatrist and the Subpoena." *Bulletin of the American Academy of Psychiatry and the Law* 1:245.

Guy, J. D., P. L. Poelstra, and M. Stark. 1989. "Personal Distress and Therapeutic Effectiveness: National Survey of Psychologists Practicing Psychotherapy." *Professional Psychology: Research and Practice* 20:48–50.

Hamilton, G. 1940. *Theory and Practice of Social Casework.* New York: Columbia University Press.

———. 1951. *Social Casework*. 2d ed. New York: Columbia University Press.

Hancock, R. N. 1974. *Twentieth Century Ethics*. New York: Columbia University Press.

Hardman, D. G. 1975. "Not with My Daughter, You Don't!" *Social Work* 20 (4): 278–85.

Henson, D. M., and J. L. Schinderman. 1980. "Therapy with Battered Women." In A. Weick and S. T. Vandiver, eds., *Women, Power, and Change*, pp. 27–37. Washington, D. C.: National Association of Social Workers.

Hogan, D. B. 1979. *The Regulation of Psychotherapists*. Vol. 1: *A Study in the Philosophy and Practice of Professional Regulation*. Cambridge, Mass.: Ballinger.

Hollis, F. 1964. *Casework: A Psychosocial Therapy*. New York: Random House.

Hornblower, M. 1987. "Down and Out—But Determined." *Time*, November 23, p. 29.

Humphrey v. Norden, 359 N.Y.S. 2d 733 (1974).

Hunt, L. 1978. "Social Work and Ideology." In N. Timms and D. Watson, eds., *Philosophy in Social Work*, pp. 7–25. London: Routledge and Kegan Paul.

Jayaratne, S., and W. A. Chess. 1984. "Job Satisfaction, Burnout, and Turnover: A National Study." *Social Work* 29:448–55.

Johnson, A. 1955. "Educating Professional Social Workers for Ethical Practice." *Social Service Review* 29 (2): 125–36.

Johnson, L. C. 1989. *Social Work Practice: A Generalist Approach*. 3d ed. Boston: Allyn and Bacon.

Johnson, M., and G. L. Stone. 1986. "Social Workers and Burnout." *Journal of Social Work Research* 10:67–80.

Jonsen, A. R. 1984. "A Guide to Guidelines." *American Society of Law and Medicine: Ethics Committee Newsletter* 2:4.

Joseph, M. V. 1987. "The Religious and Spiritual Aspects of Clinical Practice." *Social Thought* 13 (1): 12–23.

———. 1989. "Social Work Ethics: Historical and Contemporary Perspectives." *Social Thought* 15 (3/4): 4–17.

Judah, E. H. 1985. "A Spirituality of Professional Service." *Social Thought* 11 (4): 25–35.

Kagle, J. D. 1987. "Recording in Direct Practice." In *Encyclopedia of Social Work*, 18th ed., pp. 463–67. Silver Spring, Md.: National Association of Social Workers.

———. 1991. *Social Work Records*. 2d ed. Belmont, Calif.: Wadsworth.

Keith-Lucas, A. 1963. "A Critique of the Principle of Client Self-Determination." *Social Work* 8 (3): 66–71.

———. 1977. "Ethics in Social Work." In *Encyclopedia of Social Work*, 17th ed., pp. 350–55. Washington, D.C.: National Association of Social Workers.

———. 1992. "A Socially Sanctioned Profession?" In P. N. Reid and P. R. Popple, eds., *The Moral Purposes of Social Work*, pp. 51–70. Chicago: Nelson-Hall.

Kilburg, R. R., F. W. Kaslow, and G. R. VandenBos. 1988. "Professionals in Distress." *Hospital and Community Psychiatry* 39:723–25.

Kilburg, R. R., P. E. Nathan, and R. W. Thoreson, eds. 1986. *Professionals in Distress: Issues, Syndromes, and Solutions in Psychology*. Washington, D.C.: American Psychological Association.

Kirk, S. A., and H. Kutchins. 1988. "Deliberate Misdiagnosis in Mental Health Practice." *Social Service Review* 62:225–37.

Knutsen, E. 1977. "On the Emotional Well-Being of Psychiatrists: Overview and Rationale." *American Journal of Psychoanalysis* 37:123–29.

Koeske, G. F., and R. D. Koeske. 1989. "Work Load and Burnout: Can Social Support and Perceived Accomplishment Help?" *Social Work* 34:243–48.

Kultgen, J. 1982. "The Ideological Use of Professional Codes." *Business and Professional Ethics Journal* 1 (3): 53–69.

Laliotis, D. A., and J. H. Grayson. 1985. "Psychologist Heal Thyself: What Is Available for the Impaired Psychologist?" *American Psychologist* 40:84–96.

Lamb, D. H., N. R. Presser, K. S. Pfost, M. C. Baum, V. R. Jackson, and P. A. Jarvis. 1987. "Confronting Professional Impairment during the Internship: Identification, Due Process, and Remediation." *Professional Psychology: Research and Practice* 18:597–603.

Leiby, J. 1985. "Moral Foundations of Social Welfare and Social Work: A Historical Review." *Social Service Review*: 324.

Levy, C. S. 1972. "The Context of Social Work Ethics." *Social Work* 17:95–101.

———. 1973. "The Value Base of Social Work." *Journal of Education for Social Work* 9:34–42.

———. 1976. *Social Work Ethics*. New York: Human Sciences Press.

———. 1984. "Values and Ethics." In S. Dillick, ed., *Value Foundations of Social Work*, pp. 17–29. Detroit: School of Social Work, Wayne State University.

Lewis, H. 1972. "Morality and the Politics of Practice." *Social Casework* 53:404–17.

Lewis, M. B. 1986. "Duty To Warn versus Duty To Maintain Confidentiality:

Conflicting Demands on Mental Health Professionals." *Suffolk Law Review* 20 (3): 579–615.

Lightman, E. S. 1983. "Social Workers, Strikes, and Service to Clients." *Social Work* 28 (2): 142–48.

Loewenberg, F. M. 1988. *Religion and Social Work Practice in Contemporary American Society.* New York: Columbia University Press.

Loewenberg, F. M., and R. Dolgoff. 1992. *Ethical Decisions for Social Work Practice.* 4th ed. Itasca, Ill.: F. E. Peacock.

Lynch, C. G., and T. Norris. 1977–78. "Services for Battered Women: Looking for a Perspective." *Victimology* 2:553–62.

Marty, M. E. 1980. "Social Service: Godly and Godless." *Social Service Review* 54:463–81.

McCann, C. W., and J. P. Cutler. 1979. "Ethics and the Alleged Unethical." *Social Work* 24 (1): 5–8.

McCrady, B. S. 1989. "The Distressed or Impaired Professional: From Retribution to Rehabilitation." *Journal of Drug Issues* 19:337–49.

McDermott, F. E., ed. 1975. *Self-Determination in Social Work.* London: Routledge and Kegan Paul.

Meinert, R. G. 1980. "Values in Social Work Called Dysfunctional Myth." *Journal of Social Welfare* 6 (3): 5–16.

"Membership Survey Shows Practice Shifts." 1983. *NASW News* 28:6.

Meyer, R. G., E. R. Landis, and J. R. Hays. 1988. *Law for the Psychotherapist.* New York: Norton.

Miles, A. P. 1954. *American Social Work Theory.* New York: Harper and Row.

Mill, J. S. 1973. "On Liberty." In *The Utilitarians,* p. 484. New York: Anchor. (Originally published in 1859.)

Morales, A., and B. W. Sheafor. 1986. *Social Work: A Profession of Many Faces.* 4th ed. Boston: Allyn and Bacon.

National Association of Social Workers, Ad Hoc Committee on Advocacy. 1969. "The Social Worker as Advocate: Champion of Social Victims." *Social Work* 14 (2): 19.

——. 1974. *The Milford Conference Report: Social Casework, Generic and Specific.* Washington, D.C.: author. (Originally published in 1929.)

——. 1975. *NASW Standards for Social Work Personnel Practices.* Silver Spring, Md.: author.

——. 1982. *NASW Standards for the Classification of Social Work Practice.* Silver Spring, Md.: author.

——, Commission on Employment and Economic Support. 1987. *Impaired Social Worker Program Resource Book.* Silver Spring, Md.: author.

——. 1989. *NASW Standards for the Practice of Clinical Social Work*, rev. ed. Silver Spring, Md.: author.

——. 1994a. *Code of Ethics*. Silver Spring, Md.: author.

——. 1994b. *Social Work Speaks: NASW Policy Statements*. 3d ed. Washington, D.C.: NASW Press.

Paine, R. T., Jr. 1880. "The Work of Volunteer Visitors of the Associated Charities among the Poor." *Journal of Social Science* 12:113.

Perlman, H. H.. 1965. "Self-Determination: Reality or Illusion?" *Social Service Review* 39 (4): 410–21.

——. 1976. "Believing and Doing: Values in Social Work Education." *Social Casework* 57:381–90.

Peters, C., and T. Branch. 1972. *Blowing the Whistle: Dissent in the Public Interest*. New York: Praeger.

Plant, R. 1970. *Social and Moral Theory in Casework*. London: Routledge and Kegan Paul.

"Political Philosophy." 1988. In *Encyclopedia Britannica*, 15th ed., pp. 972–84. Chicago: University of Chicago Press.

Pope, K. S. 1988. "How Clients Are Harmed by Sexual Contact with Mental Health Professionals: The Syndrome and Its Prevalence." *Journal of Counseling and Development* 67:222–26.

Popper, K. 1966. *The Open Society and Its Enemies*. 5th ed. London: Routledge and Kegan Paul.

Popple, P. R. 1985. "The Social Work Profession: A Reconceptualization." *Social Service Review* 59:565.

——. 1992. "Social Work: Social Function and Moral Purpose." In P. N. Reid and P. R. Popple, eds., *The Moral Purposes of Social Work*, pp. 141–54. Chicago: Nelson-Hall.

President's Commission for the Study of Ethical Problems in Medicine and Biomedical and Behavioral Research. 1982. *Making Health Care Decisions: The Ethical and Legal Implications of Informed Consent in the Patient-Practitioner Relationship*. Vol. 3. Washington, D.C.: GPO.

Prochaska, J., and J. Norcross. 1983. "Psychotherapists' Perspectives on Treating Themselves and Their Clients for Psychic Distress." *Professional Psychology: Research and Practice* 14:642–55.

Pumphrey, M. W. 1959. *The Teaching of Values and Ethics in Social Work*. Vol. 13. New York: Council on Social Work Education.

Rawls, J. 1971. *A Theory of Justice*. Cambridge, Mass.: Harvard University Press.

——. 1975. "The Justification of Civil Disobedience." In R. Wasserstrom, ed., *Today's Moral Problems*, p. 352. New York: Macmillan.

Reamer, F. G. 1979. "Fundamental Ethical Issues in Social Work: An Essay Review." *Social Service Review* 53 (2): 229–43.

——. 1983a. "The Free Will–Determinism Debate in Social Work." *Social Service Review* 57 (4): 626–44.

——. 1983b. "The Concept of Paternalism in Social Work." *Social Service Review* 57 (2): 254–71.

——. 1987a. "Values and Ethics." In *Encyclopedia of Social Work,* 18th ed., pp. 801–9. Silver Spring, Md.: National Association of Social Workers.

——. 1987b. "Ethics Committees in Social Work." *Social Work* 32 (3): 188–92.

——. 1988. "Social Workers and Unions: Ethical Dilemmas." In H. J. Karger, ed., *Social Workers and Labor Unions,* pp. 131–43. New York: Greenwood Press.

——. 1989. "Toward Ethical Practice: The Relevance of Ethical Theory." *Social Thought* 15 (3/4): 67–78.

——. 1990. *Ethical Dilemmas in Social Service.* 2d ed. New York: Columbia University Press.

——. 1991. "AIDS, Social Work, and the Duty to Protect." *Social Work* 36 (1): 56–60.

——. 1992a. "Social Work and the Public Good: Calling or Career." In P. N. Reid and P. R. Popple, eds., *The Moral Purposes of Social Work,* pp. 11–33. Chicago: Nelson-Hall.

——. 1992b. "The Impaired Social Worker." *Social Work* 37 (2): 165–70.

——. 1993a. *The Philosophical Foundations of Social Work.* New York: Columbia University Press.

——. 1993b. "Liability Issues in Social Work Administration." *Administration in Social Work* 17 (4): 11–25.

——. 1994a. "Social Work Values and Ethics." In F. G. Reamer, ed. *The Foundations of Social Work Knowledge,* pp. 195–230. New York: Columbia University Press.

——. 1994b. *Social Work Malpractice and Liability.* New York: Columbia University Press.

——. 1995a. "Ethics and Values." In *Encyclopedia of Social Work,* 19th ed. Washington, D.C.: National Association of Social Workers.

——. 1995b (in press). "Malpractice and Liability Claims against Social Workers: First Facts." *Social Work.*

Reamer, F. G., and M. Abramson. 1982. *The Teaching of Social Work Ethics.* Hastings-on-Hudson, N.Y.: The Hastings Center.

Reeser, L. C., and I. Epstein. 1990. *Professionalization and Activism in Social Work.* New York: Columbia University Press.

Rehr, H. 1960. "Problems for a Profession in a Strike Situation." *Social Work* 5 (2): 22–28.

Reid, P. N. 1992. "The Social Function and Social Morality of Social Work: A Utilitarian Perspective." In P. N. Reid and P. R. Popple, eds., *The Moral Purposes of Social Work*, pp. 34–50. Chicago: Nelson-Hall.

Rein, M. 1970. "Social Work in Search of a Radical Profession." *Social Work* 15:13–28.

Rescher, N. 1969. *Introduction to Value Theory.* Englewood Cliffs, N.J.: Prentice Hall.

Reynolds, B. 1956. *Uncharted Journey.* New York: Citadel.

Rhodes, M. L. 1986. *Ethical Dilemmas in Social Work Practice.* London: Routledge and Kegan Paul.

Richmond, M. 1917. *Social Diagnosis.* New York: Russell Sage Foundation.

Roberts, A. R. 1984. "Crisis Intervention with Battered Women." In A. R. Roberts, ed., *Battered Women and Their Families*, pp. 65–83. New York: Springer.

Rokeach, M. 1973. *The Nature of Human Values.* New York: Free Press.

Ross, W. D. 1930. *The Right and the Good.* Oxford: Clarendon.

Rozovsky, F. A. 1984. *Consent to Treatment: A Practical Guide.* Boston: Little, Brown.

Saunders, D. G. 1982. "Counseling the Violent Husband." In P. A. Keller and L. G. Ritt, eds., *Innovations in Clinical Practice: A Sourcebook*, pp. 16–29. Sarasota, Fla.: Professional Resource Exchange.

Schechter, S., and L. T. Gray. 1988. "A Framework for Understanding and Empowering Battered Women." In M. B. Straus, ed., *Abuse and Victimization Across the Life Span*, pp. 240–53. Baltimore: Johns Hopkins University Press.

Schutz, B. M. 1982. *Legal Liability in Psychotherapy.* San Francisco: Jossey-Bass.

Sheafor, B. W., C. R. Horejsi, and G. A. Horejsi. 1988. *Techniques and Guidelines for Social Work Practice.* Boston: Allyn and Bacon.

Siegel, D. H. 1984. "Defining Empirically Based Practice." *Social Work* 29 (4): 325–31.

——. 1988. "Integrating Data-Gathering Techniques and Practice Activities." In R. M. Grinnell, Jr., ed., *Social Work Research and Evaluation*, 3d ed., pp. 465–82. Itasca, Ill.: F. E. Peacock.

Siporin, M. 1982. "Moral Philosophy in Social Work Today." *Social Service Review* 56:516–38.

——. 1983. "Morality and Immorality in Working with Clients." *Social Thought* 9 (4): 10–28.

——. 1989. "The Social Work Ethic." *Social Thought* 15 (3/4): 42–52.

——. 1992. "Strengthening the Moral Mission of Social Work." In P. N. Reid and P. R. Popple, eds., *The Moral Purposes of Social Work*, pp. 71–99. Chicago: Nelson-Hall.

Sloan, D. 1980. "The Teaching of Ethics in the American Undergraduate Curriculum, 1876–1976." In D. Callahan and S. Bok, eds. *Ethics Teaching in Higher Education*, pp. 1–57. New York: Plenum.

Smart, J. J. C. 1971. "Extreme and Restricted Utilitarianism." In S. Gorovitz, ed., *Mill: Utilitarianism*, pp. 195–203. Indianapolis: Bobbs-Merrill.

Smart, J. J. C., and B. Williams. 1973. *Utilitarianism: For and Against.* Cambridge: Cambridge University Press.

Solomon, B. 1976. *Black Empowerment: Social Work in Oppressed Communities.* New York: Columbia University Press.

Specht, H. 1990. "Social Work and the Popular Therapies." *Social Service Review* 64:345–57.

——. 1991. "Point/Counterpoint: Should Training for Private Practice Be a Central Component of Social Work Education? No!" *Journal of Social Work Education* 27 (2): 102–7, 111–12.

Stalley, R. F. 1975. "Determinism and the Principle of Client Self-Determination." In F. E. McDermott, ed., *Self-Determination in Social Work*, pp. 93–117. London: Routledge and Kegan Paul.

Strube, M. J. 1988. "The Decision to Leave an Abusive Relationship: Empirical Evidence and Theoretical Issues." *Psychological Bulletin* 104:236–50.

Tarasoff v. Board of Regents of the University of California, 33 Cal. 3d 275 (1973), 529 P.2d 553 (1974), 551 P.2d 334 (1976), 131 Cal. Rptr. 14 (1976)

Teel, K. 1975. "The Physician's Dilemma: A Doctor's View: What the Law Should Be." *Baylor Law Review* 27:6–9.

Teicher, M. 1967. *Values in Social Work: A Reexamination.* New York: National Association of Social Workers.

Thoreson, R. W., M. Miller, and C. J. Krauskopf. 1989. "The Distressed Psychologist: Prevalence and Treatment Considerations." *Professional Psychology: Research and Practice* 20:153–58.

Thoreson, R. W., P. E. Nathan, J. K. Skorina, and R. R. Kilburg. 1983. "The Alcoholic Psychologist: Issues, Problems, and Implications for the Profession." *Professional Psychology: Research and Practice* 14:670–84.

Timms, N. 1983. *Social Work Values: An Enquiry.* London: Routledge and Kegan Paul.

Trattner, W. I. 1979. *From Poor Law to Welfare State.* 2d ed. New York: Free Press.

VandenBos, G. R., and R. F. Duthie. 1986. "Confronting and Supporting Colleagues in Distress." In R. R. Kilburg, P. E. Nathan, and R. W. Thoreson, eds., *Professionals in Distress: Issues, Syndromes, and Solutions in Psychology*, p. 211. Washington, D.C.: American Psychological Association.

Varley, B. K. 1968. "Social Work Values: Changes in Value Commitments from Admission to MSW Graduation." *Journal of Education for Social Work* 4:67–85.

Vigilante, J. L. 1974. "Between Values and Science: Education for the Profession; or, Is Proof Truth?" *Journal of Education for Social Work* 10:107–15.

Wakefield, J. C. 1988a. "Psychotherapy, Distributive Justice, and Social Work, Part I: Distributive Justice as a Conceptual Framework for Social Work." *Social Service Review* 62:187–210.

———. 1988b. "Psychotherapy, Distributive Justice, and Social Work, Part II: Psychotherapy and the Pursuit of Justice." *Social Service Review* 62:353–82.

Walker, L. E. 1980. *The Battered Woman*. New York: Harper Colophon.

Wasserstrom, R. 1975. "The Obligation to Obey the Law." In R. Wasserstrom, ed., *Today's Moral Problems* (pp. 358–84). New York: Macmillan.

—, ed. 1971. *Morality and the Law*. Belmont, Calif.: Wadsworth.

Welfel, E. R., and N. E. Lipsitz. 1984. "The Ethical Behavior of Professional Psychologists: A Critical Analysis of the Research." *Counseling Psychologist* 12 (3): 31–42.

Williams, B. 1972. *Morality: An Introduction to Ethics*. New York: Harper and Row.

Williams, R. M., Jr. 1968. "The Concept of Values." In *International Encyclopedia of the Social Sciences*, vol. 16, pp. 283–87. New York: Macmillan/Free Press.

Wilson, S. J. 1978. *Confidentiality in Social Work: Issues and Principles*. New York: Free Press.

———. 1980. *Recording: Guidelines for Social Workers*. 2d ed. New York: Free Press.

Wood, B. J., S. Klein, H. J. Cross, C. J. Lammers, and J. K. Elliott. 1985. "Impaired Practitioners: Psychologists' Opinions about Prevalence, and Proposals for Intervention." *Professional Psychology: Research and Practice* 16:843–50.

Woodroofe, K. 1962. *From Charity to Social Work in England and the United States*. Toronto: University of Toronto Press.

Younghusband, E. 1967. *Social Work and Social Values*. London: Allen and Unwin.

INDEX

• • •

Designer: Andrea Ratazzi
Text: Optima
Composition: Columbia University Press
Printer: Maple Vail
Binder: Maple Vail